ATD's
Organization
Development
Handbook

BRIAN JAMES FLORES
EDITOR

PRESS
Alexandria, VA

To my wife, Ariel, and my children, Noah, Nell, and Naia,
the inspiration for everything that I do.
—Brian J. Flores

ATD Press is an internationally renowned source of insightful and practical information on talent development, training, and professional development.

ATD Press
1640 King Street
Alexandria, VA 22314 USA

Ordering information: Books published by ATD Press can be purchased by visiting ATD's website at td.org/books or by calling 800.628.2783 or 703.683.8100.

Library of Congress Control Number: 2023934786

ISBN-10: 1-953946-54-2
ISBN-13: 978-1-953946-54-6
e-ISBN: 978-1-957157-39-9

ATD Press Editorial Staff
Director: Sarah Halgas
Manager: Melissa Jones
Content Manager, Organization Development: Mallory Flynn
Developmental Editor: Jack Harlow
Cover Designer: Shirley E.M. Raybuck
Text Designer: PerfecType, Nashville, TN
Printed by BR Printers, San Jose, CA

Contents

Part 3. Workforce Design

Part 4. Leadership Preparedness

Foreword

TONY BINGHAM

The Association for Talent Development is celebrating its 80th anniversary in 2023, the year that ATD Press is releasing our newest handbook—one on organization development. It is fitting that as the association marks another milestone in its own evolution, we are publishing a book about tools and resources needed for an evolution talent development professionals may make in their own careers—supporting and contributing to organization development (OD).

When the association was formed in 1943, it was called the American Society of Training Directors, and its purpose was to educate practitioners in the emerging field called workplace training. At the time, the association acknowledged that particular skills and knowledge were needed to help adults learn at work and develop capabilities to drive a company's performance and growth.

Fast forward several decades. As the training and development field evolved, so did the society, eventually becoming the American Society for Training & Development (ASTD). However, that moniker became constraining as the society's membership grew beyond US borders and the work being done by members grew beyond training programs.

In 2014, ASTD rebranded to the Association for Talent Development (ATD). The purpose of the new name and mission of the organization was to encapsulate—and support—the growing breadth of work in the field and the many countries and cultures in which members of our global community empower growth and unleash human potential.

Another evolution was the development of our Talent Development Capability Model in 2019. When the research for that model was conducted, it became quite clear that there was an important role for TD professionals to play in creating organizational impact. The research showed that there were three domains of capabilities: personal, professional, and organizational capabilities.

Within the Impacting Organizational Capability domain is a specific capability of *organization development and culture*. It is compelling that our global research identified this set of knowledge and skills as important for TD professionals who are interested in contributing to their organizations at a higher and more robust level. For any OD effort to succeed, learning must happen.

In the past three years, we've witnessed the value of talent development increase substantially. It was learning professionals who helped companies worldwide navigate the early days of the pandemic as nearly everyone had to adapt to new ways of working, new tools to work with, and new demands to balance. The longed-for "seat at the table" has been mostly achieved; learning and developing talent are now viewed as vital contributors to an organization's success. It is incumbent on practitioners to continue to add value in strategic ways.

Increasingly, we hear that organizations are asking their TD professionals to contribute to OD initiatives. The reasons for these requests are as varied as the organizations making them. Challenging economic times, as well as times marked with disruption and change, often result in organizations looking for ways to maximize the contributions and engagement of employees, streamline processes, improve efficiencies and effectiveness, and attract and retain talent. This is the place where talent development and organization development should meet and collaborate. However, there's often been a siloed approach between TD and OD initiatives, to the detriment of organizational impact.

That's why it is time for this handbook.

Our field is being asked to transform organizations in new and exciting ways. OD is one of them. But—until now—there has never been a resource for TD professionals that connects the dots between the talent development and organization development disciplines with such a broad lens. I am excited to see how this resource serves our field—and organizations worldwide.

It's time for talent development and organization development to work together to create businesses—and a world—that works better.

Steve Jobs once said, "Great things in business are never done by one person. They're done by a team of people." I would echo that and expand it: Great things in business are never done by one department in a silo. They're done by cross-functional teams focused on harnessing that most precious resource: human potential.

Introduction

BRIAN J. FLORES

The State of Learning and Development's Role in the Organization

Learning and development professionals are naturally curious. Curious about how individuals learn new knowledge and skills. Curious about how they can best design training courses and programs to help individuals get better at their jobs. Curious about how their initiatives affect organizational results.

It's only natural that L&D professionals would be curious about the field of organization development and how the practice can help elevate L&D effectiveness as well as drive overall performance as they work to simultaneously develop the individual and create lasting impact among organizations.

L&D professionals understand that to be most effective they must extend their work beyond designing and developing one-off training workshops or e-learning courses. They are getting more involved in establishing and nurturing an organizational culture that embraces learning—not just as a requirement, a perk, or a punishment—as a necessary element embedded within the organization. To do so, they're crafting L&D strategies that align with the business and, when necessary, influence overall organizational goal setting.

L&D professionals know learning doesn't happen in a vacuum. Rather, it's influenced by what happens back on the job. And so, they have started to ensure that learning transfers. This requires getting a better understanding of what happens outside the classroom, with organizational design and employee dynamics, and focusing on the need to create a learning ecosystem and further partner with neighboring departments.

L&D professionals realize they can play a vital role in building organizational agility. When they understand what technical and workplace transformations the organization may have to undergo to keep pace with the competition, the L&D team can ensure that members of the organization—including themselves—are ready to adapt, reskill, and assume new roles. L&D professionals can enable their organizations to respond well to disruptions through managing change, leading skilling initiatives, and encouraging employees to adopt a growth mindset.

L&D professionals grasp that when talent development programs aren't accessible and inclusive to all employees, it undermines more than the L&D function—it suppresses overall employee satisfaction and engagement. As a result, they're learning more about their organization's DEI policies and how workplaces are set up to enable all to participate and feel welcome. They are working to position training and talent development as a driver of DEI in the workplace through mentoring, coaching, employee resource groups, and more.

All of this is evidence that L&D is changing, and L&D professionals have to change with it. To keep up, they need new knowledge and new skills—and new resources to help them grow.

Why You Need This Book

ATD's Organization Development Handbook is a tactical, hands-on book for those in L&D looking to make that first step into organization development or those who are a one-person band doing both. This book aims to meet L&D professionals where they are in their journey today. Although there are many books and textbooks about organization development—the effort to improve an organization's capability through the alignment of strategy, structure, people, rewards, metrics, and management processes—this volume is the first of its kind to address OD from the talent development and, specifically, L&D perspective.

More than ever, L&D professionals are taking on organization development work to propel organizational effectiveness and performance. Sometimes this happens out of choice when seeking a new career challenge, and other times out of necessity when the organization adds OD to their responsibilities. In either case, L&D professionals need new knowledge and skills—as well as insight into how to use their analysis, design, development, implementation, and evaluation abilities—to become successful in creating OD solutions.

L&D professionals will also benefit from a book on organization development if they're:

- **Seeking a career pivot.** You already know that you want to contribute to your organization in a different but similar way. You may feel bored and unchallenged in your current role. This book will give you some ideas on how to expand your skill set and seek new endeavors. See if any of the OD initiatives in the table of contents resonate with you.

- **Seeking career advancement.** If you're looking to grow from an individual contributor to a leader, especially ascending to the director level and above, one path could be moving from specialist to generalist and taking on organization-wide development implementations. Exposure and experience with these often-times high-visibility initiatives can add a new dimension to your L&D efforts.
- **Seeking career security.** Whether it's imminent layoffs during a recession or your company's underperformance for the year, seeking to grow your skill set and contribute in new ways to your organization could demonstrate validity in retaining your role. When training budgets get cut, experience in change management or employee engagement may be integral to showcase your ability to continue to provide value.
- **Seeking intrinsic value and purpose.** It can be a great gift to do work you really care about, and some of the categories of OD initiatives may be aligned with your own values. Projects related to diversity, equity, inclusion, and belonging or well-being can provide opportunities for those interested in contributing in ways that personally resonate.

No matter your reason for picking up this book, L&D professionals can benefit from the expert knowledge, key takeaways, practical resources, and lessons learned from actual case studies, to supplement much of the learning that will take place on the job.

Defining Learning and Development and Organization Development

Before going further, we need to answer the question that you're likely asking: How are we defining L&D and OD?

ATD defines *learning and development* as a function within an organization that is respon-sible for empowering employees' growth and developing their knowledge, skills, and capa-bilities to drive better business performance. The function may be organized centrally (either independently or sitting under human resources), decentralized throughout different business units, or it could be a hybrid structure (sometimes referred to as a federated structure).

Examples include:

- Soft or power skills training, like delivering effective feedback or having difficult conversations

- Discipline-based training, like how to close a sale or overcome objections
- Systems or software training, like how to use video conferencing software or an HRIS

ATD defines *organization development* as the process of developing an organization so that it's more effective in achieving its business goals. OD is a science-backed, interdisciplinary field rooted in psychology, culture, innovation, social sciences, adult education, human resource management, change management, organization behavior, and research analysis and design, among others. OD uses planned initiatives to develop the systems, structures, and processes in the organization to improve effectiveness.

As a discipline, OD takes a much broader view of the organization's ability to perform better by looking at several parts, including people growth and development. The core outcome of OD is improvement, which is brought about through change, and change is facilitated through thoughtful learning experiences.

OD initiatives are typically categorized as:

- **Human process initiatives** that include team building, interpersonal and group process approaches, and coaching
- **Techno-structural initiatives** that include restructuring organizations (such as mergers and acquisitions, flexible work design, downsizing, business process engineering, total quality management, quality of work life, Six Sigma, and Agile)
- **Human resource management initiatives** that include employee engagement, employee experience, performance management, employee development, succession planning, coaching and mentoring, career development, and diversity awareness
- **Strategic initiatives** that include organization transformation, culture change, leadership development, and attraction and retention initiatives

While L&D and OD may initially appear quite different, the lines are continuing to blur. Each discipline is continually working toward the same goal as practitioners strive to develop their organization's capability, from the individual to the greater collective.

Here are some examples of where I've seen the overlap and intersection of L&D and OD:

- **Reskilling and upskilling.** How organizations choose to tackle skilling their workforces is a clear intersection of the two disciplines. In the digital marketing space, agencies are facing the reality that more and more clients are taking their budgets and focusing on in-house solutions. In my own past experience, my company needed to pivot some of our retention efforts to consultation versus activation and that required reskilling a workforce rooted in practical execution to one that was able to speak to theory and strategy. My L&D efforts in this situation were tightly aligned to OD in that I had to understand the updated vision of the department, aid in identifying skills associated with new roles, and craft a learning plan that included changes in philosophy and strategy. This included training team members in consultative skills, as well as product training at scale to ensure everyone from associate to executive was able to identify gaps in a client's portfolio.

- **Change management.** Increasingly, L&D teams are pulled into organizational change initiatives both directly and as consultants. They have to tap into L&D principles and philosophies, like adult learning theory, and apply them in managing change. In particular, connecting the relevance of the change to the individual is critical. It's the "so what?" that helps to drive the change in the organization, and L&D teams know how to convey this in a way that is organic to employees and learners.

- **Professional development.** I can personally attest to the opportunity for a seamless transition from L&D to OD. Over my career, I've gone from corporate trainer and manager of L&D to talent and OD consultant and, most recently, to senior manager of OD. There are many transferable skills and tangential knowledge, which make it a much smaller leap than you may think. And because of the broad scope that OD encompasses, you'll have plenty of new avenues and disciplines to explore. One of the goals of this book is to show you how you can transfer these skills and knowledge.

What's in This Book

ATD and I have collected a superb group of in-house experts and consultants from the OD field itself as well as those who crossed over from L&D to OD. Thanks to their rich contributions and varied experiences, the book goes beyond the theoretical information on how to use OD strategies and structures. You'll explore the actual foundational stepping stones of OD and how to apply those to multiculturalism, upskilling and reskilling, soft skill development, team development, succession planning, and other OD programs. In addition, the book lays out how OD and L&D differ, the business knowledge you deeply need to be an outstanding OD practitioner, how to measure and evaluate each program, the tools needed to do so, and how to learn through failure.

We've organized the book into four broad parts:

- **Part 1. The Foundations of Organization Development**—how to put OD principles into action and develop organizational values that elevate the importance of diversity, equity, inclusion, and belonging and employee well-being.
- **Part 2. Organizational Design**—how to design an organization that meets the business objectives, introduce new processes and methods of working, engage the workforce, and manage change.
- **Part 3. Workforce Design**—how to build a global pipeline of talent, support work in a remote environment, and find skills solutions to workforce challenges.
- **Part 4. Leadership Preparedness**—how to develop leaders and teams and the importance of comprehensive and integrated succession planning efforts.

I hope you'll enjoy learning about OD from this book as much as I have enjoyed working on this project with my esteemed colleagues. I can tell you that for whatever reason you've chosen to pick up this handbook, and whatever made you curious about organization development, you're sure to find enough knowledge in here to get started.

PART 1

The Foundations of Organization Development

Foundations of Organization Development

ED HASAN

IN THIS CHAPTER

♦ Describe the placement of OD on the organization chart

♦ Address how OD practitioners work with interpersonal interactions to help achieve change results

♦ Summarize how the responsibilities of the OD function are identified

♦ Review the advantages and disadvantages of OD consultants working externally or internally

Introduction

Imagine that you have been experiencing nonstop headaches for several weeks. You decide to visit the doctor with the hopes of finding out the cause and, hopefully, a cure. The doctor spends 10 minutes asking generic questions about your health and stress levels but does not draw blood or run any tests. The doctor seems hurried and doesn't spend time building a relationship with you or getting to know your overall history.

Your answers indicate some work- and family-related stress in your life. The doctor says you look healthy and that stress could affect you without realizing it. The doctor has seen several recent patients who have also been having stress-induced headaches due to the state of the economy and other world events. Therefore, the doctor recommends you monitor your stress levels and take acetaminophen when the headaches occur.

Let's reflect on this scenario:

- Did the doctor attempt to treat your symptoms (the headache) or the root cause (what is causing the headache)?
- Is prescribing acetaminophen alleviating the symptom but covering up a more serious condition?
- Should the doctor have run more tests?
- Is it okay to assume that just because stress has affected some patients it must be affecting you?
- Was the doctor biased based on previous patients?

Do you agree that the doctor focused on the symptom but not the root cause? The doctor's solution (acetaminophen) could be covering up something more serious that's actually causing the headaches. In addition, the diagnosis may have been biased due to the assumptions made based on previous patients. Let's hope this scenario never happens when visiting your doctor, but misdiagnosis is consequential and could worsen an illness, have a long-term impact on quality of life, or result in death.

Unfortunately, when it comes to organizations, focusing on the symptoms of an issue rather than the root cause is prevalent, which can be understandable. The OD process is systematic and exploratory in nature, and discovering the root cause of an organization's issue requires time and patience. The root cause could be a deeply embedded, systemic cultural issue that is not easily seen, or it could be an ineffective CEO or leadership team, poorly defined goals, or lack of infrastructure and tools. Conversely, symptoms of an organization's issue—high employee turnover, low morale, burnout, absenteeism, or lack of employee engagement, for example—are often evident and easy to point out. Up and down the organizational chart, in an earnest attempt at solving problems, people will jump at what appears to be the easiest, fastest, and cheapest solution to a problem. However, without proper research and understanding of the issue, this may result in little to no changes or could even compound the issue. In fact, misdiagnosis is not only costly in terms of time wasted, but it could also affect employee morale, lead to employee turnover, or even result in closure. However, with stronger knowledge and skills in organization development, those tasked with addressing the most critical organizational problems, such as L&D professionals, can better set up their organizations for success. Therefore, it is imperative to understand what organization development is and how OD experts support organizations.

What Is Organization Development?

You will find many definitions for organization development. The Association for Talent Development defines *OD* as "an effort that focuses on improving an organization's capability through the alignment of strategy, structure, people, rewards, metrics, and management processes" and "involves an ongoing, systematic, long-range process of driving organizational effectiveness, solving problems, and improving organizational performance."

We can then extrapolate from this definition and state that OD could include the process of identifying the root cause of an issue and correcting it through a series of initiatives (Aaronson and Hasan 2018). Another way to view OD is through the effort of conducting a gap analysis—that is evaluating the gap between an organization's current state (such as low revenue or poor performance) and desired state (such as, high revenue or positive performance) and implementing an initiative to address the root cause (Clark and Estes 2008; Aaronson and Hasan 2018).

Similar to the patient analogy that was used in the chapter opening, organizations often try to implement an initiative to correct an issue's symptoms rather than assess the root cause. For example:

- Increasing pay as a way to combat high turnover
- Adding team activities and throwing company parties to boost employee morale
- Hiring more diverse individuals as quickly as possible in response to diversity and inclusion challenges, but failing to launch any inclusion initiatives

While these efforts might alleviate the symptom temporarily, they're often not enough and the symptom will reemerge. Unfortunately, this also leads to frustration from organizational leaders who don't understand why the efforts failed to deliver. As an L&D professional tasked with doing OD work or who may want to become an OD professional, it is essential to clearly define and understand OD so that you can implement initiatives that lead to successful change.

Contributing Disciplines of Organization Development

The fascinating part about the OD discipline is that it is an amalgamation of several other disciplines:

- Psychology, which is the study of human behavior
- Sociology, which is the study of society, relationships, and interactions
- Anthropology, which is the study of human beings vis-à-vis culture, social interactions, and environment
- Organizational behavior, which is the study of how people interact in organizations

Phases of the Organization Development Process

The OD process has five phases: entry, diagnosis, feedback, solution, and evaluation (Figure 1-1). However, before we review each stage, here are four things to remember:

- **Never skip or speed through a phase.** It does not matter if someone is rushing you to get the job done, if you think you have a handle on the problem and it's safe to skip steps, or if you become impatient and just want to move on. It is imperative to honor each phase to its fullest. Quite simply, you don't know what you don't know, which can be detrimental to the process.

- **Whether you are an internal or external consultant, you still need to observe all phases of the OD process** (Anderson 2019). For example, Phase 1: Entry may seem superfluous for internal consultants; however, it is a critical step to ensure that all stakeholders are on the same page.
- **Never stop at Phase 4: Solution.** Implementing various initiatives to correct a problem and simply walking away is not enough. They need to be evaluated constantly for efficacy.
- **Leading the OD process can be a time consuming and emotionally draining experience.** If you aren't careful, the pressure of the OD process could lead to frustration, stress, and burnout. You may constantly be pressured to speed up the process, quickly implement initiatives, or demonstrate immediate results. Moreover, you are invoking change that will affect people's jobs in some way, shape, or form. Even if the changes are for the betterment of the organization, people are not always receptive and may push back. Therefore, remember to pace yourself, stick to your game plan, remember the bigger picture, and don't take things personally.

Figure 1-1. Organization Development Strategy: Five Phases to Designing and Implementing

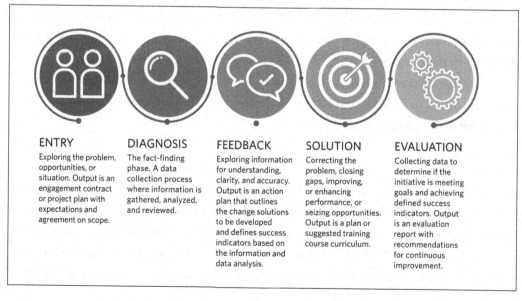

ENTRY
Exploring the problem, opportunities, or situation. Output is an engagement contract or project plan with expectations and agreement on scope.

DIAGNOSIS
The fact-finding phase. A data collection process where information is gathered, analyzed, and reviewed.

FEEDBACK
Exploring information for understanding, clarity, and accuracy. Output is an action plan that outlines the change solutions to be developed and defines success indicators based on the information and data analysis.

SOLUTION
Correcting the problem, closing gaps, improving, or enhancing performance, or seizing opportunities. Output is a plan or suggested training course curriculum.

EVALUATION
Collecting data to determine if the initiative is meeting goals and achieving defined success indicators. Output is an evaluation report with recommendations for continuous improvement.

Phase 1: Entry

The entry phase is critical because it lays the foundation for the subsequent phases and is when you learn about your client's needs and culture. Moreover, this is an opportunity for you to clearly understand and define the company's problem (or assumed problem).

A good trick is to try your best to define the problem in one or two clear sentences. For example, "The company is experiencing high employee turnover, which is affecting our ability to fulfill customer requests." If the problem statement is unclear, lengthy, or amorphous, you will run into issues in the later phases. It is also imperative for the client to review and agree with the problem statement, which leads us to a key component of the entry phase: documentation.

Create a document that clearly articulates the problem statement, the client's expectations and needs, your responsibilities, the client's responsibilities, a data gathering strategy, deliverables and deadlines, a project timeline, and other items. You should view this document as a contract that ensures a mutual understanding between you and the client of the project's goals. You and the client should also sign the document as evidence that it was reviewed and approved (Anderson 2019).

Phase 2: Diagnosis

The diagnosis phase is a fact-finding mission. At this phase, you decide on the data collection strategy and then collect and analyze data. The aim is to collect data to help assess the root causes of your problem statement from phase 1. Therefore, ensure that the data collection strategy is aligned with the problem statement.

During the diagnosis phase, you must be unbiased, disinterested, and unequivocally objective (don't forget the doctor scenario earlier in this chapter). We will discuss this phase in more detail in the data gathering section.

Phase 3: Feedback

The feedback phase is essentially a touchpoint. This is when you provide a status update for the project, including accomplishments and challenges and, most important, the results from phase 2. Phase 3 is also an inflection point because the client becomes accountable for the data you've provided. Moreover, the client should use the data you provide and partner with you to create solutions that mitigate or eliminate the root cause of the problem, as well as create key performance indicators (KPIs) that assess whether those solutions are on the right track to success.

Phase 4: Solution

People often want to jump straight to the solution phase because it involves taking immediate action to correct a problem. However, if they do, their solution often fails because the other phases were not observed. At this stage, you implement targeted initiatives designed to mitigate or eliminate the problem's root causes, close gaps, or eliminate barriers to success.

Phase 5: Evaluation

The evaluation phase is the final step. At this phase, you assess whether the initiative implemented in phase 4 was successful or is heading in the right direction by reviewing the KPIs. It is important to note that this phase is constant and not an action that occurs at a single point in time. Instead, you should evaluate the efficacy of the initiatives using different metrics or milestones at multiple points in time.

Data Gathering

Let's focus on Phase 2: Diagnosis, which is when data gathering occurs. Data gathering is key to making decisions based on empirical data, called *data driven decision making* (DDDM; Stobierski 2019). DDDM is an objective process that allows you to make decisions based on facts rather than conjecture or anecdotal evidence.

Think back to the doctor scenario provided in the introduction of this chapter. Did the doctor determine the cause of your headache using DDDM or conjecture? Moreover, did the doctor collect enough data before determining the issue? Had the doctor leveraged DDDM correctly, five initial steps would have been followed:

1. Collect initial information from the client and obtain a clear problem statement.
2. Collect data from the client through a series of tests.
3. Evaluate and interpret the data.
4. Provide a determination of the root causes based on the data collected.
5. Provide feedback and offer remedies based on the data.

For OD practitioners, the "series of tests" are the tools used to collect data, such as interviews, focus groups, surveys, questionnaires, and observations (Table 1-1). You can use one tool or a combination of several; each tool has its advantages and disadvantages. No matter which tool you select, it is critical to align your questions with the problem statement you formalized in phase 1.

Table 1-1. Data Collection Tools

	Approach	Setting	Advantages	Disadvantages
Interview	The consultant asks the participant a series of questions analogous to a job interview. Ideally, questions are prepared in advance so the consultant can modify them if needed.	• Face-to-face (preferred) • Virtual	• In-depth, meaningful conversations • Follow-up questions • More personalized approach • Obtaining verbal and nonverbal communication	• Time consuming • Resource intensive • Expensive • Lack of confidentially • Interviewer's biases
Focus groups	The consultant asks a group of participants a series of questions. Ideally, the questions are prepared in advance so the consultant can modify them if needed.	• Face-to-face (preferred) • Virtual	• Collect information from a group rather than an individual • More efficient • Follow-up questions • Participant dialogue and collaboration	• Somewhat time consuming • Somewhat expensive • Lack of anonymity • Unbalanced speaking times and participant contribution • Interviewer's biases
Surveys and questionnaires	The consultant distributes a survey containing a series of questions to participants. The questions are prepared before distribution and can't be modified after distribution.	• Internet based • Paper based (less likely)	• Less expensive • Easier to administer • Statistical analysis • More confidential • More anonymous • Target larger groups	• Not as in-depth • Not conversational • Not personalized • Lower response rate • Incorrect interpretation of questions
Observations	The consultant observes the participant's actions and behaviors in a natural setting.	• In person (in the participant's work environment)	• Natural setting • More context • In-depth understanding of the process • Build relationships	• Participants may change their behavior (Hawthorne Effect) • Observer's biases • Not effective with larger groups • Less control • Over generalizations

Adapted from Anderson (2019) and Michigan.Gov (n.d.).

Solutions

The solution phase is when specific actions are taken to mitigate or eliminate an organization's root problem. Possible solutions include 360-degree feedback, assessments, coaching, confrontation meetings, education, job aids, job redesign, mentoring, reorganization, role analysis, team building, and training (Anderson 2019; Clark and Estes 2008; Hasan and Adeleye 2021).

There are four things to remember about the solution phase:

- Jumping straight to the solution phase could do more harm than good, as you may be operating under faulty assumptions or unsubstantiated data.
- Don't fixate on a single solution—a one-size-fits-all approach is ineffective (Aaronson and Hasan 2018). Instead, view each initiative as a different tool in your toolbox. Just because a solution effectively fixed one issue does not mean it can effectively resolve all problems. Therefore, it's important to remember that you may be biased toward a particular solution, approach, or tool. Finally, while training is critical, it is not a universal tool for solving all issues.
- As an OD consultant or advisor, you should not be expected to implement initiatives independently; instead, this is a joint effort between you, the company, and the employees (Anderson 2019). As such, key stakeholders must buy into the proposed initiatives and be accountable for implementation. If you are working independently without the appropriate support, you must speak up because failure is imminent.
- Implementing initiatives will invoke change, which people won't always like and may resist. Resistance to change occurs for several reasons, including fear of the unknown, a feeling of loss of control, comfort with the status quo, lack of understanding of why change is needed, and change fatigue (Anderson 2019).

Solutions generally occur at three levels:

- Individual initiatives target one person and support their individual growth and development.
- Team initiatives target a department or group of people and support their growth and development.
- Organization initiatives target the entire organization to support its growth and development (Anderson 2019).

However, rather than viewing them in terms of levels, ATD compartmentalizes OD initiatives into four categories: human process, techno-structural, human resource management, and strategic (Figure 1-2).

Real-World Case Study

To demonstrate the importance of going through all five phases of the organization development process, I want to share a case study of a company where an OD initiative produced short-term improvements but failed to deliver lasting results.

Background

Company XYZ, a California-based tech company, has around 80 employees. The organization's makeup is primarily homogeneous with little representation from different races

Figure 1-2. Organization Development Initiatives: Four Typical Categories

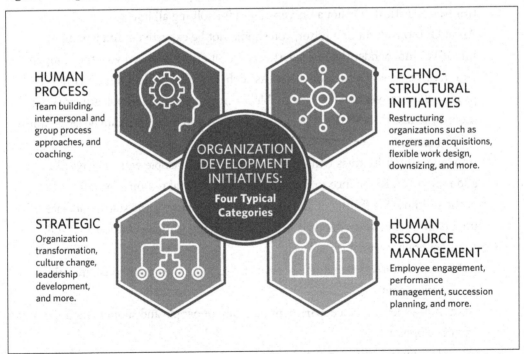

HUMAN PROCESS
Team building, interpersonal and group process approaches, and coaching.

TECHNO-STRUCTURAL INITIATIVES
Restructuring organizations such as mergers and acquisitions, flexible work design, downsizing, and more.

ORGANIZATION DEVELOPMENT INITIATIVES:
Four Typical Categories

STRATEGIC
Organization transformation, culture change, leadership development, and more.

HUMAN RESOURCE MANAGEMENT
Employee engagement, performance management, succession planning, and more.

and cultures. Moreover, the company has a high turnover rate, specifically with underrepresented minorities, which is particularly alarming.

When the new HR director was hired 18 months ago, she was perplexed as to why the organization lacked the diversity that represented the makeup of the local community. After several weeks on the job, the HR director met with the CEO to request an initiative for the company to become more diverse. The CEO, who had a reputation for being too profit-focused, initially pushed back on the notion of the organization not being diverse enough. Moreover, the CEO feared that the diversity initiative would take away focus from the company's other business needs. However, the CEO hesitantly agreed to the initiative due to fear of discouraging the HR director and to avoid the optics of not supporting diversity in the workplace.

Solution

Based on experience, the HR director knew that the organization needed to adjust its approach to recruitment if it hoped to hire more diverse employees. Accordingly, she made the following adjustments:

- Updated the company's careers page to give off a more diverse feel
- Added language in the job postings about the importance of diversity
- Posted positions on job boards that were known for their diverse job applicants

Short-Term Result

The initiative to become a more diverse company by adjusting its recruitment strategy was successful. In fact, within five months of implementation, the company hired more diverse candidates than ever. Much to the satisfaction of the HR director, the company was finally becoming more diverse.

Long-Term Result

Unfortunately, within 12 months of implementing the initiative, the strategy seemed to falter. While the company successfully recruited candidates from various racial and ethnic backgrounds, the turnover rate of those employees was still abnormally high. In other words, the company could hire diverse candidates but not retain them over the long run.

Evaluation

The HR director was dismayed and confused about why the company could not retain employees from different cultures. After weeks of reflection, the HR director decided to reach out to a colleague who was an OD specialist. During their conversation, they addressed several questions. Here is how it went:

> **OD Expert:** What was the core issue you were trying to solve?

> **HR Director:** The company had trouble hiring and retaining diverse employees.

> **OD Expert:** Did you collect any data on why the company was having issues?

> **HR Director:** No, not really. I used my past experiences and consulted with some hiring managers. I mean, it was pretty apparent that we were terrible at recruitment.

> **OD Expert:** OK, based on your opinion, what was the root cause of the issue?

> **HR Director:** We did a poor job at recruiting diverse individuals.

> **OD Expert:** That could answer the recruitment portion of your issue, but what is causing the turnover? In any case, what did you do to fix the recruitment problem?

> **HR Director:** I updated the company's careers page to reflect diversity, added language to job postings about the importance of diversity, and posted positions on diverse job boards.

> **OD Expert:** So, you fixed the recruitment issue but not the retention issue.

> **HR Director:** What do you mean?

OD Expert: Your initiative focused on the issue of recruitment and not retention. So, you were successful in hiring but could not retain them for some reason. The question is, why can't you retain them?

HR Director: That is a good point.

OD Expert: Tell me about the company's culture. Is it inclusive, and does it make everyone feel welcome?

HR Director: Absolutely, we have one of the most inclusive cultures I have ever seen.

OD Expert: OK, great, so these individuals who resigned, what did their exit interviews reveal to you?

HR Director: Our exit interviews are pretty generic. It is more of a checklist of items needed before the employee leaves and answers questions the employee may have.

OD Expert: So, there are no questions about their overall experience? For example, how their managers treat them, their view on the company's culture, and if they believe the company is inclusive or welcoming of their diverse backgrounds.

HR Director: *Sighs.* No.

OD Expert: OK, tell me about your current employees. Did you interview any of them and ask for their opinion about the company's culture? Do you conduct stay interviews?

HR Director: I mean, I talk to employees pretty consistently, but it is nothing formal. No, we don't do stay interviews.

OD Expert: So how do you know the issue isn't the culture or management?

HR Director: I just don't think the culture is the issue. Based on my experience with the CEO, management could be the issue, but I am not sure. There were some rumblings of unfair treatment toward certain employees, but no one ever complained directly to me.

Commentary

There is a parallel between the case study and the story shared at the beginning of the chapter. The doctor did not go through the appropriate steps to assess the root cause of the patient's ailment. Similarly, the HR director did not go through the proper steps to evaluate the root cause of the company's inability to recruit and retain diverse individuals. In both cases, the parties implemented an initiative based on assumptions; however, neither party validated their beliefs through data collection methods. In the end, DDDM was not used to determine the root cause and appropriate solutions. Therefore, both scenarios serve as a reminder that fixing the symptoms may only offer short-term results; however, fixing the root cause increases the probability of long-term success.

Summary

As this chapter noted, organization development is a multifaceted domain that comprises five phases—entry, diagnosis, feedback, solution, and evaluation—with a feedback loop. Each stage is critical to the OD process. Although rewarding, leading an OD process is a high-stakes endeavor that invariably involves people and change, which can be time consuming and emotionally draining.

Key Takeaways

Here are a few things to remind yourself of throughout your OD journey:

- **Focus on discovering the root cause of the organization's issue and not getting distracted by the symptoms.** Keep in mind that it is often more convenient to focus on the symptoms because they are often easy to point out, while the root cause of those symptoms isn't obvious and requires patience to bring to light.

- **Avoid skipping any of the five phases of the OD process.** You may get impatient with a particular phase or pressured by the client to rush the process. Moreover, people often jump to the solutions (phase 4) or fail to evaluate the efficacy of initiatives (phase 5). However, observing all five phases of the OD process is essential.

- **Leverage data-driven decision making.** It is essential to make decisions that are based on actual data rather than conjecture or opinions that may be biased. Otherwise, you may make consequential decisions based on inaccurate information.

- **Remember that there isn't a one-size-fits-all initiative that will fix an organization's issue.** Therefore, be careful not to bias yourself toward a particular initiative, and remember that there is a toolbox of initiatives you could implement to correct a problem.

- **Refrain from implementing initiatives on your own.** Implementing initiatives should be a collaborative effort between you and key stakeholders.

Working Inside and Outside the Organization

WILLIAM J. ROTHWELL

IN THIS CHAPTER

♦ Examine the placement of OD on the organization chart

♦ Review how OD consultants manage organizational politics

♦ Manage OD strategically and tactically

Overview

This chapter focuses on organization development (OD) and its placement on the organization chart. It also addresses how OD practitioners work with the white space—that is, interpersonal interactions—to achieve change results. Some call that organizational politics. Whether the topic is on the positioning of OD on the formal organization chart or its positioning in the informal social network that makes up the political infrastructure of the organization, both concern how OD works with, or around, the organization's command structure.

How is OD positioned on the organization chart? How can OD be managed strategically and tactically? How are the OD department's responsibilities established? How do organizational politics affect OD? What ways other than political action can work in, or around, the organization chart? What advantages and disadvantages are experienced by external and internal consultants? How can internal and external OD consultants work together? This chapter tackles these and other important questions.

Opening Vignettes: Internal Versus External OD Consultants

Let's first review two compelling vignettes to dramatize challenges faced by internal and external OD consultants.

Vignette 1

A large organization's leaders wanted to resolve conflicts between two work teams that served different geographical groups with the same insurance products. The two teams were taken off-site to a local resort for a weekend. An OD consultant from the organization called the two teams together and gave them each a flipchart. They were then asked to go to a breakout room and write down everything the team thought or felt about the other team. When they were finished, the teams came back to the main room to debrief. This was the beginning of a confrontation meeting intended to identify and address lingering issues facing the two teams.

Internal OD consultants can do confrontation meetings because they know the corporate culture and can appreciate, and work to address, cross-team politics.

Vignette 2

A large organization's leaders decided that the company needed a succession plan because most of the senior executive team was eligible to retire within two years, and their direct reports were also eligible to retire within three years. The organization's CEO brought in an external OD consultant to help the organization formulate and implement a succession plan. The CEO did not want a "cookie cutter approach"; rather, she wanted a succession plan uniquely crafted to meet the organization's needs. She wanted an OD consultant from outside the company who had worked on other succession programs to serve as a facilitator.

External OD consultants can help leaders think through their own solutions to problems—and also can, when asked, provide insights from other organizations that have faced similar issues.

Positioning OD in the Organization

Organization development may be applied by external consultants, internal consultants, and (with proper training) managers or even workers. While anyone with proper training can apply OD principles, placing an OD department or function is important for establishing the change efforts in which it is typically involved.

Organization Development Conducted by External Consultants

External consultants do not enjoy placement on the organization chart. They are usually hired on a project basis to facilitate solutions to identified problems or build on organizational strategic strengths.

Most external consultants are independent contractors or vendors. Some may work with captured companies, which are tied by contract to the organization they're providing services to. Others may be individual consultants who work on their own or in partnership with other consultants. Some OD consultants are employed by large consulting firms such as Accenture, Deloitte, or Development Dimensions International (DDI).

External OD consultants are typically given a single point of contact, a liaison, inside the organization. They are usually hired for their specialized expertise with a type of change effort—such as corporate restructuring, team building, succession planning, coaching, or implementing large-scale technology solutions.

As a simple example related to L&D, an organization's leaders wanting to implement a leadership development program could bring in an external consultant for that purpose. External consultants are thought to provide a more objective approach than internal consultants.

External consultants enjoy advantages and disadvantages over internal consultants:

- **Advantages**
  - External consultants often have immediate access to the top of the organization; this may not be possible for internal OD consultants who must follow the chain of command to get access to the CEO and their direct reports.
  - They often have the credibility that comes from the perception that they have seen how other organizations have grappled with the same problems facing the current client organization.

- ○ They are perceived as less subject to the organization's internal politics because they don't have to "take sides" or fall under the influence of canny organizational politicians.
- **Disadvantages**
  - ○ External consultants do not always work with the organization for the full duration to implement strategic solutions (which can take many years), so they may not be able to facilitate course corrections during implementation.
  - ○ They rarely know the politics of the organization and may fall victim to traps set by savvy leaders who try to turn change efforts to their personal advantage.
  - ○ They may be cast as too theoretical. (I have heard people say, "I do not want to work with those OD eggheads or ivory tower types.")
  - ○ They may be cast as mere mercenaries hired by senior executives to do their bidding—even if their bidding is harmful to others or does not make sense to employees. (I have heard people say, "I do not trust those OD people because their fees are paid by leaders whose motives are driven by nothing more than a desire to get a big annual bonus even if change efforts bankrupt the company or anger customers.")

They may not know the business or industry, the command structure, the work processes, or the challenges faced by managers and employees in the organization. It can take too long to orient them to the organization, which also costs money.

Organization Development Conducted by Internal Consultants

Internal consultants are employed by the organization. When the OD senior leader independently reports to the CEO, the OD department typically enjoys a status equal to human resources. However, this can prompt conflict if the duties and responsibilities of the OD and HR departments are not clearly delineated.

Internal OD departments may exist within HR, within or combined with L&D, or else be placed within an operating division, such as production, marketing, finance, IT, or engineering. When OD is combined with another organizational unit, its priorities are shaped by the group with which it is placed. For instance, if OD is placed within HR, then operating managers and employees may associate OD with HR—which can be positive or negative, depending on the reputation of HR in that organization.

If OD is placed with L&D, it may cause confusion about the difference between talent development efforts geared to changing individuals (by equipping them with new knowledge, skills, and attitudes through training) and OD efforts geared to changing individuals, groups, departments, divisions, or the whole organization (by equipping people with new norms and cultural interaction patterns). If OD and L&D are combined, then managers and employees may have trouble telling them apart, which can weaken or confuse the brand of either or both.

As a simple example related to L&D, an organization's leaders wanting to implement a leadership development program could rely on the L&D function as internal consultants to spearhead that effort.

Internal consultants enjoy some advantages over external consultants. They also suffer from some disadvantages not experienced by external consultants:

- **Advantages**
  - Internal consultants should already know the industry and corporate culture. They do not require extensive orientation to understand the issues.
  - They should already know the work processes and understand the workflow issues.
  - They should already know key decision makers and their agendas.
  - They usually report to a manager in another area (like the VP of HR) who is not under the authority of the client manager of the department or division the internal consultant is working with. That can be a distinct advantage.
  - They already have a track record within the organization. If they are perceived to be effective, then managers are confident in their abilities. External consultants may have to prove themselves—and that takes time and costs money.

- **Disadvantages**
  - Internal consultants may face pressure to use their department budgets to pay for expenses associated with organizational change efforts—including those that should be paid for by other departments who are their clients.

- They must deal with the bureaucratic chain of command and may have to get permission to act—but this takes time if they have to ask for permission for routine change activities.
- They may not enjoy the credibility of external consultants. (Sometimes there is an unspoken assumption that "you can't possibly be any good if you work for us." That is the counterbalance to "whatever you propose cannot work if it was not invented here.")
- Their credibility may be suspect. Operating managers may think they have more expertise in dealing with change issues than consultants, not realizing that OD requires special competencies of its own.
- They are bound to the corporate culture and group norms in ways that external consultants are not. External consultants, because they are outsiders, can get away with behaviors that may not be permitted or tolerated from internal consultants.

Oganization Development Conducted by a Team of Internal and External Consultants

Often the most desirable situation is for internal and external OD consultants to work together on the same change effort. They can enjoy synergy that is more than the sum of their individual parts. Internal consultants can offset the disadvantages faced by external consultants; likewise, external consultants can offset the disadvantages faced by internal consultants.

Both internal and external OD practitioners must demonstrate the competencies essential to success in the field (Cady and Shoup 2015; Global OD competency framework). Internal consultants must be good at developing and communicating a compelling message about what needs the OD department is addressing; external consultants must be good at finding a niche market to serve and then leverage their social media and word-of-mouth efforts to discover clients.

As a simple example related to L&D, an organization's leaders wanting to implement a leadership development program could parse out activities between the internal L&D function and one or more external consultants.

Using internal and external consultants brings its own advantages and disadvantages:

- **Advantages**
  - External consultants can get immediate access to the top of the organization chart while internal consultants can stick with the change effort.

- ° External consultants bring the credibility associated with experience in other organizations; internal consultants bring the credibility associated with experience in the client organization.
- ° External consultants may know managers from other organizations who can give testimony to the results achieved by solving problems in a certain way; internal consultants may know which managers are most likely to support a change effort to gain positive visibility or improve their promotion prospects.
- ° External consultants can bring glamor to change efforts because they may dress better or be more articulate than those inside the organization; internal consultants ground the change in the existing corporate culture and group norms.

- **Disadvantages**
  - ° Managers will question the cost of using two consultants rather than only one. They will ask if it is necessary.
  - ° Managers may try to play the external consultant against the internal consultant—or vice versa. This is a political strategy to slow down or halt a change effort.
  - ° An internal consultant might try to overshadow the external consultant out of fear they will be fired in favor of the outsider.
  - ° The external consultant might try to overshadow the internal consultant out of a genuine desire to replace them as a full-time employee with a better pay and benefits package than the consulting firm offers.
  - ° Trust issues may cause trouble in the relationship, and thus affect the impact of the external and internal consultant relationship.

Organization Development Conducted by Operating Managers

Operating managers can also apply the theories and techniques of organization development (Varney 1977). They can do this with or without assistance from external or internal consultants from outside their sphere of responsibility. Operating managers applying OD enjoy the advantage of close contact with those involved in the change effort. But there is one major reason literature on OD has traditionally emphasized the use of consultants:

People will not always tell their immediate supervisors the truth, but they may tell outsiders. Workers naturally fear the consequences of speaking truth to power or else admitting their own culpability in organizational problems. Consultants may thus discover information that may otherwise escape managers seeking such information.

As a simple example related to L&D, an organization's leaders wanting to implement a leadership development program could form a task force of operating managers to work on the program. While that group of operating managers may draw on help from internal and external consultants, they would take command of the change effort in addition to their daily work.

Organization Development Conducted by Employees

Employees can apply OD methods after they've been trained in OD. Employees enjoy close contact with organizational change efforts—and with customers, immediate supervisors, co-workers, and others with a stake in change efforts. However, not all employees want to facilitate change—they may not agree with the direction of the change; they may be reluctant to voice their reservations and authentic feelings about the change; they may lack the training to help a group agree on problems, solutions, or strengths; or they may wish to keep their own views to themselves while trying to exit an organization undergoing change.

As a simple example related to L&D, an organization's leaders wanting to implement a leadership development program could form a task force of workers to work on the program. While that group of workers might be ill-equipped for the project, they could rely on the assistance of internal and external consultants who could brief them on what to do and facilitate their efforts. Designing a learning program could be managed as an action learning project and could develop workers while simultaneously securing business results (Rothwell 1999).

Strategic Versus Tactical Organization Development

In common parlance, an OD department or function that reports directly to the CEO is called *Big OD* or *Strategic OD*. OD that reports directly to the VP of HR or some other company officer below CEO is called *Little OD* or *Tactical OD*.

Big OD has a focus outside the organization and may deal with mergers, acquisitions, takeovers, and other large-scale efforts that take years to implement successfully. Little OD focuses inside the organization and may deal with change efforts of shorter duration.

When an organization has multiple OD departments, they're often focused on different geographic locations (such as China and US or North America and South America), functions (such as IT or engineering), or specific change efforts (such as overseeing health and safety efforts or implementing an enterprise resource program).

OD can be positioned in many ways on an organization chart. Figure 2-1 illustrates what different organizational placements might look like.

Figure 2-1. Examples of Different Placements of the OD Function

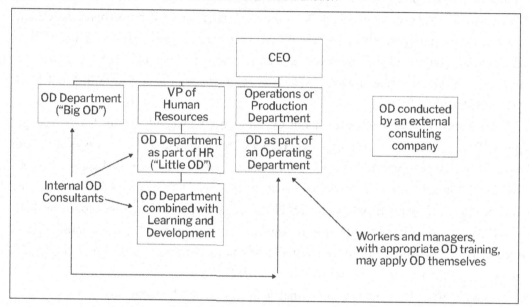

Establishing the OD Department's Responsibilities

I once asked an OD manager in China what his OD department was responsible for. His answer was amusing. He said, "We do whatever we are told to do."

OD practitioners are often asked, "What does the OD department actually *do?*" Many people tasked to set up an OD department from scratch often crave information about how the role of an OD department differs from HR and other fields of practice. They might struggle with the difference between *organization development* and *organization design*. Adding to the confusion is that some OD practitioners specialize in helping their organizations restructure and thus perform work in organization design. Organization design is, of course, the field of practice focused on how to organize (and structure) work and the chain of command. OD is the field of practice centered on humanistic approaches to *facilitating* change.

Using needs assessments, L&D professionals can distinguish between learning needs and learning wants. This allows them to separate training from management issues and create a foundation for establishing learning objectives for planned learning experiences (Rothwell et al. 2016).

But organizational diagnosis in OD works differently from training needs assessments. In OD, the stakeholders (not consultants) shoulder all the responsibility. OD professionals typically facilitate a process by which organizational stakeholders identify their own organizational problems (separating them from the symptoms) and prioritize them for action. They also help stakeholders identify their own solutions, prioritize them, establish action plans for implementation, and create measurable objectives to guide the change effort (Rothwell, Stopper, and Myers 2017).

Managers everywhere often ask about the difference between OD and change management. While OD and change management overlap, *organization development* is associated with bottom-up change in which those affected by change have a major say in shaping decisions. But *change management* is akin to project management in which the primary focus is on setting and meeting deadlines, achieving project goals, and keeping project expenses at or below budget. OD emphasizes involving people in change, encouraging support, and creating opportunities for participation to reduce resistance to change. Change management emphasizes achieving project results at all costs (Smith et al. 2014).

A simple example would help to dramatize the difference. If a company is losing money, management may want to cut costs. Change management would call for senior leaders to draw up a list of what costs to cut, which they could hand off to a change manager. The change manager would then implement the changes by applying a project plan. This approach would likely see a high level of resistance to cost cutting. But the goal is to quickly get the cost cutting change effort implemented, regardless of resistance.

On the other hand, OD would approach this problem in a unique way. OD consultants might take workers off-site so senior leaders could explain the crisis confronting the organization and why it necessitates cost cutting. Then the OD consultants could facilitate a process by which managers and workers identify a list of cost cutting measures and when and how to implement them. While nobody enjoys cost cutting, this facilitated approach typically garners more support from managers and workers than the change management approach.

The portfolio of responsibilities handed to the OD department may include:

- Facilitating mergers, acquisitions, and takeovers
- Implementing enterprise resource programs (ERPs) such as Oracle, Peoplesoft, or SAP
- Implementing executive succession planning
- Implementing integrated and comprehensive talent management programs
- Facilitating organizational restructuring
- Spearheading downsizing efforts
- Facilitating strategic planning
- Providing support to managers involved in major business startups or shutdowns

When OD reports to the VP of human resources, the focus is more often on the innerworkings of the organization. OD in HR may be handed such assignments as teambuilding for work groups, resolving management or work group conflicts, coaching executives, using instruments (such as MBTI, Disc, or others), or administering surveys centered on engagement or climate. Internal OD consultants often focus on creating and sustaining corporate culture change.

How Organizational Politics Affects OD

Politics, what some might call the white space outside the normal boxes and lines on the organization chart, is about the exercise of power. For some people, it is a provocative word that's spoken in disgust when someone's selfish interest is shown to trump reason, logic, or the best interests of the organization. Politics is about getting and keeping power, and it is a fact of organizational life. It is always present in change efforts, and to ignore it is to see change efforts fail. Change can threaten vested power interests, and that is (often) the simple reason that most change efforts fail. OD practitioners need to pay attention to the impact of change on stakeholders and what steps those stakeholders might take to preserve their power and their staff, budget, job title, or other resources. Thus, they must both understand the politics of their organization and be well equipped to navigate it.

Michael Jarrett (2017) groups organizational politics into four metaphors—the weeds, the rocks, the high ground, and the woods—which are helpful in conceptualizing how to navigate them:

- **The weeds** refer to informal groups of people who form around shared interests. These groups can act to further change efforts—or block them.

- **The rocks** refer to how people interact and how symbols of status (like job titles) can influence organizational actions. Using the rocks in a change effort might involve forming task forces to study an issue, which can help build a change impetus or delay a change idea for so long that it suffers a quiet death.
- **The high ground** refers to how organizational rules, policies, procedures, and other relics for control are used. Sometimes bureaucracy can be used to demonstrate the need for change based on a change in policies, procedures, or other control mechanisms. Bureaucracy may rely on policies, procedures, or rules to help or hinder change efforts.
- **The woods** refer to the power of the unspoken norms and rules of behavior governing the organization. What interactions are permitted, and what interactions are frowned upon? For instance, is it acceptable for a manager to go to lunch with a direct report? Norms may help or hinder change, and learning those norms is important in fostering (or impeding) change. (I was once reprimanded by an operating manager for sending out a survey because I didn't ask his permission first. It didn't matter that I had the CEO's permission.)

Practical Advice to OD Practitioners on Managing Politics

Politics is about influence. Who can influence others? People with perceived power can exert leadership in ways that those of lower status or power cannot. Organizational politics stems from many feelings. Among them are an unwillingness to work, an unwillingness to adjust to change, personal relationships (who likes whom), jealousy, lack of trust, and struggles for rewards or promotions (Bhasin 2021).

OD practitioners must cope with the traditional organization (as depicted on the organization chart and in relics such as job descriptions and planning documents) and the political organization. Professional OD training does an excellent job of preparing people to deal with traditional organizations but is less effective in preparing OD practitioners to deal with organizational politics. This often requires effective mentoring by shadowing savvy organizational politicians and gaining consulting experience.

To manage the white space of organizational politics, OD practitioners should identify the formal leaders who appear on the organization chart as well as the informal leaders who seem to garner the most support from others. In addition, they should develop a political strategy for change by posing such questions as:

- What are the most critical issues to the organization's formal leaders? What issues are most important to the informal leaders?
- How can you (as an OD practitioner) and your department help the formal and informal leaders achieve progress on their important issues?
- How can you and your department avoid making enemies? Build alliances?
- What other steps can you take to collaborate more effectively with individuals and groups in the organization?

Use Tool 2-1 to organize how to develop an effective political strategy for managing change efforts.

Tool 2.1. Working the White Space of Organizational Politics

Directions: Use this worksheet to organize how you may manage the white space of organizational politics in change efforts. For each question appearing in the left column, brainstorm answers in the right column. There are no "right" or "wrong" answers, though some answers may be better than others. When you finish, share the completed worksheet with others in the OD department. Try to find mentors in the organization who might be better at company politics than you are. Share your answers in the right column with those mentors and listen to the advice they give you.

	Questions About Organizational Politics	How Would You Answer?
1	Who are the most important *formal* leaders in the organization? (Formal leaders appear on the organization chart.)	
2	Who are the most important *informal* leaders in the organization? (Informal leaders are those who regularly secure the most support and exert the most influence in the organization.)	
3	What are the most critical issues to the *formal* leaders of the organization? To the *informal* leaders?	
4	How can you and your department help the *formal* leaders address those issues?	
5	How can you and your department help the *informal* leaders address those issues?	
6	What can you do to avoid making enemies?	
7	What can you do to find organizational allies and/or champions to help you achieve your goals and make change efforts successful?	
8	What other steps can you take to collaborate more effectively with individuals and groups in the organization?	

Other Ways to Work in or Around the Organization Chart

OD practitioners can work within the system—that is, use their authority based on their placement on the organization chart—to help facilitate change efforts. They can also rely on skillfully applied organizational politics in their bid to facilitate change. However, there are even more ways OD practitioners can work in or around the organization charts while serving as change agents.

Many change efforts rely on various strategies to enable change, such as:

- Creating temporary organizational councils, committees, task forces, or groups to enable change
- Changing the work responsibilities of managers and workers in the organization
- Changing the job performance requirements of managers and workers
- Creating new functions or departments to lead the charge for change
- Establishing and empowering informal political coalitions militating for change
- Building dream teams of superstars to formulate and implement change efforts
- Creating virtual or informal communities of practice to enable change

All these strategies—and there are others—can be used by OD practitioners to formulate, implement, and continuously improve change efforts and work within or around the organization chart.

Creating temporary groups to provide an organizational structure to support change is a well-known approach. Many decision makers task a special team or steering committee to study or benchmark an innovation, shape proposals for implementation for review by senior leaders, and conduct special activities to support change. When this temporary organizational structure is used to build or support change, it is called a *shadow organization chart approach* (Banerjee 2021). In short, the temporary structure casts a shadow of the formal organization chart, but it focuses the attention on one change effort—such as implementing a new succession program, a new customer service program, or a new health and wellness program.

Change in an organization can also be supported by an *embedded change approach* (Banerjee 2021). This involves building change responsibilities into organizational policies, procedures, employee handbooks, job descriptions, and individual performance review plans. Responsibility for the change is cascaded in the organization from the top of the organization chart to the bottom. Any policy or procedure that impedes the change implementation is revised so policy and procedures consistently support the change.

So if someone says, "I don't want to be involved in that organizational change because it is not addressed in my job description or key performance indicators," their manager can respond with, "Have you checked your job description or KPIs lately? They have been updated and you're now accountable for your role in making the change happen!"

Another approach, called the *structural approach,* is to create a new box on the organization chart to provide a focal point for a change effort. For example, if the organization's leaders wish to give prominence to quality, they create a quality department; if the leaders wish to give prominence to diversity, equity, and inclusion (DEI), they create a DEI department; if the leaders wish to give prominence to talent development, they create a talent development function. When a change is institutionalized on the organization chart, it communicates a commitment to that change and provides a function that can spearhead policy formation, procedures, training, and communication.

The *dream team approach* draws on high potential workers from across the organization. Taking its name from the world of sports, a dream team draws on the best player from each team in a sports league to create a super team of best players. Likewise, when this approach is used for change efforts, leaders draw on people from various levels on the organization chart as well as different departments, geographical locations, and backgrounds. Each person is chosen based on their reputation, influence, and likelihood of rapid promotion. For instance, team members could be pulled from the C-suite, middle management, frontline supervision, the nonexempt ranks, a union, and HR or OD.

Teams should be limited to no more than 12—and seven is the best number. A challenge is to keep the numbers low but the quality exceedingly high. Each member should be a high-potential worker. However, it often helps to add one team member who is a vocal critic of the change and will constantly challenge the group's opinions to avoid groupthink (Janis 1983).

The *community of practice approach* is not as clear-cut as other methods described. There is no effort to identify and select targeted individuals to serve on a steering committee, task force, or other group; rather, members self-select and join based on their support for a change effort. For instance, if the organization's leaders wish to build a corporate university, they may create a community of practice around that change effort. Workers can join—or not join—as they wish.

Communities of practice may be formed and work together on-site (residentially), online (virtually), or use blended approaches to meet and discuss the changes advocated. Virtual teams can draw from members inside and outside the organization that originally founded the community of practice (see Rothwell and Cho 2021). Members try to advocate for change inside the organization or in society more broadly. For instance, a community of practice may be formed to inspire job-related professional development, to encourage religious study off the job, or to advocate for social change efforts to address an issue like climate change.

Many ways to organize for change exist and they can be used together or in isolation. They may be used with formal and political efforts to drive and sustain change.

Measurements and Results

How can we measure and evaluate the relative success and the results of the OD function in an organization? While answering that question could fill an entire book (see Jones and Rothwell 2017), there are two basic ways to think about it:

- **The political or informal way of evaluating the relative success of OD in an organization.** Simply ask this question, "Has the OD function been gaining or losing staff and resources?" If the staff and budget are growing, then its influence is also growing. But if the staff and budget are declining, then OD's influence is diminishing.
- **The more traditional approach of measuring success by looking at specific change projects.** One way to do that is to establish measurable change objectives (targets) at the outset of any OD initiative. Experienced OD practitioners will facilitate discussions with their clients early in the discussion about the amount of money that problems are costing the organization and how much the change project will cost. This provides the information to conduct cost-benefit measures (return on investment) before, during, and after the OD initiative.

Since OD initiatives may last longer than a year, practitioners may also wish to establish scorecards that permit regular conversations with OD clients about how the initiative is progressing (Phillips and Phillips 2011). It is highly desirable, but also difficult, to relate the relative success of OD change efforts to organizational success—particularly when looking at the business impact of OD efforts on achieving the success of the organization as measured by its balanced scorecard metrics. One way to do that is to devise strategy maps that relate the success of OD efforts to organizational goals (Kaplan and Norton 2003).

Summary

As this chapter noted, OD may be applied by external consultants, internal consultants, managers, and (with proper training) workers. While anyone with proper training can apply OD principles, for efforts to work in an organization, they depend on the placement of OD and the assignments it is given. External consultants work from outside and are usually assigned a liaison from inside the organization; internal consultants work from inside but may hold a position in one department while collaborating with other organizational units.

Change can also be driven in ways that go beyond formal or political action—such as relying on approaches to organize for change. Among those approaches are the shadow organization, the department organization, the functional approach, the dream team approach, and the community of practice approach. Any or all these approaches may be used in isolation or in combination.

Key Takeaways

Here are a few things you can do to manage the white space of organizational politics:

- Learn who is an informal and formal leader based on the organization chart.
- Establish good relationships with formal and informal leaders (often by helping them accomplish goals of value to them).
- Monitor existing and emerging problems of importance to the formal and informal leaders.
- Determine how informal and formal leaders regard key issues.
- Try to avoid making enemies while also building support from formal and informal leaders.

Developing Organizational Values

CATHERINE W. COREY

IN THIS CHAPTER

♦ Adapt the needs assessment approach to your current values effort

♦ Engage your employees in developing organizational values

♦ Integrate values into everything the organization does

Signs and Signals

Company values provide guiding principles for all aspects of decision making. Sure, mission and vision have long aided in this purpose and are also key for decision making, but values speak to how the work *gets done*. Values outline how people treat one another while working to advance the mission and vision.

Many of you are familiar with the values that companies discuss when it comes to customer service. State Farm promises to be there like a good neighbor, offering quality service and relationships, mutual trust, integrity, and financial strength. Others provide a specific set of behaviors that apply to everyone, including employees and external stakeholders; for example, Starbucks promises a culture of warmth and belonging where everyone is welcome. And while you may not be able to identify exactly what a company's values are, you can absolutely tell when they aren't in place or exist in words only.

As a learning and talent development professional, this is most evident when you're asked for training solutions, but the problem isn't clear and the time for exploration and diagnosis isn't encouraged or even allowed. You may find yourself getting requests from departments for topics like trust or communication. Conversations around "the way we do things" are also very common at this particular point in organizational growth. In the very beginning, new organizations are simply trying to survive. It's about keeping the lights on, finding capable people who are willing to take a chance on a new venture and wear multiple hats, and securing initial investors and clients. You're all in the trenches, and the bond of simply trying to get through each week together is enough to overlook issues because the successes seem pure and sweet. The initial team typically develops a shorthand for how work is completed and learns how to work with, around, and in spite of one another, for better or worse.

This chapter will focus on how to use your expertise as a talent development professional to either design or recraft your internal organizational values. We'll cover how to recognize when it could be helpful (or necessary!) to work on your organization's values, explore pitfalls to avoid and the specific strengths that will help you, and, finally, walk through a successful case study.

Why Values Matter

For many organizations, the focus is often on mission and vision. The *mission* describes the business and the needs you're meeting while the *vision* describes where the organization is going and what the future looks like. Those tools are incredibly helpful because they ensure everyone is following the same map and knows where they're headed and why. So, what about values? *Values* outline what is most important to you as you continue the journey, and are necessary to help you prioritize when discussing how you get the work done. Without a values plan and discussion, you may find that your organization is headed in the wrong direction or no direction at all.

As a TD professional in your organization, you're likely aware of the external values your organization has regarding clients and stakeholders. Not that those aren't important or may not overlap, but you've also likely noticed a distinction between those values and types of internal values discussed here. And if the waters are still a little muddied, not to worry—you'll soon get some great examples of how internal values have been done well and what to avoid.

The absence of clear and agreed-upon values matters most if you've reached a major crisis point in how your organization is developing. Perhaps your organization is facing an intragroup conflict caused by an emotional response from one or more team members when a core value is violated, even if you don't know it. Leaving organizational values unstated or murky opens the organization to clashes because people will fill in gaps with their own personal values. And violations of your own core values aren't things that just irritate you. They are things that make your blood boil, make you withdraw, or make you start a conversation with a friend or trusted colleague with, "Can you even *believe* that?!?!"

For instance, equity and access is one of my core values. I once worked with an organization that was undergoing a renovation project and wanted employee input on furniture choices. The organization asked who I thought should go on the shopping expedition. I felt that the people in the call centers who spent all day at their desks and more junior employees who didn't have as much freedom to move around the building to work should be included in the decisions based on how much time they actually spent at their desks each day. I also thought it was a chance for employees who didn't get to travel for work to do so and participate in a process that was important to them. I was overruled and they took C-suite executives instead. I was livid. My core values had been stepped on in favor of hierarchy (which is decidedly not a core value of mine).

On the other hand, I have a more pliable relationship with time. I do not see lateness as a reflection of how people feel about me and my priorities. I believe things come up in life and that no one is really thinking about me and my (or our) plans that much. I also know there are people for whom punctuality is a core value and that's how they show their respect for those in their lives. However, I do keep note of who those people are, and I do my best to be on time and try not to disappoint them!

So, at the organizational level when you find yourself getting more requests for training regarding conflict issues, there's a good chance it's actually an organizational values issue. If this happens, it may be time to create, revisit, or find firmer footing on existing values.

Creating Values—What Else Could You Do?

I once worked for a company, let's call it Widgets, that had hung up a giant poster board with old organizational values printed on it and maybe 60 or 70 signatures in red and green. But the prime feature was the giant X across the whole board that someone had clearly unsuccessfully tried to remove. It was one of my favorite things in that office and had a fantastic origin story: At some point before I was brought in to work with the staff on engagement (which ended up including values work), Widgets had been dealing with internal conflict and friction. Recognizing that they needed a values solution, they implemented one. The company's board and executive leadership got together and came up with values that any organization would be proud to include in their work: respect, communication, concern for others, and excellent service. They proudly printed several giant poster boards displaying the new values and unveiled them at the end-of-year all-staff and holiday party. Everyone was encouraged to participate and show their support for the new values by signing the poster in festive colors. Then they planned to display the boards on different floors of the office. What could go wrong? Fortunately, I am here to dissect the situation so you won't have to learn these things the hard way.

Specifics

There is nothing wrong with respect, communication, concern for others, or excellent service. However, these values are also so generic that they don't speak to anything in particular that anyone at Widgets is doing. Which means I can safely tell you this story because, by changing its name, no one will know which organization I'm referencing. Nothing about any of these words are specific enough to tap into an emotional reaction that causes values conflicts—or resolutions.

So, when considering your values, don't just write down general words. Instead, start by asking these questions:
- How can you tap into the passions of your team?
- Where are your people in your values?
- What are you fiercely defending?
- How are you driving progress?
- What is unique to your organization or industry?
- What puns or word play are available to you? (Fun is not against the rules!)

Inclusion

These values were presented by Widgets leadership for Widgets staff, which makes it tough to see how respect, communication, and concern for others were being modeled. Because they were decided on by one subset of staff and presented to another subset of staff, these values immediately created a divide—as well as questions. Sure, leadership was signing on to the values, but they had been in the room when they were created and had participated in the conversations about what was important.

But the rest of the Widgets team hadn't had any input. True values are cultivated and discovered. You can't just tell people what they value—not successfully, anyway.

When considering your organization's values, think about how they have been developed or how you plan to develop them. Then ask:

- Who is involved in the conversation?
- Who is leading the discussion and effort?
- What opportunities are there for participation?
- Are people aware of the values development process?
- Is the values development process clear and transparent?
- Where can people find information about what's happening?

Process

Finally, the rollout was flawed too. The end of the year all-staff party was traditionally a festive occasion to celebrate the end of the year and recognize achievement, which is why the Widgets leadership thought it would be a great opportunity to launch and celebrate the new values. There was a photo booth, delicious food, a signature cocktail, a selection of beer and wine, and a DJ to contribute to the jovial mood; they also set up a station for signing the new posters. Unfortunately, two staff members who had been let go that morning were also invited to the party. At some point, after some drinks, one of the newly unemployed people grabbed a marker and drew a giant X across one of the new values posters.

It was not exactly the rollout leadership was hoping for—but perhaps it was what they should have anticipated.

When considering your values, take into account the process of values work and ask:

- What else is happening in the organization when you want to kick off your effort?
- What is the mood or tenor of the different levels and teams within the organization?
- Where are you in the calendar or fiscal year? How might this influence energy or availability for participation?
- What have you learned from past efforts? Or from the absence of past efforts?
- How else could the effort be viewed by those not in the know about what's happening?
- How might these changes be viewed? What change management theories could be useful in your effort? (Hint: Check out chapters 8 and 9!)

The values those former employees crossed out on the poster board were still in place when I showed up. However, I honestly didn't know that for a long time because they weren't mentioned or ingrained into the organization's daily work. Those values weren't mentioned during onboarding, they couldn't be easily found on the intranet (I'm not sure they were even posted), and they certainly weren't supported with any training or development. I only found out about them when the poster board showed up. The rollout legacy continued.

From Training Values to Developing Values

Well-developed values can make training a whole lot easier. Ill-defined values can have exactly the opposite effect, which is where the unique lens of talent development can come in handy. For instance, being asked to work with a team on customer service objectives where the value is "empowerment to own the issue" as opposed to "respect" provides a much clearer picture of the goal.

Empowerment to own the issue will involve avoiding transferring calls; doing what needs to be done in the moment; tracking issues, follow-up calls, or emails; pulling in necessary resources to resolve challenges; and establishing a clear issue lead. A value of *respect* ends up in a much murkier place. Who is defining respect? What are you respecting? An existing process? Hierarchy? The client? Operating hours? What happens when two of those things clash? Respect as a value ends up needing much more clarification.

When looking to develop organizational values, a background in talent development sets you up well to provide guidance for this process. Just as one-off training and development opportunities can bring success, goals are clearer, objectives are easier to meet, and the process flows much more smoothly overall with a more strategic plan. The same is true when it comes to developing values.

Here you can adapt the needs assessment approach for evaluating training and development gaps to understand more about what's behind the current values effort within your organization. Looking at organizational challenges, strengths, and training opportunities can help you outline the possible paths forward.

Challenges

A common occurrence in the early stages of organization and team development can be the "technically good but culturally challenging" employee. Behavior that might have been overlooked before but has now become an issue seems to rise to the surface. It can be difficult to address if there isn't a mechanism to do so, like with performance objectives. This is when organizational values come in handy. No longer can an employee be technically good without meeting values expectations because they're integrated throughout the organization, including in job descriptions and performance evaluations. So not allowing team members to use the bathroom outside their assigned break time, for example, would be in direct violation of the value "putting people at the heart of everything we do." (Unfortunately, that is based on a true story.)

Strengths

However, it's not just what's not happening or where there are opportunities for improvement within the organization that can point to possible values. There may also be things that already attract people to your organization that make it a desirable place to work. What are those things for you? What have you heard other team members discuss? Is your organization an especially great place to grow your career?

Perhaps your focus on understanding and meeting community needs is what attracts clients and even turns some of those clients into dedicated employees. Or do you have a reputation for being on the cutting edge of discovery, taking calculated risks to advance the knowledge in your industry, and ultimately creating powerful new solutions? You might also find that employees value being able to contribute meaningfully to the work the organization is doing while being seen as their authentic selves, and like that what they do outside work is valued just as much as what they bring to the table for the organization. Homing in on what current team members value about working at your organization can help define what's most important both now and going forward.

Training

You can also evaluate what's important to your organization by reviewing your training and development opportunities. An organization with which I was working during the beginning of the COVID-19 pandemic wanted to make sure we were staying connected and doing what we could for staff. Like many organizations, once we understood that we were going to be working remotely for a while (a privilege we were fortunate enough to have), we realized that our carefully crafted 2020 training plan would need to be completely redone.

We took a break for the first few months and offered other, more casual opportunities to connect. However, once people stopped enjoying Zoom happy hours, we started a new line of professional development offerings we hadn't had before. We brought in a licensed psychologist for optional sessions like changing relationships, stress management, mental health, and dealing with uncertainty. We featured topics that applied to the work environment, but more importantly to us at the time, also applied to whatever relationships were important to our staff, wherever stress was showing up for them, and so on. It was one of the ways we put people at the heart of everything we did, starting with our staff. Between a quarter and a third of the company regularly attended those sessions, showing we were relatively on the mark for the time.

That is one way to put values in action through training. However, it's also easy enough to test possible values through training as you're working to develop them. If you suspect a value based on innovation may be fundamental to your organization, hosting a lunch & learn or a webinar to augment current training offerings can help test that theory. Alternatively, if you suspect making individual contributions is important to the fabric of your organization, consider inviting staff members to recommend their favorite podcast or book and why they enjoy it (it could be for fun or related to a business or development concept). It's possible to get creative and supplement your current training plan without having to pause everything else you're doing. Plus, you don't have to do it all on your own.

Engaging Staff in Values Development

Given what you learned regarding specifics, development, and process from the less-than-successful values effort at Widgets and considering that you need to assess what's important to your organization, you now have most of the building blocks you need. Now let's walk through a process I've used to add the element of employee engagement to help develop organizational values. For the sake of stepping through this, I'll talk about the process and how it went at a different company, which I'll call Gadgets.

The Core Group

When we started the values process at Gadgets, there were already values in place, although much like Widgets, they didn't have traction with staff. So, the first thing we did was recruit a core group of staff to help lead the process. Not only was this an opportunity for staff to get involved, which was helpful because I couldn't do all the work myself, it's also one of the first two steps recommended by leading change expert, John Kotter. Back in 1995, Kotter summarized his research from more than 100 organizations into an article detailing why change efforts so often fail. His first two observations included not creating a strong enough sense of urgency and not establishing a vocal and visible enough team to lead the effort—what Kotter called a guiding coalition. While it's clearly critical to have the head of the organization on board, one person can't do it all. True support and sustainability for any change effort needs to come from all levels. Additionally, while Kotter separates creating a sense of urgency and establishing the leadership group as separate items, I have found that in practice, they often go hand in hand. Creating the core staff leadership team gets people more invested as a part of the process, generates more urgency as the team coalesces, and forms greater urgency from your champions as part of that process.

When building your core team, there are several factors to consider. One of the first questions will be how you want to build your team. Will you be selecting people, asking for applications, or a combination of both? Each option has its advantages and challenges. Selecting people ensures you'll have a balance across all the characteristics you want for your team and can be a quick way to get started, but it isn't necessarily as transparent a process as some might hope. Applications can ensure that everyone who is interested has a chance to raise their hand so you get a sense of who's interested in the process, but there may not be enough spots for all those interested, and you may end up needing to do some creative recruiting to ensure an inclusive mix of staff. A combination of selection and application (often billed as a nomination process, including self-nomination) can allow for more transparency regarding the process but can take the longest time and, along with the application process, also requires a selection process that is as clear to staff as possible. Which process you use will depend on your organizational culture, both current and aspirational, and it may be worth a discussion with a few staff members in different positions if you don't already have an established process. This will be the staff's first exposure to your values process, and they'll be paying attention.

Regardless of the process you choose, there are a few key demographics to consider. Access to senior leadership is important for access to resources and the ability of employees to prioritize the work, as is showing leadership support for the development of your values. Having a couple senior team members act as champions on your core team will help accomplish these objectives and give more junior team members the opportunity to work with leaders with whom they may not normally get to interact. Champions at all levels will be important to consider, so examining your organization's hierarchy and determining how many different levels of leadership and individual contributors you need to include will be important.

Another key demographic to consider will be the persuasive skeptics. You obviously do not want to include anyone with the potential to actively work against your values initiative, but you might want to consider people who have been through past culture efforts, have institutional knowledge, or are fans of the phrase "That's not how we do things here," or "We've tried that before." These people are your hidden gems. If you can get one or two of them to invest in your values—both as creators and champions—not only will your efforts have more credibility, but you'll also have an easier time bringing along other skeptics. The key to identifying these people is they're still invested—they still attend events and programs, raise their hands for things (perhaps stubbornly), and have connections and friends at work. Their knowledge of how things are and were before can be incredibly valuable along the way when exploring what to avoid.

Another consideration when building your core team is how the following demographics are represented:

- Senior leadership
- Leaders from each level of organizational hierarchy, including individual contributors
- Persuasive skeptics
- Departments or functional areas
- Branches, locations, on-site, or remote employees
- Tenure with the organization
- Survey demographics, such as age, gender identity, race, ethnicity, partnered status, or parental status
- Percentage of staff represented through the core team while still being manageable

At Gadgets, we ended up using a selection method to form a core team of 16 people, which represented approximately 7 percent of the full staff at the time. And because we used a selection method to get up and running quickly, it was especially important to ensure we planned multiple opportunities for staff outside the core team to participate in the exploration and creation of our values.

Involving the Full Staff

Once our core team was established at Gadgets, we began planning our timeline and how we could involve as much of the full staff as possible in the creation of the new staff values.

Allowing Time

A full-scale effort takes time, both in planning and execution. The core team began by identifying when we were hoping to launch our new values, which was in the fall. This timeline worked with the organization's calendar, and gave us about seven months to work. While that may seem like a long lead time, we knew that we'd lose about six of those weeks to a national conference.

When discussing how companies fall short regarding communicating their vision for change, Kotter (1996) references the misalignment between the words and actions of organizational leaders. Committing a significant amount of time to how the employee experience should be at your organization is one of the ways to begin building a strong message for integrating your values into the daily work at your organization—the values won't be added or on top of the work you're doing. They will be the way work gets done.

Back at Gadgets, we carefully laid out a four-stage strategy to meet staff members where they were and provide opportunities to engage that could happen simultaneously and build on one another. We sent out regular communications detailing the opportunities to get involved as they approached, reminding people to sign up and reiterating the timeline. In addition to emails, the core team relied on internal newsletter updates and appearances at all-staff meetings throughout each stage.

Stage 1: Broad Thinking

In stage 1 of the process, staff were able to share their input on the project through conversation circles, one-on-one conversations, and a corkboard space.

Conversation Circles

Small groups of staff (no more than 15) were invited through an open sign-up process to discuss the future of the organization and how things could look. They were asked to bring an article, an idea from a podcast, something they'd heard about at another organization, or something they'd been thinking about for a while. These discussions were moderated by core team members, and ideas were collected in a confidential manner unless participants expressed consent to having their name tied to an idea.

One-on-One Conversations

Core team members were given a coffee gift card as a thank you for their participation and an incentive to take five other staff members off campus for confidential conversations (this could also work virtually using e-gift cards). These other staff members were chosen from different teams, tenure, leadership position, and even personal relationship status to engage in a 30-minute chat regarding their experience with Gadgets. The conversations loosely followed the start, stop, and continue method, asking what practices and experiences staff enjoyed, wished didn't exist, or would like to see at the company.

Before having these conversations, members of the core team received training from HR on how to listen for any significant issues or handle anything that might need to be addressed formally. Again, all conversations were confidential, and the information was collected in aggregate unless participants understood that an issue would need to be addressed.

Real Life Pinterest Board

We placed a corkboard on the wall in a common area of the building to serve as a visual mood board. Staff members were asked to use the board to share words, phrases, photos, articles, and anything else they found inspiring.

Other real-time feedback ideas include using beans or buttons to fill voting jars representing words or phrases that resonate with staff, hosting an online intranet poll to test out ideas, or setting up a drive or folder on the organization's intranet to share materials.

Stage 2: Quantitative Data

We used surveys to collect quantitative data in stage 2. Because Gadgets had a sporadic history of conducting employee surveys, the core team decided to start an annual survey using the Gallup Q12 as a baseline. This tool is most helpful when used annually to compare results. While the first year wasn't necessarily going to provide a lot of data, the tool's implementation was able to show the company was now committed to annually checking in with staff. By working with a third-party firm to ensure confidentiality, we were also able to add several questions (in addition to the 12 from Gallup) that were geared toward what we had learned in the first stage.

This survey allowed us to do two important things. First, we could reach a broader audience using the online survey format—almost 90 percent of staff participated in the survey. Second, we were able to narrow our focus on some of the themes we were hearing and start testing wording and phrases. We heard that people liked producing Gadgets with a helpful influence on the world, they liked being asked for their opinions, they enjoyed the people with whom they worked both internally and externally (clients and vendors), and they believed in making real change both at Gadgets and in the community.

Stage 3: Creating

During stage 3, we moved forward by sharing an initial draft, reviewing through focus groups, and then testing our results.

Drafting

Based on all the information we had from stages 1 and 2, the core team was able to begin organizing the feedback and data into an initial draft statement. This required the group to organize, edit, let things sit, and then come back to it to review again. Finally, we had one succinct paragraph that blended everything the team had heard. The group was delighted and very proud of the work we had done.

However, by the very fact that the values statement isn't included here, you can probably guess that the process wasn't over yet. The statement still needed to be vetted by staff and approved. Thankfully, we had planned for this.

Focus Groups

Once we had the final draft of our statement (of which we were very proud), we held three focus groups that were open to anyone from the full staff who wanted to offer feedback. That first meeting was the definition of the air getting sucked out of the room. The core team was so excited as we shared the values statement back to staff because it reflected everything we had heard over the past several months. But all we got were a lot of polite nods and smiles. Yeesh.

Finally, toward the middle of our first group session, someone spoke up and said, "It's just so . . . long. You know what I liked? The ground rules we had in our first conversation circles. They were simple."

Just like that, the proverbial lightbulb went off for the group. We had been trying too hard to pull everything together into a single values statement, when really, the staff liked clean, distinct statements. The ground rules we had used in the conversations circles were statements like "What's said here, stays here," "We listen to understand, not to respond," and "We understand and appreciate that not everyone has the same experience." They had addressed what would guide our conversation, and in doing so, what we valued. They helped us understand how to behave, and that was what staff members were hoping for out of their values—simple, clear, inclusive statements about what to expect from one another.

Testing

By the close of the final focus group, we had created a reworded set of values to test with the Gadgets staff. Nothing changed from the content, but the way it was presented had changed significantly. Rather than pulling everything together into a single paragraph, we crafted the following statements:

- **People** are at the heart of what we do.
- We are **passionate** about our work and community.
- We believe in the power of **innovation**.
- We are paving the way for a better **future**.

These four statements captured the essence of the team's five months of work. We had identified the themes of people, passion, innovation, and a focus on the future, and had done so by focusing on the heart of the organization, a commitment to work and the community, and the power Gadgets had to create a better world. The final two focus groups had an entirely different energy from the first, and their enthusiasm was mirrored by that of the core team.

Stage 4: Rollout

The best way to introduce new values to staff will be different for each organization. At Gadgets, more than 90 percent of the staff participated in the creation of the values, so the process certainly wasn't a secret. It was energizing to come back with the results of their work. We planned a skit for the all-staff meeting, created swag so everyone could easily display the values on their desks and the apparel they could wear to the office, and posted the values and the story of how they evolved to a place on the intranet that was easily accessible.

The core team also alluded to other future initiatives for the organization because it wasn't just about having the new values and being done. As Kotter (1996) had seen in many organizations and warned against, we did not want to celebrate victory too early and take our foot off the gas. There was work to do to integrate these values into the culture and ensure the organization had moved solidly in the norming stage.

Integrating Values in Other HR and L&D Initiatives

Much like the work necessary to develop a strategic plan or create a training and development program, the effort that goes into developing values can be heavy enough that once done, it can be tempting to check the box, deliver the final product, and move on. But as dangerous as it is to declare victory too early, not integrating values into everything the organization does will also hamper the results you're seeking.

Performance Evaluations and Goal Setting

As a talent development expert, you're likely very familiar with performance evaluations and goal setting because that's where much of professional development either stems from or works toward. This is a prime spot to include values because you measure what matters to you. For organizations doing away with performance evaluations, another option is working values into the goal setting process. How will your team members demonstrate organizational values in their work? A training session on values-based goals can not only help with this but also serve as a way to further discussions around your values and help keep them top of mind for managers.

Recruiting and Retention

Many job descriptions have a section about the organization in them, which can be a perfect place to showcase your values. Work with your recruitment team to begin job descriptions with the organization's mission and vision statements; discussing the work you're doing along with your values will help give candidates a sense of what the culture is like and what they can expect when working with you. It can also help with retention by recruiting better fits from the start. Additionally, when it comes to retention, if the values are included in job descriptions, staff members not living up to organizational values can be put on performance improvement plans for specific actions related to living your values.

Staff Engagement Teams

If your organization isn't used to taking a values-based approach, the more integration you have, the more opportunities staff will have for the values to become habits. It will be easier for them if they're able to personally interact with the values, rather than simply reading about them or hearing them mentioned from time to time.

Staff engagement teams can be a powerful way to help integrate your values and let your staff develop opportunities that resonate most with them. At Gadgets, our staff engagement teams fueled passion for the work by arranging for tours of other Gadget-related businesses and speakers from the industry to help us understand the bigger picture and our role in it. They also stoked the passion for community involvement and put people at the heart of what we do by creating local volunteer opportunities and fundraising drives. There was even an engagement team committed to wellness and a better future for employees, which hosted walking tours, taught yoga on-site, and held brain breaks to care for mental health.

Employee Surveys

At Gadgets we used the Gallup Q12 survey to measure employee engagement. During my time with the organization, we were able to see steady growth each year in not just overall scores but also in participation in the survey. One year saw 93 percent participation from staff—almost unheard of at the company we used to manage the survey—creating an interesting finding in and of itself. We knew that number would be hard to maintain, so we didn't worry when the next year didn't match it; however, we did keep an eye on it as an indicator of whether survey participation would be a downward trend. Additionally, as people got more comfortable with the Q12 and how we used it at Gadgets, we could share more information about engagement by team and level, allowing us to be more transparent as an organization and seek more input on possible solutions to challenges staff were having. We were doing our best to live our values by putting our people at the heart of what we did and moving toward a better future as those responsible for organization development.

Evaluating Your Efforts

How you evaluate your efforts will depend largely on where you started and what you were hoping to accomplish. The great news is that you likely automatically built in many measures you can use to help evaluate your values programs. For example:

- How many goals were based around values?
- How many training and development opportunities were values-based post-launch?
- How many new hires listed your values as something that attracted them to your organization?

And of course, you can also use the specific measures regarding knowledge and implementation from each of your training and development programs. You'll also be able to use any survey measures as well as the number of staff involved in your development process and maintenance efforts. There are many ways to measure and evaluate your progress based on what is most important to you at the time. Quantitative and qualitative data is everywhere if you're willing to look for it.

When evaluating *where* and *how* to integrate your values, you can ask:

- How do we measure performance?
- What does training about our values look like?
- How are managers held accountable for values leadership?
- What opportunities are there for continued staff engagement and leadership?
- How are our values communicated to job candidates and new hires?
- What regular communication channels exist to share stories about the values in action?
- What changes need to be made to elevate our values?
- How will we celebrate wins around our values?
- What types of training and professional development requests do we get each year?

Summary

As a talent development expert, you're uniquely positioned to take on values development within your organization. By applying your assessment, diagnosis, and evaluation skills, and expanding on your knowledge of group performance and change management, you'll be equipped to take your team from dealing with conflict that seems to arise from mysterious disconnects to one that's rooted in clear values. And as you strengthen your norms and integrate your values across the everyday work, your success in supporting the peak performance of your organization will be stronger than ever.

Key Takeaways

Here are a few things to remember as you help your organization develop its values:

- **Keep an eye out for the signs and signals that values work might need to be done.** Where is your organization in the group development phases? Is it cycling back through? Are new pockets of teams beginning to form or storm?
- **Understand how values work with your mission and vision.** Do you have a clear understanding of not just *where* you're going and *what* you're bringing to the world, but also *how* you and your colleagues are doing so?
- **Consider specifics, representation, and process.** How are your values specific to your organization, who is represented, who is involved in developing your values, and what process will you use?
- **Tap into your training expertise for success in developing organizational values.** How can you assess your organizational challenges and strengths and use training to explore pockets of opportunity and norms?
- **Remember, your strongest asset is your staff.** Developing a core team of champions to assist with your values efforts will not only make your job easier but will also ensure you end up with values that resonate and stick.
- **Integrate your values into new and existing processes.** What existing processes can support the inclusion of new values that detail how you work? What new processes, forms, training, or materials need to be created to help support the integration of your values?
- **Measure and evaluate what's most important.** Consider tracking employee engagement around your values using surveys, participation rates, goal evaluations, and anything else your organization has identified as key to performance.

CHAPTER 4

Diversity, Equity, Inclusion, and Belonging

LAKISHA C. BROOKS

IN THIS CHAPTER

♦ Recognize the differences in diversity, equity, inclusion, and belonging

♦ Implement psychological safety in your organization

♦ Formulate a DEIB change management strategy

♦ Use demographic and learning measurement data to create DEIB goals

Few ideologies have transformed the landscape of the modern workplace as much as diversity, equity, inclusion, and belonging (DEIB).

DEIB was born out of a need for incorporating organizational diversity training in the 1960s as an increasing number of multicultural employees began to enter the workforce (Abassi and Hollman 1991). These training courses were mainly oriented toward covering the best legal interests of corporations, as they implemented sensitivity training programs to prevent the possibility of being sued for discrimination (Paluck 2006). Therefore, they were not adequate to transform awareness of multiculturalism in the workplace in a beneficial way.

The turn of the 21st century saw the push for organizational sustainability—a shift away from focusing on short-term profits at any cost to society to a triple bottom line and an ethics-driven workplace focused on conscious social, economic, and environmental impact (Gimenez, Sierra, and Rodon 2012). Although profit is always the goal for an organization, this shift encouraged companies to become people-focused and think more about employee well-being.

The social component of organizational success has also become increasingly important, bringing about a rise in social justice initiatives and awareness of multicultural inequality. In fact, justice has arisen as another component included in conversations about DEIB (DEIBJ). *Justice* refers to replacing harmful systems of inequality with institutions that are fair, equitable, and allow diversity to flourish (Ahmad 2021).

DEIB has seen its share of successes and criticisms; however, it is a vehicle for organizational transformation that provides measurable benefits for companies by addressing the multicultural needs of employees. As organization development (OD) practitioners, you have a pivotal role in influencing DEIB in your organization, whether you're acting as a change agent or a DEIB champion. Furthermore, OD practitioners can implement DEIB training, integrate a lived DEIB culture, and develop a DEIB strategy that drives results.

In this chapter, we'll start with some definitions of our key terms. Then, we'll shift to how you as an OD practitioner can make DEIB work in your organization and how to keep your efforts from failing—in many ways, this involves a lack of change management. We'll wrap up with some tips for measuring the effectiveness of these efforts.

What Does DEIB Actually Mean?

The terms *diversity, equity, inclusion,* and *belonging* are often used interchangeably despite having different definitions and influences on organizations. To avoid any confusion, let's discuss some key terms: *diversity, intersectionality, equity, inclusion, belonging,* and *psychological safety.*

Diversity and Intersectionality

Diversity refers to the varied background and cultural makeup of employees, including aspects such as age, disability, sexuality, gender, sex, sexual orientation, religion, race, ethnicity, socioeconomic background, veteran status, and pregnancy status. The term *intersectionality* was coined by Kimberle Crenshaw in her renowned essay, "On Intersectionality." *Merriam-Webster* defines it as "the complex, cumulative way in which the effects of multiple forms of discrimination (such as racism, sexism, and classism) combine, overlap, or intersect especially in the experiences of marginalized individuals or groups." As the world becomes more diverse, it's important to understand that employees will have more than one perspective of how they experience the world and perceive discrimination, prejudice, or bias due to the intersectionality of their cultures.

OD practitioners can use intersectionality to determine trends within certain populations and design programs tailored to that specific audience. For example, an organization may plan to implement a women's leadership development program. Their goal is to increase the number of women in senior level and executive roles because they've found that only 15 percent of those roles are held by women. While this may seem like a great initiative, the organization must make sure to examine the roles held by *all* women; otherwise, it may exclude marginalized women who don't have a fair and equitable chance to hold a senior level and executive role. Additionally, although 15 percent of senior level or executive roles within the organization are held by women, further research may reveal that only 2 percent of those roles are held by women of color. This is an example of intersectionality, where gender and racial identity intersect to cause discrimination toward women of color.

Equity

Equity refers to an organization's ability to provide fair opportunities for all employees regardless of their differences or cultural backgrounds. This is different from *equality*, in which everyone is given the same opportunity. Equity means recognizing employee differences and using that information to provide better access to opportunities. For example, an employee who is disabled may need to work remotely, use different equipment, or receive different accommodations than other employees to have equitable access to perform their job.

Be sure to ask the employee what accommodations they need. This should be done in the early stages of their employment experience, such as during recruiting, interviewing, or onboarding. However, regardless of when this is done, make sure the employee discloses their disability first—never assume a person needs accommodations or has a disability. Lastly, create a safe space for an employee to share.

Inclusion

Inclusion is an organization's ability to foster a "supportive, collaborative and respectful environment that increases the participation and contribution of all employees" (Min 2021). All employees need to feel included within the workplace (in terms of their needs and issues) and be able to have conversations and discussions pertinent to their experience. When marginalized employees lack a sense of inclusion at work, they believe they're undervalued and their voices are not heard.

Inclusion means all employee's voices are included and made to feel important. This is fostered through listening to employees and providing opportunities for marginalized voices to contribute to team efforts and educate others.

The Evolution of DEIB in Organization Development

Through shifts in social awareness, several events contributed to the evolution of DEIB in OD.

- In 1948, President Harry S. Truman desegregated the US Armed Forces by signing Executive Order 9981, marking the first time Black and White soldiers would serve side by side (Evans 2020).
- The Civil Rights Act of 1964 effectively ended public segregation and prohibited "employment discrimination on the basis of race, color, religion, sex or national origin."
- The Women's Rights and Equality movement of the 1960s and 1970s made strides in the push for equal opportunities and pay for women in the workplace (Burkett 2022). These events changed the landscape of the workplace, challenging organizations to make their hiring and employment practices less discriminatory.
- On May 25, 2020, George Floyd, a Black man, was arrested at a convenience store in Minneapolis, Minnesota. During his arrest, he died after Officer Derek Chauvin kneeled on his neck for more than nine minutes (History.com Editors 2021). Floyd's death was captured on video and sparked worldwide outrage setting in motion the largest racial injustice protests since the Civil Rights movement (Silverstein 2021). This contributed to a growing outcry for marginalized people to be more respected and recognized in every area, including at work. As a result, more organizations began to align their brands with social awareness issues and implement DEIB strategies.

Belonging and Psychological Safety

Belonging, a psychological need we all have, refers to the feeling of being accepted in a place or group. In the workplace, *belonging* means that employees feel welcome and secure at work and able to bring their whole selves to their jobs. Organizations must have a sense of cultural awareness for belonging to be meaningful. *Psychological safety* at work means that employees can express their identity without fear of personal repercussions or negative impact to their career.

We can help build a sense of belonging and psychological safety through educating employees on cultural awareness, employing a diverse team, and making inclusion a regular practice.

When DEIB Strategies Do Not Work

DEIB training is on the rise and many organizations are using it as a tool to change their cultures. However, these strategies must be intentional, well thought out, and well executed to be effective. Often organizations have good intentions, but issues such as scrap learning, a compliant or social justice focus, or a lack of planning or resources can prevent their goals from being realized.

With so much DEIB training taking place, scrap learning is a potential risk. *Scrap learning* refers to how most employees fail to retain the information delivered in a training or fail to implement it. According to an article from the Association of Talent Development, "less than 20 percent of learners never apply what they learn in a training program back on the job, and another 65 percent try to apply what they learned, but revert back to their old ways" (Phillips 2016). This is a great opportunity to use L&D skills and incorporate them into OD work. Practitioners need to ensure that not only learning objectives are in place but on-the-job objectives are also included. These on-the-job objectives should have practical applications that learners can implement in their day-to-day work activities. Bloom's Taxonomy provides a great method for writing objectives that can translate into actionable items. Additionally, training material must be relevant, and follow-up and reinforcement are necessary. Otherwise, the time spent planning and delivering training content becomes a waste of time and money.

Many organizations understand that DEIB is an important aspect of today's workplace, but instead of taking an authentic, intuitive approach to DEIB change, they are simply compliant with their efforts. In taking an "it's the right thing to do" approach, these companies risk alienating valuable employees who want to truly be heard and see change. This also happens in organizations that implement DEIB efforts as an act of social justice. For example, a company's decision to hire a Black person to a C-suite leadership role during the height of the Black Lives Matter movement may be seen as virtue signaling, rather than an authentic display of DEIB progression. (We will discuss virtue signaling later in the chapter.)

Despite their best efforts, some organizations lack the money, time, and personnel needed to fully implement their DEIB strategy. Some don't properly budget for DEIB initiatives because they do not truly understand the value they bring to the organization. The work is either siloed or only included because it is the "right thing to do." Other reasons include allotting staff for more pressing or important projects. A *Human Resource Director* survey found that "only 34 percent of respondents reported having enough resources to support their DEI initiatives" (Corrigan 2022). Nonetheless, these organizations can still make plans for future changes and foster an inclusive environment.

Case Study: Avery Manufacturing

Avery Manufacturing, a 100-employee business with one corporate location in Pennsylvania and one warehouse location in Kentucky, was concerned about the lack of racial diversity in its corporate office in Philadelphia. In contrast, their Kentucky location was more diverse and reflected the demographics of the surrounding community. As the organization expanded into new markets, they wanted their brand to be more reflective of diversity. They also wanted to become a bigger part of their community and a place that employees could be proud of. To address existing challenges and identify possible opportunities to being a more DEIB-focused workplace, Avery brought in an external OD consultant.

Some of the challenges Avery faced were:

- The organization had not been intentional about diversity.
- A lack of communication between corporate and the warehouse limited their ability to share perspectives that could improve products and processes.
- They needed to attract more diverse candidates during the recruitment process but didn't know how.
- They needed to be able to identify diverse candidates while alleviating unconscious bias.
- Avery's website only showed white, male employees.
- 100 percent of employees surveyed skipped the question regarding the diversity of leadership.
- 47 percent of respondents were not aware of the company's diversity goals.
- 38 percent of respondents had witnessed behavior or heard comments that were discriminatory or biased.
- A lack of or poor communication was the top reason respondents said was hindering productivity.
- The company had a reactive approach to gender concerns and issues.

However, these challenges also presented several opportunities for the company, including:

- Taking intentional steps in the right direction toward diversity
- Creating diverse employee resource groups (ERGs)
- Partnering with external organizations to build relationships to help with brand reputation and hiring and retention
- Increasing diversity intelligence and awareness

The lack of communication between locations and leadership and employees at Avery allowed the organization to develop blind spots in its view of diversity. While they only identified a lack of diversity within their corporate office, several other improvements would increase diversity efforts and help the organization to expand. For example, strategic diversity goals included increasing morale and employee experience and engagement, building a diverse talent pipeline externally and internally through leadership programs and community partnerships representing marginalized groups, boosting diversity intelligence through education, decreasing employee turnover, and building the company DEIB reputation externally and internally.

Making DEIB Work in Your Organization

Implementing DEIB in your organization can lead to many positive outcomes, such as higher morale, productivity, and revenue. However, to experience these and other gains, you must take several steps to make DEIB work in your organization:

1. Create a need.
2. Set effective goals that can be measured.
3. Establish a lived culture.
4. Cultivate an environment for learning and development.

1. Determine the Need

A major tenet of making sure that DEIB works within your organization is determining the need. This can be accomplished by interviewing employees using surveys and questionnaires and creating focus groups based on the responses.

Questions should be worded using inclusive language and designed to gather demographic information. For example, instead of using the pronouns *him* or *her* in your survey questions, use *them* or *they*. Additionally, when it is necessary to address people in the disability community, refer to the individual as a person with a disability instead of a disabled person. This focuses on their person rather than the disability. Surveys should also feature closed and open-ended questions asking about the employee's experiences and concerns regarding DEIB at work. For example, "As an employee at Company X, have you ever witnessed or experienced any form of bias, exclusion, or other discriminatory behavior? If so, please share, if you are comfortable."

You can then turn this information into quantitative data based on the survey, questionnaire, or focus group answers. Quantitative data will include a summative or statistical value for information gathered, such as employee age, race, ethnicity, amount of time employed with the organization, leadership demographics, retention rates, pay rates, participation in ERGs, and how many employees answered yes or no to certain questions.

Lastly, use this data to create a targeted SWOT analysis briefly detailing the organization's DEIB strengths, weaknesses, opportunities, and threats. Table 4-1 presents an example of a DEIB SWOT analysis.

Table 4-1. An Example DEIB SWOT Analysis

Strengths	Weaknesses
• Inclusive holiday • Leadership is committed to DEIB by providing resources (time and money)	• Lack of communication regarding diversity goals and values • No formal process for hiring diverse talent
Opportunities	Threats
• Growing in various markets online • Creating ERGs	• Competition for top talent • Turnover rate 31% (industry standard is 27%)

2. Establish Goals

One of the first places to strategize DEIB goals is from the diversity audit, which you can use to determine the needs within the organization. The results should have revealed pain points (Brooks 2020). In addition to determining the need, the SWOT analysis can also help in establishing realistic organizational DEIB goals. Before completing the SWOT analysis, the organization may want a more diverse leadership team that includes more women and minorities. However, after editing and reviewing the SWOT analysis data, the organization may discover that they first need to address weaknesses in their recruiting and hiring process. Other DEIB goals can include diversity training, the creation of

ERGs, making accessibility or inclusion-based changes, or allocating a specific amount of money toward initiatives (Hall 2022). Regardless of the method used to establish them, goals should always be SMART (specific, measurable, attainable, realistic, and timely). For example, "We would like to decrease the turnover of our young talent (under 35) by 10 percent over the next 24 months."

An organizational scorecard is also an effective method for setting DEIB goals and keeping you on track. A typical scorecard consists of four areas: internal business processes, learning and growth, customer, and financial. Although DEIB-related goals can fall into one of these areas, some organizations instead create a separate DEIB scorecard. Brooks Consultants recommends creating a separate DEIB scorecard and provides a template companies can use. This DEIB scorecard includes the following areas:

- Policies and procedures (Example: Decrease number of sexual harassment complaints)
- Demographics and representation (Example: Women and people of color on executive board)
- Supplier diversity and procurement (Example: Awarding more veteran-owned businesses with vendor contracts.)
- Recruiting and retention (Example: Increasing the number of young professionals at HBCUs in technology roles)
- Company internal commitment and culture (Example: ROI of diversity training)
- Company branding and reputation (Example: Increasing average yearly net promoter score for customer satisfaction)
- Diversity intelligence (Example: Hosting four required diversity training workshops for managers)
- Customer profile and external partnerships (Example: Increasing the number of partnerships with organizations that focus on underserved communities)

It is not necessary to include each of these areas in a scorecard; depending on the size or type of organization and where it is in the DEIB implementation process, some areas may not be relevant. For example, a company in the beginning stages of their DEIB strategy may not be ready to set goals related to their customer profile or demographics. Regardless of which scorecard areas you use or what goals you set, make sure they align with the organization's overall goals. To do this, it may be ideal to speak with the executive team to gain insight to the company's strategic plan.

When you are establishing your DEIB goals, you want to ensure you are setting a benchmark. Benchmarking standards can come from industry standards, trends, internal and external experts, research, previous experience, and case studies. If you are rolling out a new program or initiative, it may be harder to set a benchmark because there is not historical context to use. In that case, you will need to use experts or case studies from organizations in your industry.

3. Make DEIB Part of the Culture, Not a Silo

DEIB should be treated as a business strategy rather than an obligation or a task to mark off on an HR to-do list. When DEIB is a silo, it will miss the mark and be ineffective. Consider these companies that got into hot water over racially insensitive marketing campaigns (Pfeiffer and Mayes 2018):

- Pepsi featured reality television celebrity and model Kendall Jenner handing a police officer a Pepsi in the middle of a protest during the Black Lives Matter movement.
- H&M featured a Black boy on the website wearing a hoodie that read "Coolest Monkey in the Jungle."
- D&G ran a commercial showing a Chinese woman dressed in their luxury clothing struggling to use chopsticks to eat Italian food.

These are the types of mistakes that can destroy a brand's reputation. When DEIB is the culture, these sorts of events are not likely to be approved and marketed for the world to see!

Having DEIB as part of a lived culture within an organization starts with leadership. There must first be a commitment from leadership to not only support DEIB efforts, but to be immersed in the process. For example, I worked with a great organization that created a mentoring program to help develop and retain high-potential young talent. Not only did their CEO support the program by greenlighting it, she also participated as a mentor in the program's second year. She demonstrated a commitment to DEIB by living the company's values. When employees see company leadership participating, they are more likely to become involved themselves. The program is now entering its third year and has become a staple in the organization. It is part of their lived culture.

Another example of DEIB becoming part of the culture is moving from performative acts or virtue signaling to intentional and purposeful efforts. Performative acts—like changing a logo for a cause or sharing a social media post about a holiday—may seem like the "right thing to do," but won't be effective if they're not coupled with work to make a difference or enact change. However, if an organization changes its logo to rainbow colors in June to show support for the LGBTQIA community and also offers gender neutral restrooms, creates an LGBTQIA employee resource group, implements a policy for using preferred pronouns, and includes same-sex couples in parental leave for births or adoptions, then the logo change is simply part of the organization's lived DEIB culture rather than a performative act.

We discussed psychological safety earlier in the chapter, but it's worth returning to here because psychological safety must be present within your organization's culture before DEIB efforts can take hold. Experts such as Amy Edmonson and Timothy R. Clark identify additional methods OD practitioners can use to create a sense of psychological safety.

One way to establish a baseline for assessing your current climate is by asking employees and yourself to reflect on these statements developed by Edmonson (1999):

- If you make a mistake on this team, it is often held against you.
- Members of this team are able to bring up problems and tough issues.
- People on this team sometimes reject others for being different.
- It is safe to take a risk on this team.
- It is difficult to ask other members of this team for help.
- No one on this team would deliberately act in a way that undermines my efforts.
- Working with members of this team, my unique skills and talents are valued and utilized.

When reviewing these statements, you must be honest and transparent. You also to have consider the risk that you take as leaders if you are not actively encouraging psychological safety within your organization. An internal Google study showed that companies with a higher sense of psychological safety also have a higher rate of more diverse teams. Additionally, they retain employees at a higher rate if they have psychological safety in place.

Once you have determined your current organizational state, it is time to act. Have open dialogues with your talent through townhalls, roundtables, and ERGs. In a remote work environment, virtual platforms such as Yammer, Microsoft Teams, Zoom, and Slack are great options to host meetings. If people are not comfortable with sharing their opinions openly, anonymous surveys can serve as an alternative. Open conversations and dialogue are not limited to frontline employees; managers also want to be open about their own mistakes.

Timothy Clark's four stages of psychological safety are useful for tracking your organization's progression toward being a psychologically safe place to work (Clark 2020):

- **Level 1: Inclusion safety.** This level relates to a sense of belonging. As noted in Maslow's Hierarchy of Needs, talent need to believe they are valued and accepted for their differences.
- **Level 2: Learner safety.** This relates to growth and development. Talent can learn and explore freely through a holistic process of discovery, feedback, and engagement.
- **Level 3: Contributor safety.** This level relates to making a difference and contributing. Talent wants to know that they are part of a greater cause. They want to contribute ideas, thoughts, and concepts that will be part of the problem solving or creative process.
- **Level 4: Challenger safety.** This level relates to challenging the status quo. Talent wants to feel safe being a disruptor and asking questions.

4. Leveraging DEIB Training

All too often, DEIB training is conducted as a one-off event so the organization can mark the diversity checkbox. Even if these training sessions are well put together and cover pertinent information, the organization must go beyond a single event if it wants true change to occur. But training can work! In fact, when done well, training not only provides an educational foundation for diversity issues, but it also increases team unity, builds competence, boosts morale, and helps retain employees. Training captures the collective attention of your employees and sets a standard for what the organization deems as important to team development.

Nonetheless, training is only a component of organization development—not the completion of a DEIB transformation. Organizations must integrate what they've learned into their overall OD strategy. This means reinforcing training objectives through the creation or improvement of DEIB systems, structures, and processes in the organization (van Vulpen 2019). Furthermore, training should also go through a DEIB audit to evaluate the diversity of facilitators, learning styles, accessibility, technology, inclusive language, and images.

Consider two examples: An organization in the US is leveraging training to introduce DEIB initiatives. At the end of each training session, an HR professional highlights additional initiatives and efforts the organization is spearheading. This strategy capitalizes on the momentum and "high" generated by the training program to ignite excitement for other DEIB projects. Meanwhile, another company with sites across the US is hosting DEIB training for their leaders and frontline staff. The intention is to use these sessions to not only increase diversity intelligence, but also make employees aware of blind spots and biases to help increase employee engagement and sense of belonging. For managers, the goal is to increase retention on their team.

5. Going Beyond Training

After employees are trained, organizations can reinforce and support DEIB objectives by improving recruiting and retention processes; creating affinity groups, ERGs, or business resource groups (BRGs); and developing leadership development programs, mentoring programs, partnerships, and external DEIB partnerships. Many organizations rely on human resource management and talent development practitioners to assist in the development of these groups and programs because they have the data to back the need for them. This data comes from people analytics, surveys, training program evaluations, or focus groups.

To improve recruiting and retention processes, organizations can assemble hiring committees made up of diverse or minority employees, who can make hiring decisions with DEIB objectives in mind (Taing 2013). Affinity groups and ERGs are employee-led groups made up of people with similar cultural identities and interests that provide a space for discussing employee concerns and advancing DEIB efforts (Bortz 2020). Affinity groups can also include allies (those who are not a member of the group but are advocates for their concerns within the workplace). BRGs are similar to ERGs but have a clear business objective, are more formally recognized by organizations, and are designed to attract and retain diverse employees (The Intersect Group 2021).

Leadership development and mentoring programs help continue the employee learning process by providing ongoing support to strengthen areas of DEIB weakness. Additionally, talent development practitioners can help design leadership development or mentoring programs that can improve recruiting and retention efforts. One form of DEIB leadership that organizations can structure is a champions program, made up of employees who advocate for DEIB within the organization in various ways (Papini 2021). This group can organize and promote events, make sure employees feel included, and model DEIB practices.

Lastly, it is wise for organizations to understand that they have their own internal biases. Partnerships with organizations that focus on DEIB and external DEIB consultants provide opportunities for employees to learn from the strengths of other organizations and DEIB experts who have successfully implemented DEIB initiatives and strategies. This can help provide fresh perspectives and identify DEIB blind spots within the organization.

Change Management and Diversity

An effective DEIB strategy includes a well-organized plan that details how and when changes will be implemented, and how that change will be measured. Implementing DEIB strategies, however, can be a daunting task. What if it is handled incorrectly and an organization wastes time and money? What if employees resist the changes?

Using a change management methodology can provide structure for changes and prevent potential problems. There are several effective change management methods to choose from, but the Lewin, McKinsey, ADKAR, and Kotter methods are used most often (Brooks 2021). John Kotter's Change Management model is an eight-step process and one of the most recognized methodologies for organizational change. (This is the method I use in my DEIB strategic work.) Kotter (2021) organized this method after studying how various organizations attempted to execute change, and I have found that it perfectly aligns with how to implement a DEIB initiative. The eight steps are:

1. Create a sense of urgency.
2. Build a guiding coalition.
3. Form a strategic vision and initiatives.
4. Enlist a volunteer army.
5. Enable action by removing barriers.
6. Generate short-term wins.
7. Sustain acceleration.
8. Institute change.

These steps can be used as milestones to encourage employees and drive change forward during the development and application of a DEIB strategy.

Let's look at an example of how to use Kotter's change management model in your DEIB initiatives (Brook 2021).

1. **Create urgency.** This involves determining the need for a DEIB initiative—through a comprehensive audit that includes focus groups, questionnaires, record assessment, cultural competency continuum, and a SWOT analysis—and building a compelling business case.

2. **Form a powerful coalition.** This involves building a team of diversity champions, leaders, and sponsors who can help you gain buy-in and create or implement the DEIB initiative.

3. **Create a vision for change.** This involves asking where you see the initiative going and how it will make a difference in the organization as well as identifying possible sources of resistance or disruption.

4. **Communicate the vision.** This involves communicating the vision to others outside your coalition with a message that includes information showing that the change is purposeful, desirable, and feasible. You might involve chief diversity officers, diversity council leaders, and other leaders to communicate the vision.

5. **Alleviate and remove barriers.** This involves understanding the emotions and feelings of those affected by DEIB changes. They might not understand the need for a DEIB initiative and, as a result, don't agree with or want it to occur at all.

6. **Create short-term wins.** This involves realizing that rolling out a new DEIB initiative can be an enormous task and celebrating quick, small wins can generate momentum. Don't be afraid to communicate your successes with stakeholders within the organization.

7. **Build on the change.** This involves taking the momentum from small victories and building on it—encouraging the organization to adapt to the change and make it stick.

8. **Anchor the changes in corporate culture.** This involves making the DEIB initiative part of the lived corporate culture, which occurs when the vision is implemented, behaviors are changing, and impact is taking place.

Measuring Your DEIB Efforts

Many organizations struggle to determine how to measure DEIB efforts because they can be viewed as an intangible endeavor, such as increasing morale, or because they may be tied to performative acts, such as changing logo colors for a cause.

The factors to measure are the ones aligned with the quantitative and qualitative data gathered from a SWOT analysis, including things such as the cultural makeup of employees and their roles, the number of ERGs, turnover rates, and employee perceptions of diversity and experiences with discrimination. To track progress, this data needs to be converted into organizational benchmarks that are reviewed within a specified timeframe, such as monthly or annually. These benchmarks are then organized and tracked on a DEIB scorecard, which includes a visual representation of the organization's progress toward DEIB goals. Comparing the change in benchmark progress over time allows the organization to calculate the return on investment (ROI) of the DEIB strategy implementation. There are several metrics an organization can look at to calculate ROI, but examples include changes in performance, profitability, retention rates, and dollars spent on DEIB efforts (Guild Education 2021). The Phillips's ROI Methodology goes into greater detail about calculating ROI and converting intangible measures into monetary values. ROI represents the fifth level of evaluation in that evaluation framework.

The Kirkpatrick's Four Levels of Training Evaluation is another methodology that can be used to measure the impact of DEIB initiatives (Kirkpatrick Partners nd). Here's a quick summary of the four levels:

- **Level 1: Reaction** measures the degree to which participants found the training favorable, engaging, and relevant to their jobs.
- **Level 2: Learning** focuses on the degree to which participants acquired the intended knowledge, skills, attitude, confidence, and commitment.
- **Level 3: Behavior** is where outcomes begin. This is when you measure the degree to which participants apply what they learned during the training when they are back on the job.
- **Level 4: Results** centers around the degree to which targeted outcomes occur as a result of the training and the support and accountability package.

Summary

As seen over the past century, shifts in the public's awareness of diversity will always bring about a push for change in society and the workplace. The movements surrounding racial and gender equality brought much needed change to the employment environment, and it's hard to imagine how completely different things were decades ago. These efforts introduced the idea of equality in the workplace and paved the way for the need to recognize the importance of equity. Now, with the social justice movement at fever pitch, its influence on the evolution of inclusion and belonging in the workplace is refreshing.

Still, an OD practitioner cannot seek to implement a DEIB strategy in a silo. The work to recruit, hire, retain, and engage diverse employees must be done, or the efforts will fall short, miss the mark, or simply not work. It is ironic, but not surprising, that DEIB efforts, which contribute to the growing knowledge base around what makes employees different from one another, are not causing more division but instead are having a unifying effect. This speaks to the universal need for every person to feel seen, heard, valued, and welcome in the world and at work. Change is happening at a rapid pace, and organizations that do not authentically embrace diversity, equity, inclusion, and belonging will ultimately become a relic of the past.

Key Takeaways

Here are a few things to remember when implementing a DEIB strategy:

- **Clearly define what diversity, equity, inclusion, and belonging mean for your organization.** Because there are many definitions of diversity, equity, inclusion, and belonging, it is helpful for you to determine what they mean for your organization. Without a clear definition or idea of these terms, your DEIB initiatives won't be effective and may even cause chaos.

- **DEIB must be integrated into your company's culture and not become siloed.** DEIB can quickly become something an organization implements because it is the "right thing to do." When this happens, resources are typically scarce and momentum gets lost. Instead of focusing on the right thing to do, make DEIB part of your lived culture. It should start with leadership and cascade down. Leaders can volunteer to become mentors or support initiatives that affect underrepresented communities within the organization.

- **An effective change management strategy can help alleviate possible barriers and obstacles when implementing a DEIB initiative.** Change is hard because it requires entering the world of the unknown. Integrating any DEIB initiative will come with obstacles and hurdles. Regardless of your change management method, be sure to have strong champions and allies in your team. They will be instrumental in communicating the vision and intentions of your DEIB initiative.

Well-Being and Caring for the Whole Person

DEEPTI GUDIPATI AND CATHERINE W. COREY

IN THIS CHAPTER

♦ Understand this moment in time and what it means for workplace well-being

♦ Define the meaning of well-being and what the definition unlocks

♦ Identify those responsible for creating a culture of well-being and the steps they can take to implement it

Introduction: Where We Are Now

The COVID-19 pandemic showed us the importance of the link between well-being and caring for the whole person as we began evaluating what it meant to live our lives holistically. No longer do we think, "This is what I do at work, and this is what I do at home." We don't have two selves—a professional self and a personal self—even though sometimes we might like to and organizations might wish we lived that way.

The movement started before the pandemic with rising awareness of the fallacy of work-life balance. When we discovered that it wasn't actually an achievable concept, especially given (or despite) technological advances, we started trying to implement boundaries: no-meeting Fridays, email servers that turn off at 7 p.m., and clear channels for specific types of communication. Yet, after more Americans worked at home in 2020 than ever before, a record

24 million people quit their jobs between April and September 2021 (Sull, Sull, and Zweig 2022). These jobs were both blue- and white-collar jobs, indicating high levels of disengagement across industries.

There was once a time when employers could credibly sell the myth that it was possible to leave our personal lives at the door when we stepped into the office, but our recent experiences of having to invite work into our homes or tolerate health risks and exposures by going into the office have stomped that fallacy out of existence. One of the many things emerging from the collective trauma of the COVID-19 pandemic is an expectation that health matters, alignment of priorities is important, and that our humanity comes with us to the workplace. Supporting our ability to bring our whole self into the workplace is going to require some significant shifts in resources and leadership.

The message could not be clearer: Employees want more from work and are willing to leave if they don't get it. A 2021 study conducted by Donald Sull and his colleagues found that toxic culture was the strongest predictor of attrition and was 10 times more likely to predict turnover than compensation. The study defined *toxic culture* as consisting of key attributes such as failure to promote diversity, equity, and inclusion; workers feeling disrespected; and unethical behavior. This same research also discovered that companies that scored high on innovation also had higher levels of turnover than their traditional competitors. While this finding requires further study to fully understand, the initial hypothesis is that consistently needing to innovate requires a more relentless focus on work and less focus on other aspects of life and the whole person.

Now that nearly two decades of millennials and have entered the workplace, along with Gen Zers, we have already begun to see large disruptions in what employees are seeking from employers. The global pandemic simply gave us all a new perspective—whether on life, work, how we spend our time, or even how the world operates. That's where we are as the two of us write this chapter. It's hard to say where we'll be when you read this, but what we know right now is that organizations and OD practitioners need to listen. And we need to pay attention to what people are saying and truly care for them as whole people so that we'll be ready, no matter what comes next.

When we think about caring for the whole person, there isn't one good case study to share because it looks different for every individual. However, there are common dimensions that come together to create well-being and a sense of safety and belonging, which we will define and discuss in this chapter. Supporting an authentic, whole presence requires understanding what we mean by workplace well-being, examining and ridding ourselves of toxic work culture, and investing in comprehensive resources and programs that invite well-being and resilience at a systemic level.

What Is Well-Being?

The research on well-being is broad and multidisciplinary, coming from a diverse array of industries such as healthcare, psychology, public policy, and economics. A comprehensive literature review of 99 different models and studies of well-being identified two core theories that support most existing research on the topic: Diener's model of subjective well-being and the World Health Organization's (WHO) definition of health (Linton 2016). The WHO defines *health* as "a complete state of physical, social, and mental well-being." *Subjective well-being* (SWB), according to Diener's work, is the combination of life satisfaction, the presence of pleasant affect, and the absence of unpleasant affect. For our purposes, let's consider *holistic well-being* as the ability to live longer, happier, and more productive lives and *workplace well-being* as the role that the workplace has in supporting the subjective well-being of employees.

The literature review also identified 196 potential dimensions of well-being that were then categorized across six key domains: mental, social, physical, spiritual, activities and function, and personal circumstances. This was further supported by research from Gallup and the National Wellness Institute, which identified multiple interconnected elements to achieving a state of well-being, including career, social, emotional, financial, physical, and community. Finally, a study of 2,200 workers of large employers conducted by Optum and the National Business Group on Health found that workplace well-being involved five primary dimensions: physical, social, financial, community, and mental.

Achieving well-being is about understanding how these elements or dimensions interact in our lives: how engaged we are with the work we do, how fulfilled we are in our relationships, how secure we feel in our finances, how physically healthy we feel, and how connected we are to our communities.

Dimensions of Well-Being: Implementation in the Workplace

It can be overwhelming (and unnecessary!) to tackle every dimension of well-being all at once. However, as you think through each dimension individually, you may be surprised to see how much your organization is already doing.

- **Career:** What makes sense for your team and industry? One of the teams we worked with hosted a workshop and brought in an expert on LinkedIn profiles. Because many of the team members were outward facing and connected with outside stakeholders, this gave them a chance to walk through all the parts of their profiles and provided a personal benefit as well as a professional one.

- **Social:** While it may seem easy enough to buy lunch or host an in-person or virtual happy hour for your team, being social means something different to everyone. Truly thoughtful and structured opportunities that give people something to do can help engage newer folks, introverts, extroverts, and those who prefer having prompts to make conversation. (We love seeing a hosted brain break with a little something for everyone.) Depending on your organization's size, you can set up different rooms or tables with jigsaw puzzles, a few board or table games, articles for people to read and discuss, adult coloring books, building blocks, or craft projects. It not only is a chance to take a break, but offers a little something for everyone and gives people a chance to learn about on another. Done virtually, Zoom rooms can provide similar opportunities using different invite links. Other visual options include encouraging pets to join in real time, setting up a Discord channel for your organization's gamers, creating a one-time online trivia activity, leading a yoga session or guided meditation, or asking people to post a photo from their last walk.

- **Emotional:** During the pandemic, another group we worked with hired a psychologist to come in and speak regularly with their staff. It was an acknowledgement of the very real issues that people were facing. Topics included navigating changing relationships, dealing with ambiguity, and handling stress. Mental health first-aid training courses are also available and can be a great companion to traditional first-aid courses.

- **Financial:** While your organization handles payroll for its employees, your vendors may offer additional support and expertise in this area. Does your retirement plan offer information on planning for the future? Might it be possible to invite a representative from your bank to talk about the differences between loan options and types of debt? What would be most helpful to your team?

- **Physical:** Initial thoughts tend to center around stand and stretch prompts for desk workers or physical safety for those in the field, but what are some more creative ways you could help integrate physical care and well-being into the workplace? Where can you save them time and money and encourage behavior? Things like on-site flu shots are a great example. Can you host seminars about physical health and well-being, a CPR class, or basic first-aid training that are also open to employees' family and friends?

- **Community:** Getting involved in the community can take lots of forms. At another organization, a team of employees set calendar events for the year and alternated donation drives and volunteer opportunities to help their colleagues participate more broadly in the community's well-being. The employees selected causes and organizations they had personal connections with, such as a hospital that had helped one as a child, a local school where several staff members' children went, and donating to a diaper bank during a shortage. Does your organization provide time off for such activities, either done as a team or individually?

Creating a Culture of Well-Being

Certainly, we as individuals have a responsibility to manage our own wellness and well-being. But if most of our time is spent working or in a state of work (what we used to consider "at work"), employers have a responsibility to recognize and honor the power they have to shape and influence well-being in their employees and the wider societies within which they exist. And as the world continues to shift and reshape, we are seeing significant trends that point to employees demanding and seeking workplaces that honor their humanity and invest in resources that enable well-being among their people.

Workplace well-being is an essential foundation to all the other elements of well-being. Financial security, for most of us, is tied to our workplace. The ability to invest in health and wellness is tied to the resources we can access and the time we can devote away from work. Social and community connections are also highly defined by how our work is structured.

This means going beyond basic wellness programs like gym memberships, recognition awards, and one-off well-being L&D programs. When employers invest resources and nurture these areas to create a culture of well-being, they invite workers to bring their whole selves to work. Organizations with cultures of well-being also see increases in personal well-being, productivity, and loyalty among their workers.

A Culture of Well-Being, or Just a Well-Being Program?

If a toxic culture is what encourages people to leave, what are the cultural settings that encourage them to stay? What is the organizational responsibility to create that culture? What is your responsibility as an OD practitioner in creating a culture that attracts and retains employees?

Culture is often one of the most misunderstood elements of an organization. For example, one of the organizations Catherine used to work with wanted to focus on wellness. Like many organizations, this one partnered with an outside company who specialized in wellness, invested a decent amount of money in the initiative, set goals, and offered incentives to staff members to participate. A culture of wellness had been established! We had something to share with the board, a percentage of the HR budget allocated to it, and a program we could share with potential candidates when they asked us about wellness.

The program had all the elements that should contribute to a culture of wellness and well-being. It was inclusive in terms of physical health, prevention activities, mental health, and meeting people where they were. The second year also included a staff team designed to both engage more grassroots support and ensure the program was meeting the needs that staff really wanted. The problem, however, was that culture can't be created on its own.

Culture is an outcome of the work—not a goal itself—and is developed over time through a series of consistent behaviors and patterns. After interviewing several chief executive officers who had overseen massive change efforts, Jay W. Lorsch and Emily McTague (2016) rightly observed that "cultural change is what you get after you've put new processes or structures in place to tackle tough business challenges like reworking an outdated strategy or business model. The culture evolves as you do that important work."

When we were creating our wellness initiative, we skipped right to the end and just declared that we'd like people to be healthy. But we didn't do any of the important work to actually figure out what that might mean. What flexibility did employees need? What challenges were they facing? What did they need to help their families or loved ones? How could we as employers uniquely help? Most importantly, what would wellness and well-being look like to them?

While some of the established metrics were met (such as total participants in the program and number of participants who reached the incentive milestones), the broader changes didn't stick. Well-being was not incorporated into other aspects of the organization—it wasn't in other policies, staff members weren't looking for ways to implement wellness into their own programs and events, and we had trouble getting staff to participate when we asked for input or held wellness events. Our team had failed to do the long-term work of creating a culture of well-being before declaring success. We simply created a standalone program.

Who Determines Culture?

Culture isn't something that exists at an organizational level. It's made up of the behaviors and patterns of individual people, which is where organization development comes in. Wellness and well-being are often owned by HR by virtue of being tied to health benefits, which can be a great place to start. Sull and his colleagues (2022) note that the dangers of a toxic workplace include mental health issues and an increased likelihood of major health issues like coronary disease, diabetes, or arthritis. Obviously decreasing these symptoms is in everyone's interest.

However, it's not just up to HR, and well-being isn't just about health. Addressing potentially toxic behaviors needs to begin long before mental and physical symptoms appear. Individual supervisors have a great deal of power to help create an employee experience that contributes to a culture of well-being. Encouraging team members to show up as their authentic selves can be a key step in creating workplace wellness. Through coaching, training, and other targeted L&D programs, organizations can prepare their managers to have these authentic conversations.

Managing or supervising staff is often added as a line in a job description right above "other duties as assigned." Through an OD lens, however, shifting that responsibility from one that happens after other primary job functions are done to the top of a manager's priority list can make all the difference. Imagine redesigning all your job descriptions so that any supervisory position begins with a section outlining expectations to shift and strengthen the culture you want to create, not just managing people. Your supervisors' responsibilities could include coaching team members to excel based on their ability to bring their authentic selves to work, experience a genuine sense of belonging, and explore their unique potential for growth—all in pursuit of aligning their individual goals to those of the organization.

You might add a personal check-in reminder to take a more holistic view in your performance review process. What changes might be coming up in your direct report's personal schedule? Is there anything they're particularly excited about that's happening outside work? In addition to formal processes, consider getting together groups of supervisors to talk about how they're connecting with their direct reports. What have they been noticing that seems to help people show up as themselves? Have they implemented any interesting ways to foster connection in groups, one-on-one, or virtually? You may have more tools at your disposal than you realize to start shifting the patterns of how people interact.

A 2021 scholarly literature review about authenticity in the workplace found that "maintaining an authentic self at the workplace is important to develop a connection with the inner self which is prominent in making employees healthy and promot[ing] well-being at the workplace" (Mehta 2021). Encouraging discussions about outside interests, not making assumptions about family or living situations, asking for pronouns, and treating everyone's time as equally valuable (caregivers vs. noncaregivers) can go a long way to helping employees feel free to show up as themselves.

Going beyond individual supervisors, what policies—spoken or unspoken—may be in place that are reinforcing a narrow band of acceptable behavior in your organization's culture? What do your employees see when they look at company leadership? What kinds of visible diversity do they see? What behavior is rewarded and what's brushed under the rug? Who gets promoted, given key projects, or has prime face time? What language is used or avoided? How are mistakes handled? What happens to those who speak up?

At another organization, Catherine was on a conference call with the CEO, three members of volunteer leadership, and one other staff member. The CEO and the volunteer leaders identified as male, and the other staff member identified as female. About halfway through the call, one of the volunteer leaders started to berate Catherine for something he believed she had done wrong, raising his voice and calling her names. Catherine's female colleague looked at her, eyes wide—not in disbelief that he was yelling at her (he had a reputation), but that no one was saying anything. After what felt like an eternity, but was probably more like 30 seconds, Catherine interrupted. She said she appreciated the feedback, but it seemed like the conversation wasn't going anywhere productive. She'd be happy to continue the discussion later, but she was ending the call. Then she hung up and left the room. The three other men on call checked in with her later to say how sorry they were and how inappropriate that was. However, they did so individually when they wouldn't have to worry about losing face in front of their colleagues or leadership.

Encouraging Authenticity at Work

How can we help leaders and supervisors encourage authenticity at work? Here are a few discussion points to share. What else would you add?

- **Start from a place of curiosity.** Do this by not making assumptions. Engage in conversation to find out what hobbies people have, what they enjoy outside work, where they live, what they value, and even with whom they spend their time. Don't assume that everyone lives within a nuclear family setting, newly married young women will eventually go on maternity leave, or that colleagues who are not married or without children have time to pick up extra work. White straight men may very much want to participate in your inclusion and equity efforts, while people from underrepresented populations may be tired of being asked to lead those efforts or are more comfortable participating outside of work. Conversations based in genuine curiosity will help people discuss their interests and life situations.

- **Use inclusive language.** Using inclusive language begins from a place of not assuming everyone is in the same situation. Be mindful of heteronormative language that may indicate an expectation or preference for mixed gender couples. For example, referring to spouses when discussing benefit plans may leave out people who are partnered rather than married or supporting a dependent rather than a partner. Terms like minorities automatically indicate a majority and can lead to othering of whole groups of people. Use person-first language, like people experiencing homelessness, people who are incarcerated, or those living with schizophrenia rather than homeless people, prisoners, or schizophrenics.

- **Revisit organization norms and policies.** Policies like asking everyone to specify their pronouns (note the evolution to simply "pronouns" versus "preferred pronouns" to indicate that pronouns just exist, rather than are preferred) is an inclusive way to let everyone indicate how they want to be addressed, not just those who feel like they may need or want to share it. Allotting company time for mental health needs and ensuring the time is used appropriately can also be incredibly effective. Rather than hunkering down and white knuckling through stress or turmoil, encouraging leaders to help team members label their emotions and feelings will show leaders care while also helping employees manage those emotions. Additionally, while organizational leaders are helping normalize emotions in the workplace, they can also be working on policies and solutions to deal with the root issues causing that trouble.

That toxic culture left Catherine feeling alone to defend herself against the injustice of the discrimination and was just one of the reasons she left. The company's unspoken policy said that staff would take whatever treatment volunteer leaders thought appropriate. While unspoken, it was evident in actions as the entire senior staff turned over within two years.

Even with all the privilege Catherine has as she moves though the world, there was still a very basic element of who she was that was not welcome at that organization: a female member of staff with a voice.

Strategic Resilience

Thinking about where to start in shifting patterns and behaviors around well-being can be overwhelming. Marta Morais-Storz and colleagues (2018) beautifully outlined why we so often feel set up for failure. Classic definitions of resilience are built on responding and survival—a crisis presents itself, and we adapt and move forward. It's exhausting because we're constantly in a defensive position. Morais-Storz and team also raise a critical problem with this traditional definition of resilience: If we don't survive, we die. This strict binary approach to resilience is unnecessarily terrifying and artificially inflates the stakes. Rather than viewing survival as a winner-takes-all result, they more eloquently state that "destruction, however, does not necessarily mean death, but rather, the unlearning that must precede learning and metamorphosis. What is important in a world of turbulence, complexity, and uncertainty, is the organizational ability to reinvent itself where the ultimate goal is resilience itself."

We have all had plenty of experiences with organizations that do not practice resilience well. Deepti has been fortunate to work for an organization that exemplified systemic resilience in practice in many ways. One that stands out in her memory was a program that allocated professional development dollars that employees were free to use in any way they wished to increase their capacity and resilience to perform their jobs effectively. This meant anything from taking a spa day, to travel, to professional training and courses. Deepti was free to define resilience in whatever way she wished. The possibilities those unrestricted funds opened up were tremendous—she was able to invest in intellectual and skills development through courses while also spending some money nourishing her mental health and well-being.

Organization development gives you the chance to take on this beautiful opportunity of unlearning to help with metamorphosis, and it doesn't all have to happen at once. Behavior change can begin at the policy and procedure level, allowing for explicit new expectations. Training and other L&D efforts in which you may have been involved can support these new initiatives as well as different approaches to organizational policies and procedures. Coaching leaders to adapt to new ways of doing things, seeing blind spots, and integrating feedback gracefully can be powerful tools. The vantage point offered by organization development allows you to see both the strategic overview and the tactical opportunities to execute on that vision. When was the last time you spent real time with your staff reviewing the purpose behind your policies and procedures—not just the final product?

Holistic Security

Catherine once had the opportunity to be involved in an active assailant training due to another building occupant. To be compliant, the exercise would have to be implemented building-wide. The organization had done fire and evacuation drills before but nothing of this sort. While they could have simply gone down the traditional resilience path and responded to the crisis—add an active assailant training to the portfolio, survive (hopefully quite literally), and then move on—they chose a different path.

This training mandate became a turning point for the organization in terms of policies and procedures. The organization embraced the chance to unlearn the way they'd always done the required biannual fire drills and safety protocol sign-offs. Catherine and her team took the extra time necessary to look at the organization's security as a whole, top to bottom. Nothing was off limits for the discussion from key cards to inclement weather to online threats to garage access. It was a massive undertaking that involved HR, facilities, legal, IT, the executive office, outside vendors, building tenants, outside contractors, and many, many hours. But in the end, they ended up being able to position the organization to be much more proactively resilient in the face of many more threats than they could have envisioned, far past an active assailant.

One of the accomplishments Catherine is most proud came of out of that effort: a policy regarding intimate partner violence (IPV) or domestic violence. It was an opportunity for the organization to completely care for the whole person in many ways. First, statistically, she knew the policy would apply to employees in the population whether the organization was aware of it or not. According to the National Domestic Violence Hotline, an average of 24 people per minute experience rape, physical violence, or stalking by an intimate partner in the United States. That equates to more than 12 million women and men over the course of a single year. Additionally, on average, one in three women and one in four men will experience rape, physical violence, or stalking by an intimate partner in their life. Out of those experiencing IPV, 96 percent who were employed reported experiencing problems at work due to the abuse, and 33 percent of women killed in US workplaces between 2003 and 2008 were victims of current or former intimate partners.

It is simply not possible to have a holistic security policy or business continuity plan without a policy on IPV. This is a prime example of a behavior that helps develop a culture. When members of your workforce may not be safe at home or at work, which may then also result in danger to your other employees, you have not cared for the whole person. Organizations are in a unique position to alter work schedules, change direct deposits, advance salary, change work locations, or make connections to support organizations that may not be possible through other avenues.

These were new policies and a very different way of working to be sure. Catherine and her team were upfront in the introduction of the new security policies and their purpose. There was no specific threat—they were simply working to be proactive. They focused on cyber security, which was familiar, and took the time to talk about changes to the building, work up to drills, let people know what was coming, and introduce new resources. And the day after they introduced the IPV policy, a supervisor come to Catherine's office ready to talk about a team member she'd been concerned about. This was the purpose of the policy.

Modeling and Permission

There is a lot about self-care that has been co-opted by "shoulds." I should treat myself to a day at the spa, a weekend away, or the latest tech gadget to make my life easier. I should be sleeping more, eating better, getting more exercise, meditating, catching up with friends, or making time for myself. Basically, self-care would be fantastic if only there were 104 hours in each day.

Part of the beauty of self-care is that it is for the self, and no one knows the self better than the individual involved. However, that does present a challenge at the organizational level when trying to meet the needs of numerous staff members. So rather than presenting shoulds and mandates, how can you in your role as an OD practitioner help leaders within your organization model the behaviors you want to empower?

One of the most powerful things to do is first remove shoulds and replace them with wants. What do team members want? What would be useful to them when it comes to recharging? It may end up being something from the should list, but *wanting* to do something is very different than doing it because you think you *should*. Do employees feel like they should use their paid time off (PTO) for travel, one week at a time, because that's the acceptable way it's modeled? Or do they know they can take a Wednesday off simply because they want to? Early adopters of unlimited PTO, for instance, reported having to institute minimum requirements for PTO as opposed to maximums because their cultures were not supporting the use of PTO as they had hoped. When it comes to how time and resources are used, employees will pay more attention to what leaders do as opposed to what they say.

And while leaders can't model every possible behavior, you can absolutely help your leaders model listening and a yes first attitude as opposed to a no first attitude. When team members express their wants, is what they're asking doable within your current system? If not, why not? Sometimes there are specific reasons that roles or individuals have restrictions; hopefully in those cases the reasons were clearly outlined upfront. However, if the answer is "because," then you've entered no first territory.

Remember how we discussed the increasing willingness of employees to leave their jobs if they're not getting what works for them? Well, what are the costs (both real and opportunity) to saying no to a request versus saying yes? Especially in this hybrid world where some staff are remote and some are on location, what are the guidelines around that? Are they transparent and well-known? Do leaders model equity for caregivers and those who live alone? The need for flexibility with work can be just as important for employees with children or aging parents, people volunteering in their community, attending school, traveling, caring for their mental health, or making time to see friends and family.

As OD practitioners, our job is not to prioritize life choices but to ensure we create environments that empower individuals to do what they need to do and advocate for what they want.

Summary: A Necessary Shift for Organizations

We are experiencing a shift in what people expect from their employers around health, wellness, and the ability to fit work in along with other priorities—not the other way around. True workplace well-being must go beyond gym memberships and affirmations of support for work-life balance. It is imperative that organizations begin investing in systemic resources and policies that support well-being and care for the people who make their organizations run. Consider the dimensions of workplace well-being as a place to begin—physical, social, financial, community, mental, and emotional.

With the financial health dimension, organizational support could come in the form of helping with healthcare costs; access to advances on paychecks; or resources for childcare, student loans, or housing. Or the mental health dimension—tangible ways to manage stress, access treatment, and invest in personal resilience are all important to employees. Additionally, what opportunities do you have as an OD practitioner to help your leadership redirect work or get creative with cross-training, job sharing, or project streamlining? Efforts to relieve work stress can have a tremendous impact on mental health and show that you're really listening to employee needs.

We have offered examples and reflections on different ways to dismantle toxic cultures and build habits that support and foster well-being, creating new cultures. We recognize that what is possible and feasible is different for each organization. The algorithm for the best way to do that for your company is yours to create. How might you build systemic well-being around these dimensions? Which ones make sense for you? What do you want to prioritize? What models make sense for you?

Key Takeaways

Here are a few things to think about as you work to foster a culture of well-being in your organization:

- **Where is your organization now?** How has the COVID-19 pandemic influenced your industry? Your specific team? What generations are in your workforce? What issues are you hearing that are important to your people, both inside and outside the workplace?
- **Define what well-being means in your world.** With so many possible definitions of well-being, using the dimensions of well-being presented here and focusing on what's important to you and your team can help provide a specific road map for your well-being plans.
- **Take an honest look at your current culture.** What type of culture is created by your current patterns, behaviors, and policies? Where are your strengths and opportunities for growth and change? Who is going to feel empowered to help with those opportunities for change?
- **Support strategic resilience.** Where can you move away from a win or perish mentality? What norms might need a review?
- **Practice the why.** When writing or revising your policies, procedures, and training content, taking the time to share the "why" of it all will not only help connect the dots for employees but also help illuminate any blind spots. Are you missing any related or supported policies? Should there be an extra training or job aid resource?

- **Ensure that leaders understand how to model, encourage, and grant permission.** Change and culture evolve from a series of behaviors. Cultures of well-being won't emerge unless your leaders model self-care, encourage their teams to truly bring their authentic selves to work, and give employees permission to ask for what they need when they need it.

PART 2

Organizational Design

CHAPTER 6

Business Alignment: Designing an Organization to Meet Business Objectives

BETH MESSICH

IN THIS CHAPTER

♦ Identify the multiple components of business alignment and how to account for them in your organization design

♦ Analyze current and future states to determine the key organizational changes needed to meet the business goals

♦ Create a process for ongoing business alignment to address shifts in company strategy

Effective organization design starts with business alignment. You may have heard this boiled down to the idea that strategy drives structure. There is truth to that statement, but it's not that simple. You need to understand more than just the strategy, and you need to do more than just create a new organizational chart to support the growth and success of the business. Organization development (OD) practitioners need to understand the company's mission, vision, and values, and consider a multitude of factors, including the workforce capabilities needed and the scope of behavioral change that alignment requires.

While mission and vision largely remain stable, strategy and goals do not. Volatility driven by a host of internal and external causes is a very real factor. Companies are faced with disruptive and unpredictable events—COVID-19 and natural disasters resulting from climate change are recent examples—that force them to reevaluate and pivot their strategy on an ongoing basis. Consequently, business alignment is a continuous improvement process that challenges us to create organization designs that are resilient and flexible.

The good news is that as the lines between HR, L&D, and OD have blurred, you likely have begun doing at least some of this work in your current role. You've already honed your strategic planning and thinking, needs assessment, and gap analysis skills as an L&D expert. This chapter will help you shift into an OD mindset, describing the factors you need to consider to ensure the business is set up to deliver on its strategy.

What We Mean by Business Alignment

Business alignment (also referred to as strategic alignment) is the process by which we assess whether a company is set up to deliver on its strategic goals. The fundamental question to ask is, "Is the business set up for success?" You and the organization's leadership need to be willing to examine many elements to understand the full picture of alignment. These include job scopes and organizational structure, IT and systems, policies and processes, funding and budget allocation, and people practices.

Your role in the business alignment process can vary depending on the size and structure of the organization. Ideally you will be brought in as part of the strategic planning process so you can influence and inform how the plan is created, ensuring business alignment from the beginning. More frequently, OD practitioners are brought in after the plan is developed, either to help implement it or because the organization is not meeting its strategic objectives.

Regardless of whether you are building the strategy or supporting one that already exists, you will first want to ground yourself in some core tenets of the business.

Mission, Vision, and Values

As you think about organization design, it is important to understand the company's mission, vision, and values. Let's start with some distinctions:

- **Mission** is the organization's reason for existing; what we do (tactical).

- **Vision** is the future state that the organization wishes to achieve; what we will do (aspirational).
- **Values** are the core principles that guide the organization and help to shape its culture; how we do it (behavioral).

The mission, vision, and values shape the purpose and goals that make up the strategic plan. They can inform performance standards, metrics, and behavioral expectations, which ultimately translate into organizational design. Keep in mind, not all companies have a mission statement and a vision statement, and not all organizations explicitly articulate their values.

Let's review the mission statement and core values for the outdoor apparel retailer Patagonia, which are posted on their customer-facing website. Note, they do not show an explicit vision statement:

- **Mission:** We're in business to save our home planet.
- **Values:** Build the best products; cause no unnecessary harm; use business to protect nature; not bound by convention.

Now let's consider some business alignment questions Patagonia's leaders may ask:

- How will we maintain the right level of continuous leadership focus and budget allocation required to deliver on our mission and live our values? Do we need a specific role (not the CEO) tasked with leading and championing this work?
- What are the ways in which we can ensure that we "cause no unnecessary harm"? What processes, policies, and oversight need to be in place?
- How will we "use business to protect nature"? Does this require both internal-focused and external-focused resources?

Keep in mind that an organization's subgroups (departments, functions, even individual teams) may also have their own mission and vision. These will likely be an expression of how that group delivers on the company's mission and vision and can be quite helpful as you get to the specifics of organization design at that level. For example, it is possible to imagine that Patagonia's product design team could have a mission to create products that lead to a more sustainable future and a vision to set the standard for sustainable product design in the industry.

At this level, some of the business alignment questions that you could consider are:

- What type of technical experience or training does the product development team need to help them to unlock sustainability innovation?

- How will we determine which processes, practices, and technologies are proprietary? Could keeping these things proprietary conflict with our vision to set the standard for the industry?
- Does the right technology exist, or do we need to build new technology?

Make note if a group-specific mission and vision conflict with the company mission and vision (for example, if the company mission is focused on sustainability, but the design team mission is focused on creating fast-fashion products). This points to a lack of alignment in the organization, which you will need to address and resolve before you continue with the organization design.

Strategy

Next, review the strategy. You should be looking for two things: the strategic plan and the yearly goals. They are similar, but here is the distinction:

- **Strategic plan** is long-term.
- **Yearly goals** are short-term.

The strategic plan is a document that outlines some or all of the following: long-term company goals, actions that the organization will take, who is accountable, metrics to determine success, resource allocations, prioritization, and desired outcomes. It can come in the form of a three-, five-, or even 10-year plan, although a strategy of that length is becoming less common given the speed of change in the world today.

Yearly goals are the organization-level goals that the company sets out to achieve in a fiscal year. They should ladder up to the long-term strategic plan. If they don't, you may have identified another lack of alignment that needs to be resolved before moving on.

Note that not all strategic plans or goals documents are created alike, and there is no one set template to use. This means that the information you are looking for may not be presented in the clearest or most thorough way. Regardless of formatting, they should have some specific components including mission, vision, and values; a SWOT (strengths, weaknesses, opportunities, and threats) analysis; long-term goals; objectives by year; and action plans.

If you are brought into the strategic planning process from the beginning, part of your role can be to ensure that the goals in the plan are comprehensively defined using the SMART framework. Having fully fleshed out goals is like the difference between being given a hand-drawn map to get to your destination versus using the step-by-steps instructions in a digital navigation app. Both will get you to the same place, but the app will get you there more efficiently and with less risk of error.

As I review a strategy, I find it helpful to follow the same basic principles that I use when I conduct a learning needs analysis:

- Understand the goal.
- Identify the desired performance outcomes.
- Identify the conditions and resources needed.
- Identify the current conditions and resources.

The intersection of those last two bullet points is critical—compare the current state to the future state, identifying the gaps between the two. A helpful clarifying question to ask yourself at this stage is, "What needs to be true for us to be able to meet this strategic objective or goal?"

Watch Out For

As an L&D professional, you are likely already familiar with goal setting structures and processes. A solid plan or goals document should use a SMART framework or something similar. It will be harder to determine alignment needs if the goals and objectives are too broad, poorly defined, or do not have expected timeframes. In this case, you may determine that the strategic plan or goals document itself requires revision and further definition.

SMART goals are:
- **Specific:** Well-defined; clear
- **Measurable:** Metrics or data targets; a concrete way to evaluate
- **Achievable:** Within scope; ambitious but attainable
- **Realistic:** Improves the business; has reasonable budget and resources requirements
- **Timebound:** Milestones and completion dates

Information Gathering

Now that you are clear on the strategy, you still have some information gathering to do. Gary Neilson, Jamie Estupiñán, and Bhushan Sethi (2015) outline a simple framework of formal and informal elements to assess and include when building your organization design:

- **Formal (tangible)**
  - Decisions
  - Motivators
  - Information
  - Structure
- **Informal (intangible)**
  - Norms
  - Commitments
  - Mind Sets
  - Networks

It is helpful to talk to people throughout the organization at different levels and in different roles about how things are now and whether the current elements support where the organization wants to go. You can conduct individual interviews, host listening sessions, or send electronic surveys to gather information. Remember to continue comparing the current state and the desired future state to identify gaps that you will need to account for in your design.

Build on these exploratory questions to get to the information you need:

- How are decisions made in the organization? What needs to change to create more autonomy in the decision-making process?
- What are our talent practices (for example, talent reviews, succession plans, critical roles)? What resources do we think we need to make the outcome of these processes more actionable?
- What are the most important objectives and key results (OKRs) for the company, function, or team? As we move to a focus on [XYZ], what OKRs will be most important to determine success?
- What are the existing business processes? What business processes get in the way of our ability to operate efficiently?
- What are the unwritten rules of getting work done around here? How would people need to change their behaviors to shift to a new way of working?
- What makes people proud to work here? What will inspire, encourage, or convince people to stay with the organization for years to come?

- What concepts do we commonly rely on as we get work done across the organization? Where are our actions not in line with our beliefs?
- What does collaboration look like here? What would help teams operate in a more agile way?

Some practitioners place a premium on formal elements and systems over informal ones; however, in my experience, this is a mistake. While the formal system may be more explicit, the informal one is often more ingrained and powerful. For example, norms are the unwritten rules of an organization. You will not find them on the employee portal or in a policy manual, but they inform how things get done in the organization—and everyone knows what they are. They represent how people intuitively act and are reinforced by the organization's culture. Therefore, these informal norms can be a more reliable predictor of behavior.

Watch Out For

If you work in a global organization, you will want to dig even deeper and consider cultural norms as well. For example, in US organizations, the norm is to hold meetings to have discussions and make decisions. In Japan decisions are made during individual conversations prior to the meeting. The meeting itself is when the decision is formally approved (Story 2018). In the US the idea of meeting before the meeting might be considered inefficient and unnecessary. In Japan, it is essential. Not exploring and accounting for differences in cultural norms can cause unintended friction and disruption.

Designing the Organization

Use the information you've gathered to round out your picture of the current state so you can create a design that effectively realigns the organization. Use the formal or informal framework questions outlined earlier to ensure you've explored all the necessary elements. Keep in mind, you are designing an organization that will set the company up to deliver on the strategic plan. You need to account for and address the gaps between the current and future state.

Don't let current limitations influence how you design the organization as it needs to be. For example, you may determine that the current compensation model is limiting the company's abilities to get the right talent to do the work. Rather than assuming that the compensation model will not change, design the model required to deliver results. Your objective is to figure out what is needed to solve the issues. Leadership will have to decide if they are willing and able to support the changes required to implement the new design. (More on that in a minute.)

Structure Comes Last

It is tempting to think primarily about team structure—designing the right organization chart. Of all these factors, the structure should come last. It is only once you have defined every other aspect of organization design that you can determine the structure of the team.

Why design the structure last? Because a new structure will not solve the business problems. It's all the other elements—decision rights, systems, processes, behaviors—that will solve the problems and determine the structure that the organization needs.

For example, if one of the obstacles you identified was that decision making takes too long, you need to address it in your design. You determined that the root cause was that too many levels of the organization needed to weigh in to reach a final decision. So, you design a more streamlined decision rights framework to support speed and efficiency. Creating a flatter structure—a more compressed hierarchy with fewer layers—is one way to enable that framework. You need the inputs from all the other elements before you can design the structure.

Just because the structure is last doesn't mean that it isn't important. Again, it is an enabler of success. Creating and maintaining the right structure—that is, having a process to approve or deny changes to the structure—is critical.

The Human Element

Organizational structure means people. Unless you are building an entirely new team, there will be an inherent tension because there are people in jobs in the current structure, and those jobs may not exist—or exist in a different form—in a new organization chart. When the jobs change, what happens to the people?

The reality is, you need to design for organization's needs first, people second. This isn't to say that people are not important. It's quite the opposite. The organization structure will only be successful if the right people are in the right roles. You will define the right roles by defining the responsibilities, capabilities, and experience required—even for jobs that already exist—agnostic of the people who may currently be in those roles.

Watch Out For

In my experience, leadership can have a difficult time thinking about the design of a new structure without simultaneously factoring in the current team. As a result, we end up designing around the people, not the actual talent needs. Why does this happen? First, we want to retain talent. It is expensive when people leave. We lose institutional knowledge, and it can affect both productivity and morale. Second, it can feel heartless to focus on structure first, people second. I mean, let's face it; no company wants their message to be that the structure is more important than people. However, putting structure first *is* caring about people. You are thinking about the long-term health and growth of the organization, which has an impact on everyone in the organization.

Once you create the structure, including reporting relationships and job descriptions, you can go through a process to place existing employees into new roles based on their qualifications. It will be incredibly helpful if the organization has solid talent practices in place. Being able to consult up-to-date talent review information, succession plans, and critical role or people lists will make the process for placing people into the organization chart much easier.

If those things do not exist, you will need to devise a process to assess talent. It is important that this be a systematic, evaluative process and not a subjective exercise. In addition to having legal ramifications (labor law violations, impacts on protected classes, and issues of discrimination and bias), a subjective process will fail to put the people with the right skills and capabilities in the right roles, negating the work you did to create the appropriate structure.

When you complete the placement process, you will likely have to contend with two issues: open roles and people who have not been placed. It's easier to deal with open roles. In most instances, your talent acquisition team will post these roles and fill them using the hiring processes and practices in place.

For existing employees that you have not been able to place in the new structure, you will need to decide on next steps. If there are no roles in the new organization that align to their skills and capabilities and no open positions for which they are qualified in another part of the organization (a different department or another brand or company in the portfolio), you may have to terminate their employment via a reduction in force (RIF).

Retaining Top Talent

You may find that some top talent in the organization—identified high-potential experts and leaders—do not fit into the new organizational structure. You simply do not a have a role for them. Companies do a lot to attract and retain top talent. Ideally, you do not want to lose people due to a shift to the organizational structure. You still need to evaluate the person's capabilities against the need of the organization, though, and make some tough decisions.

I don't necessarily have an add-water-and-stir approach to decide what to do in this situation. Here are some questions that may help:

- Is this person's specialty something we still need in the organization? (Are they a supply chain expert, but we have decided to fully outsource supply chain management?)
- Are they a specialist or a generalist? Are they a utility player?
- What is the opportunity cost if we don't keep them in the organization?
- What is the impact if we create a role just to retain them? On the person themselves? On the organization?
- While they do not fill a role that we have now, could they fill a role we anticipate having open in the next six months to a year?
- Are they bench talent for a critical role in the organization?
- Have we realized the return on investment that we made in them? (Did they get a signing bonus, relocation cost, or other incentives?)

Sharing the Design, Gaining Approval, and Moving to Implementation

Now that you have asked all the questions, explored all the options, and designed the plan, you are ready to share the plan for approval.

When sharing your design with leadership, make sure they understand all the factors. Here are some ways to handle the conversations with leadership:

- Highlight where the current state is falling short, identifying all the gaps (in processes, policies, resources, talent, and so on) that need to be filled to get to the future state.
- Call out any barriers or restrictions (such as regulatory controls that cause inefficiency but cannot be skipped).
- Highlight behavioral changes and training needs that will be required. (For example, in the current state, leaders do not provide much feedback, and when

they do, they do not do it well. The future state will require leaders to provide ongoing, high-quality feedback to continually manage and upskill their team.)

Watch Out For

As you present the design, expect push back. Two common concerns are budget and time requirements. Be clear about the impact that trade-offs will have on the plan's effectiveness. At the same time, know that trade-offs will likely be required. It will also be helpful to have a list of non-negotiables—the things that, if not included, will greatly diminish the likelihood of success. Then note the things that will have a far less negative impact on the outcome if they're either eliminated or pushed to a later time. If leadership insists on trying to push forward with unrealistic expectations—the same design with half the budget, for example—be prepared to speak honestly and clearly about the resulting likelihood of failure.

In addition to sharing the design, you will share your recommended implementation approach. It is helpful to prepare two or three options, noting which one you think is optimal and why. Your goal is to present the design, answer the questions, overcome any objections, and agree on an implementation plan and timeline. With that done, you are ready to implement the plan to realign the organization.

Continuous Improvement and Adjustment

With the organization design implemented, your work is done, right? Actually, successful business alignment isn't an end state so much as an ongoing process. Change, predicted and unanticipated, comes quickly from both internal and external sources.

We live in a volatile, uncertain, complex, and ambiguous (VUCA) world. While VUCA may sound negative, the effects can be negative or positive. The onset of the COVID-19 pandemic is a perfect example. From a strictly economic standpoint, this unprecedented and ongoing event had drastic—and drastically different—impacts on different segments of the business community. In some cases, it had both positive and negative impacts on the exact same businesses:

- Some restaurants had to permanently shut their doors due to the closure of indoor dining. Other restaurants were able to increase profitability by expanding their delivery service or greatly increasing their seating capacity by adding outdoor dining spaces both during the height of the pandemic and ongoing.

- Home exercise equipment retailers experienced increased demand early in the pandemic due to the closure of gyms. Two years on, many had to cut their sales projections as people went back to in-person workouts.
- To make up for lost sales, some clothing retailers pivoted to designing and selling masks, creating an entirely new product segment for themselves. As infection levels and government mandates fluctuated, some companies found they had overinvested in masks and had to pivot again to avoid being left with stock they could not sell.

In all these cases, the business environment changed rapidly. Leaders quickly reassessed business alignment (even if they didn't consciously realize that was what they were doing) just to stay afloat, and found themselves needing to do it again and again as the situation continued to evolve.

I was working at a global retailer that instituted significant reductions in force—up to 25 percent of staff in some parts of the organization—to cut expenses a few months into the pandemic. Later that year, when restrictions eased and pent-up demand drove sales back up, they found themselves trying to quickly hire people to fill roles in nearly every function in the organization. In the process, they lost efficiency and market share.

While the COVID-19 pandemic presents an extreme example, the need to continually monitor, evolve, and improve the organization design is a constant. Determining who in the organization is responsible for ongoing business alignment is critical. Often it is a responsibility shared across multiple people and groups in the organization without any one individual or function being accountable for overseeing end-to-end business alignment (Trevor 2018).

In your role as an OD practitioner, you can build processes and accountabilities for continuous improvement and business alignment into the organization's design to ensure that the company will be able to continue to deliver on its strategic objectives despite ongoing disruption and change.

Summary

As an L&D expert, you need to leverage many of the assessment, data collection, needs analysis, and strategic planning skills that you use in your work every day to create business alignment with organizational design. By shifting to an OD-focused mindset, you will help set your organization up for success, ensuring the implementation and maintenance of the organization design is flexible enough to adjust to this constantly evolving world.

Key Takeaways

Here are a few things remember about business alignment:

- **Business alignment requires you to understand a multitude of elements in the organization.** This includes foundational aspects of the business such as the mission, vision, and values; the current state of everything from policies and processes to people practices and systems capabilities; and the company strategy. Alignment requires a comprehensive approach.

- **As you consider both the formal (tangible) and informal (intangible) elements in the organization, don't underestimate the power of the informal.** The norms are the unwritten rules of the organization, which are often a more reliable predictor of behavior.

- **You will continuously use your needs analysis skills to compare the current state to the future state.** Your organization design will have to address the gap between the two to ensure successful alignment.

- **Structure comes last.** You may be tempted to start with structure, but until you determine the requirements for things like decision rights, systems, processes, and behaviors, you do not actually know what kind of structure the organization needs. Structure is an enabler.

- **Successful business alignment isn't an end state so much as an ongoing process.** Given the speed of change in an increasingly volatile world, ensure that you build a continuous assessment and improvement process into your organization's design.

Lean and Agile

RANDY MATUSKY

IN THIS CHAPTER

♦ Recognize the importance of continuous improvement in your talent development portfolio
♦ Understand the basics of Lean and Agile
♦ Name the initial steps you can take to begin your continuous improvement journey

If you have ever worked in a department of one, you know the level of challenge it can bring. Each stakeholder has a different set of priorities, senior leadership is expecting you to move the needle on key business metrics, and the detail of managing all the different projects may leave you feeling as though you need an additional team member or two. This is something many in the learning and development (L&D) field know rather well. According to ATD's *2022 State of the Industry* report, there were an average of 457 employees per talent development (TD) staff member (not adjusted for outsourcing) in 2021. Thus, the average TD professional is working to support more than 450 employees. It's no wonder you're busy.

Many organization development (OD) professionals have a similar experience. Unless they're working for very large global organizations, OD professionals are members of small teams, sometimes even teams of one. Speaking personally, I am currently working for a global organization headquartered in Germany with just under 3,000 employees. The German headquarters has a five-member OD team, while I support all of North America as an OD team of one. I'm lucky because I can occasionally partner with my German OD colleagues, but for the majority of the time, I need to act independently.

Being the sole OD professional supporting all of our North American locations is daunting. However, by leveraging continuous improvement (CI), I'm able to empower the organization's teams to mobilize and become change agents, which allows me to deliver on more projects. There are many CI models and methodologies out there, and they all have their own unique strengths and weaknesses. Michael Boose, a former manager and mentor of mine, first introduced me to this amazing world when he gave me a copy of Eliyahu Goldratt's book *The Goal: A Process of Ongoing Improvement.* It explores the Theory of Constraints (TOC), which is a wonderful model for pinpointing bottlenecks in a development pipeline.

For the rest of this chapter, I will explore the two CI models that I use the most frequently: Lean and Agile.

Lean

The Lean methodology for continuous improvement was developed from the great work at Toyota following World War II. Toyota was facing an extremely challenging situation, dealing with the economic and social fallout of the war. Through the leadership and guidance of Kiichiro Toyoda, son of Toyota founder Sakichi Toyoda, and Taiichi Ohno, a Japanese industrial engineer, the Toyota Production System (TPS) was born.

TPS is not just a method for efficient work—it's a philosophical approach to the nature of work. At its core, TPS strives to eliminate the three Ms in the work system: *Mura* (unevenness), *Muri* (overburden), and *Muda* (waste). In a perfect state, if all three were completely removed, we would be left with a work system that is balanced, efficient, and produces nothing but value for the customer. This is the ideal state that we must continually strive for, hence the continuous aspect of CI.

Where to Begin

Toyota has been working with TPS for nearly seven decades. That's a long time for improvement and maturation. It can be daunting to take such a complex system and figure out where exactly to begin.

However, before I discuss some of my thoughts on how to kick off your CI journey with Lean, I want to explain one important thing: There isn't one true definition or vision of a Lean system. One reason for this is that it is constantly changing to meet the changing needs of the customer. Organizations that believe their implementation of Lean is perfect risk developing a fixation on the training and the Lean tools, and they will quickly end up producing more waste (*muda*) for their employees and internal teams. Lean is personal to the organization, so my advice is to jump into it with a learner's mind. Don't get wed to one specific approach or try to copy exactly what Toyota did. Make it your own!

Katsuaki Watanabe, senior advisor at Toyota, told *Harvard Business Review* that "there's no end to the process of learning about the Toyota Way. I don't think I have a complete understanding even today, and I have worked for the company for 43 years" (Stewart and Raman 2007). The Lean journey is a lifelong journey, so I advise beginning by educating key leadership. Your C-suite does not have to be make up of Lean experts or master black belts, but they do need to understand the core concepts of Lean and the influence it will have on the nature of work for their divisions. If senior leaders are not behind you, it will make implementing Lean nearly impossible. Provide adequate training on Lean, highlighting the core philosophy and how it will influence daily work. Make sure that all senior leaders are aware of their roles in supporting the initiative and how they can provide value, such as through the removal of any roadblocks that teams may face. They must act as champions for CI.

Once senior leadership is onboard, I recommend having frequent communication with the entire organization, especially at the beginning. Some employees may have misconceptions you'll need to address, such as the idea that Lean implementation will lead to a reduction in force. Any organization that is looking to use Lean as a way to reduce headcount is missing the entire purpose of continuous improvement. Employees who have experienced Lean before may have had a negative experience and need reassurance that this time will be different. Ideally, you want to win the employees over by sharing all the benefits of Lean, including more efficient processes, better project visibility, reduced lead times, and an increase in team morale. Be clear with your employees from the start and help answer their "What's in it for me?" questions. This will allow them to feel part of the movement.

I also recommend selecting a few teams that share your drive and enthusiasm for CI and Lean and asking them to become early adopters. Running a few Lean improvement workshops or events with teams that have already bought-in allows you to establish some early quick wins. This will give you motivation to keep moving forward, and these teams can become champions of the process and share the benefits they are experiencing with the rest of the organization.

A 5S is a great tool you can use to reduce waste in a workspace (Figure 7-1). The goal is to create an orderly workplace that is not just organized but also incorporates visual cues as a

Figure 7-1. The 5S System

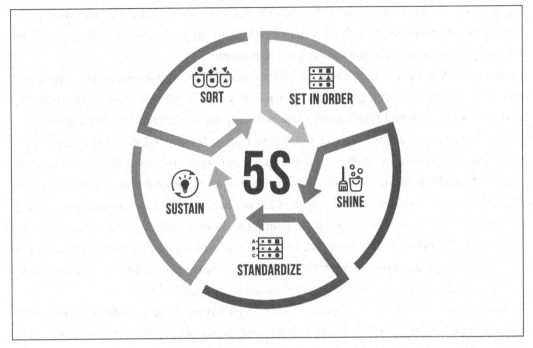

mean for operational excellence. The five steps in a 5S workshop are sort (*Seiri*), set in order (*Seiton*), shine (*Seiso*), standardize (*Seiketsu*), and sustain (*Shitsuke*).

Two important notes about the 5S system:

- **Make sure to involve the entire team.** I have heard stories of Lean teams coming into a workplace, running the 5S on their own, and then inviting workers to come and see their new workspace. A 5S must be led by the workers in the space. They are the ones working there, which means they are experts on what an efficient space will look like. This also communicates that everyone can and must make improvements, not just the team leads or the Lean facilitators.
- **Do not overlook the last step, sustain (Shitsuke).** We have all experienced this at home—cleaning and organizing a room, just to see it revert to the way it was a few weeks later. Create a system to ensure that the space remains orderly and optimal. Something as simple as a cleaning schedule with a checklist to record when the room was last inspected will help. Overlooking sustain will only lead to more waste creeping into the workspace.

PDCA Cycle

The last section focused on the important question of where to begin your Lean journey. One critical component of every Lean transformation is a solid understanding of the PDCA cycle, so I want to focus on that for a moment. The PDCA cycle stands for plan, do, check, and act (Figure 7-2). Because it was first proposed by Walter Shewhart and later expanded upon by William Edwards Deming, it's often referred to as either the Shewhart Cycle or the Deming Cycle. You may also see it written as PDSA (plan, do, study, act). For my purposes, I will stick to PDCA.

The PDCA cycle gets to the heart of what continuous improvement is. Deming believed that all business processes need to exist in a continuous feedback loop so teams can examine, identify, and improve any steps that need refinement. The team will begin by designing or revising any specific steps in the process, such as those causing bottlenecks. Once created, those plans will be implemented and tested. Checking requires the team to measure the performance of the newly applied actions, making sure that they are meeting expectations. Finally, the team will verify the results of the new process. If the results are good, and the

Figure 7-2. PDCA Cycle

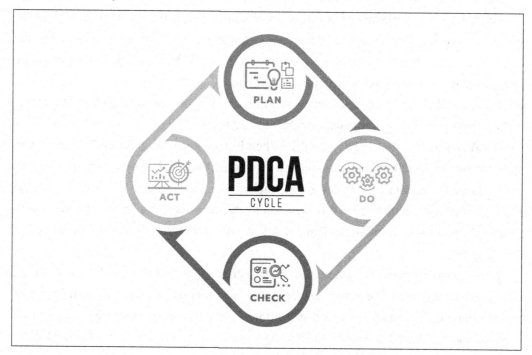

process has improved, then the new steps will be implemented and become the norm. If there is no improvement, then the team starts over.

The PDCA cycle highlights the importance of continuous learning and experimentation. It's often used to help implement large change initiatives and as a proven method for problem solving. PDCA is a very important tool for anyone looking to work in the organization development field.

Muda

One of the main goals of the PDCA cycle is to eliminate as much waste in the process as possible. Waste is referred to as *muda* in Japanese, and it represents anything that does not add value to the customer. When I'm explaining this concept to students for the first time, I often compare it to a river. The river represents your processes, and the water flowing by represents the output and products from your team. An ideal river, just like an ideal process, will have no resistance. The goal is a perfect state of flow. But problems exist in the real world, and the things that slow down the flow or get in the way are muda. Thus, in our analogy, muda depicts the rocks that clog up the river.

Muda or waste can be broken down into seven groups (Table 7-1).

A simple way to remember these seven wastes is through the acronym TIMWOOD. When I'm teaching this concept to teams, I often add an eighth waste to the list—skill or the waste of untapped human potential—making the acronym TIMWOODS. Not fully tapping into the full capabilities or skills of employees is a waste that can easily lead to disengagement and burnout. As organization development consultants, it's your job to help ensure that none of these wastes are getting in the way of real value-added work.

PDCA is a fixed cycle, similar ADDIE. When instructional designers and course developers follow the ADDIE model, they begin by analyzing the problem or situation; then they design the instructional material, develop it, implement it, and evaluate it. Once a step in the ADDIE process is complete, they can move on to the next one. It's a similar approach with the PDCA cycle, the only difference being that they will begin the cycle over again once completing a pass.

If you ever participate in a Lean workshop or a kaizen event, there's a good chance you will use a value-stream map. These maps are a popular Lean tool that represents a visual guide of a work process. The map breaks process steps into three important categories: value-added steps (typically in green), non-value-added steps (typically in red), and non-value-added but business necessary steps (typically in yellow). The ultimate goal is to remove as many non-value-added steps as possible.

Table 7-1. Seven Types of Waste

Muda	Definition	Examples
Transportation	Transportation waste involves unnecessarily moving material from one spot to another. Think of printing a document and then sending it to another division by courier.	Physically transporting printed training materials to the desks of the participants.
Inventory	Inventory waste pops up when a space is poorly used. Overproduction often leads to a build-up of excess inventory.	Printing too many training packets, which then have to be stored.
Motion	Motion waste refers to the unnecessary movement of people. The field of ergonomics tackles this waste by ensuring that all jobs are designed to fit the physical needs of each individual.	Unnecessary prework or training activities that do not support the workshop's learning objectives.
Waiting	Waiting occurs when there is a delay in the process. There are many reasons for waiting to occur, such as a machine breaking down or a delay in shipping.	Not starting the workshop on time and making participants wait.
Overproduction	Overproduction is producing more items than the customer wants or producing those items too early, which means they will need to be stored and become inventory. Overproduction often leads to additional waste in the system.	Offering too many workshops, far beyond the actual demand.
Overprocessing	In the project management world, it's called gold plating. Overprocessing means perform-ing unnecessary processing steps that are not required by the customer. Overprocessing can lead to waiting.	Requiring every single team member to participate in the editing process for an upcoming class.
Defects	Defects require correction, which take up time and resources. Defects can be especially dan-gerous if they are discovered by the customer because it can damage the brand's image or reputation.	Printing training material with spelling and grammatical errors.

Belt System

The number 1 question I received during my time facilitating Lean workshops was "Will I receive a belt for this class?" The belt system is useful when used for resource planning on Lean projects and as a way to mark your point on the CI map, but in my experience, it is often overemphasized. Continuous improvement is an ongoing journey—the business environment never stops changing, nor do the needs and wants of our customers. I have met too many people who, after receiving their green belt in Lean, end their studies because they think they have mastered it all. If you approach continuous improvement with a certain sense of curiosity and a belief in true lifelong learning, then you will get much more out of it than those who just want to add that belt to their resume.

With that aside, let's review the Six Sigma belt system (Figure 7-3).

Figure 7-3. The Belt System

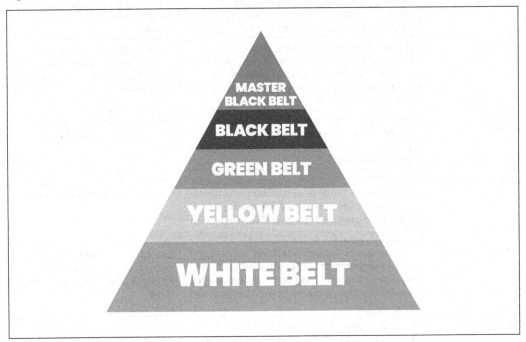

This can be handy when managing CI projects because it allows us to quickly see just how skilled individuals are in the organization:

- **Master black belts** are the Mr. Miyagi's of the organization. They are experts in the CI methodology—they know how to use the tools, they understand project management fundamentals, and they act as mentors for the black belts.
- **Black belts** are CI experts but don't have as much experience as a master black belt. They spend 100 percent of their time running and leading CI projects and mentoring the green belts.

- **Green belts** are trained on a majority of the tools and techniques and are placed in charge of straightforward CI projects. They assist the black belts by gathering data for the larger projects. Green belts typically spend 20 percent of their time working on CI projects.
- **Yellow belts** are trained on the basic tools and techniques of Lean and are often asked to participate in smaller-scale CI projects. Their time working on CI initiatives varies depending on the needs of the green and black belts. A typical yellow belt training lasts two to three days.
- **White belts** have received an introductory training on Lean and CI tools. They understand the PDCA cycle and may be able to use some of the easier tools. Many organizations choose to start at the yellow belt level rather than the white belt. A typical white belt training lasts two to four hours.

The belt system is a useful tool for those who will be helping to schedule the organization's continuous improvement projects or workshops.

Insights Through Pain

Where should you begin? That's a tough question to answer. Some Lean consultants will say that it's important to start with training so that everyone in the organization is speaking and living Lean. Other consultants will swear by beginning with a 5S initiative. I believe it depends on the needs of the teams you are working with—they're the experts on the processes and will know where the pain points are. So I suggest you begin with the leaders, and then partner with the teams and listen to their suggestions.

What if I flip the question around and ask instead what things to avoid? By learning from my mistakes, you can increase the likelihood your Lean initiative takes off and is sustainable for the long term.

The biggest pitfall to avoid is trying to jump straight to a solution by applying some sort of quick fix. I get it; I was guilty of that as well, especially when I was first starting my CI journey. The beauty of Lean and the PDCA cycle is that it forces you to properly analyze the problem, figure out the root causes, brainstorm possible counter measures, and test those measures out to see if they help. Jumping to the solutions might sound nice, but doing so before you really understand the root cause can complicate the process even more.

The second pitfall to avoid is thinking that CI or Lean training will automatically lead to process improvements. I made this mistake early in my CI journey while developing and facilitating Lean workshops. I found the experience to be exciting and energizing. Participants were leaving the workshops with a new set of tools, and I was convinced that they would go back to their teams and begin making countless improvements. Unfortunately, it didn't really play out that way.

Of course, the actual content in the training program is important—in many cases it represents the participant's first exposure to the CI methodology. It is crucial that you create an engaging learning opportunity. However, if you don't provide any support when they return to work, chances are that very little will change. That's why it's important to provide ongoing coaching to help participants use the tools back on the job. In addition, management needs to understand how a process improvement project works, and how they can help ensure any roadblocks are removed. (I recommend offering a workshop directly aimed at management.) Don't make the mistake of thinking that once participants have been trained, your job is over. In many ways, your job is just beginning.

One more point concerning the training—don't overtrain! If you are passionate about Lean and continuous improvement, you might make the mistake of trying to teach your participants absolutely everything you know. Don't do that. Training people at too high a level too soon is a waste of resources and may actually sabotage your efforts. Only provide the necessary training, at the appropriate level, when the teams need it. For example, when people are just beginning their journeys into CI, they should only receive entry-level training.

The last pitfall to avoid is focusing too much on the tools. It's understandable because the tools are exciting and offer a new way to approach problems on the job. But don't forget the other core element of Lean—respect for the people. Many North American organizations failed to truly establish a culture of continuous improvement after visiting Japan in the 1980s to study what was happening at Toyota. Why? Because they only focused on the tools. Don't overlook the people. Don't force or push the methodology onto them. Make them an important part of the transformation and include them in every step along the way.

Agile

When applied properly, the Lean methodology can do wonders for linear processes. But what about nonlinear processes that don't currently exist in your organization? Being successful in today's fast-paced business environment means constantly reinventing processes and programs. Linear process improvement tools are excellent for improving business models, but you need something slightly different for creating new business models. This is where Agile comes in.

History of Agile

At the Snowbird Ski resort in the Wesatch mountains of Utah, a group of 17 software developers met in 2001 to discuss their industry and the challenges of using the waterfall process to manage complex software projects. The waterfall approach requires chunking activities into sequential phases, with each new phase only beginning once the previous phase has finished.

A typical waterfall approach begins with gathering technical requirements, then moves to design, execution, and verification, and finally ends with maintenance. However, things come up, scope changes, and risks arise when managing a project, which means you need the ability to be flexible and jump back to a previous phase. Some types of projects—such as software development projects—are nonlinear and have a higher rate of change. Trying to manage a nonlinear project in a linear fashion is nothing short of a nightmare!

Well, those 17 software developers wanted a solution, so they created the Agile Manifesto, which highlighted the elements of software development that provided the highest value. This document would go on to truly transform project management around the world.

The Agile Manifesto

The Agile Manifesto's website (agilemanifesto.org) has not changed since the day it was published, making it a relic of the project management world. It comprises a list of working values, which are categorized by level of importance:

- **Individuals and interactions** over processes and tools
- **Working software** over comprehensive documentation
- **Customer collaboration** over contract negotiation
- **Responding to change** over following a plan

For the founders and original writers of the Agile Manifesto, the values on the left (in bold) are more important than those to their right. This does not mean that processes and tools or comprehensive documentation are not important; it just means that in an ideal setting, individuals and interactions and working software should be prioritized.

What I love about the Agile Manifesto is that it highlights the importance of taking the time to figure out what you truly value about your work, and then prioritizing those elements.

This could be beneficial for someone relatively new to working in the OD space because it highlights those elements of the OD field that you hold in the highest esteem. Personally, two OD values I tend to prioritize over others are encouraging and embracing a spirit of continuous improvement and responding in a timely manner to real-world business problems. These values guide me; they help ensure I am involving everyone on the team in the OD initiative and that I have a constant connection to the business' problems.

Scrum

There are many different approaches to Agile, including Crystal, Kanban, Extreme Programming (XP), Dynamic Systems Development Method (DSDM), and Feature Driven Development (FDD). I'll focus on the most popular framework, Scrum, in this chapter.

The term *Scrum* comes from the sport of rugby. During a game, the scrum is what happens after a stoppage, when the players group closely together, lower their heads, and attempt to gain possession of the ball by concentrating their efforts and strengths as a unified team. In many ways, this is very similar to how the Agile form of Scrum works. If a project is stopped due to changes in the scope of work (let's say, due to changes in customer demand or need), the Scrum team will come together and focus all their energy on one specific task or two during a predetermined period of time, which they call a sprint. The ultimate goal of the Scrum framework is creating a team that can work as a unified group. An L&D department may use a Scrum approach to respond to the changing needs of the client or customer, even if that means going back to development to create a new curriculum or training activity.

Some of the framework's core values include transparency, inspection, and change. Teams must be fully transparent—this includes among team members, between the team and the project manager (who is called the Scrum Master), and between the team and the customer—with a clear understanding of what *done* means for the project. I refer to this as the DOD (definition of done). Inspections must occur often, ideally at the end of every sprint period; if any quality errors are found, then the goal must be to find the root cause. Finally, Scrum teams must welcome change. In the traditional waterfall project management approach, change is seen as the enemy, but not so in Scrum. Change allows the team to adapt to trends in the market, and keeps them in close contact with the customer.

Sprints typically last two weeks, but some Scrum teams prefer to work with three- or four-week sprints. I wouldn't recommend going past the four-week mark, and I wouldn't go below two-weeks. My advice is to consider the nature of your work and your team's level of comfort with the Scrum framework. If you find that sprints are lasting too long, and the team is not adjusting quickly enough to changes from the customer, then modify the cadence and duration of the sprints. As the Scrum Master, your goal is to serve the team and ensure they have everything they need to be successful.

Most Scrum teams hold a daily Scrum, often called the daily standup, which is a 10- to 15-minute meeting that occurs each day of a sprint. The whole team participates—including the product owners, developers, and Scrum Master—and each person answers three questions:

- What did I work on yesterday?
- What am I working on today?
- What issues are blocking me?

These questions quickly reveal what everyone is working on, the status of certain tasks, and if there are any roadblocks. An advantage of having the entire team present is that you can benefit from the team's collective knowledge and strengths when there are issues or if someone's experiencing a roadblock. This also helps build team unity and overall trust.

The retrospective, another common event Scrum teams hold, occurs at the end of a sprint. It's meant to be used as a moment of reflection for the team. As the Scrum Master, you will want to ask what went well during the sprint and what things could be improved on. I prefer to keep these retrospectives short because the goal is to quickly reflect on what is working and what isn't. Just make sure that you are consistent and run a retrospective at the end of every sprint.

Insights Through Pain

Agile can be a great tool, especially if you are working with project teams that deal with a high level of change. But Agile can also be very difficult to properly implement in an organization. Three common pitfalls that I have experienced with Agile include using it with teams that lack the necessary experience or proper training, scaling Agile to the entire organization, and using Agile on every project, even those that would be better suited with another framework.

It can take teams years to truly master working in a scrum or Agile environment. In a previous role, I helped coach project managers who were transitioning to Agile development teams, and I saw their struggles firsthand. Many aspects of Agile are very contradictory to the more traditional ways of working. For example, the focus on change and how it is actually a positive thing can be a difficult paradigm shift for some people. I would advise any OD professional who wants to incorporate Agile into their organization to provide coaching for teams and project managers.

Once Agile starts to take off within the organization, your focus can shift to scaling it to other teams and other areas of the business. This is when many organizations hit a wall. Scaling Agile is extremely difficult, even for companies that have been using it for many years. Agile and its workflows tend to favor small, intimate work teams. Taking that culture and style of work and scaling it to a very large group or division can prove tricky, if not impossible. My advice is to start small with a project team that really understands the technical aspects of the job and is well-aware of the functions of the business. Use them to introduce Agile to the organization, and make sure to coach them along the way. Baby steps are key for adapting Agile into a company.

Finally, don't try to use Agile with absolutely every single team in the company. If the only tool you have is a hammer, then everything looks like a nail. Agile should be one tool in your toolkit, not the only tool. While Agile can work wonders for nonlinear projects, such as software development, the outcome is typically less positive when used by teams working in very linear environments. Don't force it where it doesn't belong.

Summary

Even if you are an OD professional working in a team of one, I highly recommend adding Lean and Agile to your development toolkit. These powerful continuous improvement methodologies will allow your teams to continue to grow, even as you are working with other teams in the organization. Just remember that no methodology is perfect, and your teams will need continual coaching and support, especially during the initial period of adaptation. But if properly supported, Lean and Agile can add great value to the teams you support.

Key Takeaways

Here are a few more things to remember about Lean and Agile:

- **Include senior leadership early on in the CI journey.** Ideally, a senior leader will take on a sponsor role and help spread the positive word about your CI program. Let them act as the change champion.

- **Your strongest asset is your staff.** It's always good to seek the help and support of a CI expert, but don't rely on them too much. Your staff owns the processes, so they'll also know best how to improve the system.

- **Don't try to boil the ocean.** Appreciate the fact that less is more. Embrace the strategy of keeping it simple, especially if you are just launching your first CI initiative.

- **Go to the *Gemba* as often as you can.** *Gemba* is a Japanese word for "the real place"—it's where the work is performed. To find out how the work really is done, you must go to the place where the work happens. Do not solely rely on process documents; don't assume that the work follows the steps laid out in the binder or workbook. Most of the time, they do not.

- **Remain system agnostic.** Personally, I like Lean. It was one of the first CI approaches I discovered, and it's the one I use most in my field. But there is value in all the other CI systems. Challenge yourself, and don't get stuck on just one approach.

- **Have fun and never stop learning.** Your CI journey should be fun! Get everyone involved, and let people take ownership where they can. If it's not fun, it will never stick.

Fostering Employee Engagement Through OD

HEATHER R. YOUNGER

IN THIS CHAPTER

♦ Create a culture of active listening where employees feel engaged, supported, and motivated to contribute

♦ Secure the support of the C-suite for employee engagement initiatives

♦ Tap into the power of strategic alliances for long-term, sustainable success

Engagement of employees is one of the most important determining factors in the success of an organization development initiative. The truth is that organizations can't realize their vision if they don't have engaged employees. But as the number of people who are consciously disengaging at work or choosing to quit continues to rise, the true costs have never been more apparent (Ito 2022). One study estimates the total cost of disengaged employees in the US is between $450 and $500 billion each year (Fechter 2020).

If you're an OD practitioner, you've likely come across employee engagement in one form or another in the course of your work. Fostering employee engagement will help the organization retain employees, improve productivity, and reduce turnover. The question is, how do you connect that goal with your day-to-day responsibilities so you don't miss out on the full potential of the organization's workforce?

This is a particularly pertinent question if you have transitioned into an OD position as an L&D professional. Suddenly, you need to adjust your focus from training employees in the tactical and technical skills they need to thinking about the organization as a whole in a more strategic way. That might feel daunting at first, but remember that this is an exciting opportunity to make changes and expand your impact. This chapter will help you do just that. I'll start with some personal development actions you can take to set you up for success and then delve into how you can take a listening approach to employee engagement initiatives.

Shift Your Thinking

When you're beginning to think about how you can tap into the full potential of every employee as an OD practitioner, it's essential that you see your role for what it is. While L&D professionals are tasked with operating as functional experts who are responsible for developing people in certain areas, organization development requires you to see yourself as a strategist and not just a tactician—someone who is tuned into the big picture with a focus on the organization's overarching goals and health. When it comes to employee engagement, this means thinking about how you can engage employees at a strategic level and how that will influence hiring practices, customer interactions, the bottom line, and more. When you can shift how you see yourself, you'll transform the way you lead the organization to reach its goals.

It's also important that you maintain realistic expectations of what's possible for you and the organization to achieve over a set period of time. After securing my first role in organization development early on in my career, I recall feeling thrilled that I had the opportunity to make real progress by building rapid momentum. I thought I'd be able to do that quickly, so I could show immediate positive results. What I didn't foresee was that progress would sometimes mean taking two steps back for every three steps forward. Had I accepted the role with a more realistic mindset, I wouldn't have become disillusioned and frustrated.

The pace of change can be slow, so celebrating the small wins is just as essential for maintaining morale and momentum. Be sure to practice balancing your expectations with what you can realistically accomplish.

Not only that, but don't forget to ask yourself, "What does success look like for me, personally?" Success looks different for everyone, and understanding your personal goals will help you stay focused and motivated to continue, even if progress takes longer than you'd like. Identifying the source of your personal motivation is important. When you understand why you want to do the work you do, you can focus forward and use your mission and vision as something to aim toward.

Prioritize Self-Care

When you prioritize self-care, you improve your ability to bring your best self to the work you do. In organization development, it's easy to overpromise, only to exhaust yourself trying to deliver those results. When you weave self-care into your workday, you can better set realistic goals that help you make consistent progress.

Self-care might also look like establishing a workout routine every morning to clear your mind, keeping a regular appointment with a mental health professional to talk through challenges, or practicing daily affirmations. It should energize you and help you show up as the best version of yourself. You don't need to aim for perfection, but you should aim to work from a place of self-awareness and emotional intelligence, so you can remain mindful of your impact on others. After all, employee satisfaction is at the core of employee retention and engagement.

Choosing self-care can often feel like an internal battle—especially when there are more pressing tasks on your to-do list. But it's important. For example, when I work out each morning before my kids wake up, I find it to be a valuable time for quiet reflection that gets me into the best frame of mind for the day ahead.

Commit to Self-Leadership

Committing time to self-leadership will help you evolve as you grow your skills in the service of others. When you prioritize your development in this area, you'll find yourself better equipped to intentionally influence the way you think, feel, and act toward certain objectives, which is a critical factor for individual and organizational success. In their book, *Self Leadership: How to Become a More Effective, and Efficient Leader From the Inside Out*, Ana Kazan and Andrew Bryant (2013) explain that "Self-leadership is having a developed sense of who you are, what you can do, where you are going, coupled with the ability to influence your communication, emotions and behavior on the way to getting there."

The good news is that we can all become better at how we lead ourselves. That means finding congruence between who you are and who you want to be, so you can close the gap and grow in alignment with your values. This also means staying consistent in your efforts to evolve your mindset, so you can respond in the right way to different situations and positively influence people around you—rather than inadvertently create confusion or conflict.

In your OD role, you set the tone for the organization. So, own your growth. Have the courage to admit when you could strengthen your leadership skills and commit to your personal and professional development. That could look like regularly investing time and energy into reading books, listening to podcasts, watching TED talks, enrolling in courses, or hiring a coach to help you develop. This is particularly important if part of your employee engagement strategy is to foster learning and growth. When you prioritize your own self-development, you help your direct reports see the value in it, which should inspire them to follow your lead.

In your role, you'll constantly face obstacles and transitions, and your mindset will influence how you respond to them. So, prepare the best way you know how. Protect your energy, manage your reactions, and continue to make key decisions—even in times of uncertainty—that create the conditions you need for success.

Devote Time to Active Listening

Once you have some self-development in the works, you can turn your focus to engaging everyone else in the organization.

In contrast to L&D, which is focused on talking to department managers about what they or their teams require, when you assume a role in organization development, you must think in terms of what the organization requires as a whole. That means having more inclusive conversations, building cross-organizational alliances, and using a framework to facilitate listening at every level.

Think about who might possess valuable information that could help you do your job more effectively. Consider interviewing them and listening to what they have to say. Catalog your thoughts, notice themes that come up, and never be afraid to dig a little deeper beneath the surface.

In my first organization development role, I made a point to meet with people who had been in that role before me or who were indirectly connected to it. I spent a lot of time asking these folks questions to figure out which employee engagement strategies they had tried in the past, and which ones they hoped I might try in the future. Their answers provided an excellent foundation on which to build.

Don't stop with internal conversations. Consider obtaining a key customer's perspective, if possible. Ask yourself, "Who's on the front lines with a clear view of what's happening?" Talk to them before you put any kind of strategic plan together to bolster employee engagement.

An employee engagement survey is another way to uncover underlying challenges as well as what's working well and can be built on. Surveys are a great place to start because they give employees a voice and help show how their insights contribute toward positive change. They feel included and important. Meanwhile, the results provide real data you can use to help people more quickly buy in to your recommendations.

Be warned: Employees may be hesitant to complete your survey if they don't trust that anything will be done about issues they raise. It's up to you to break that cycle and be someone who will actually take action. While you don't have to act on every single thing, compassionately communicating what you decide to do, or not do, will help you close the loop between the employee feedback and your response. The result is that people will feel heard and recognize that their perspectives matter. Your internal communications team, if you have one, can be an excellent ally in this process, and I recommend involving them at the earliest opportunity.

This investigative stage may take up to three months, which might be hard for the C-suite, who will more than likely want quick wins and results right away. It's important that you not only understand the priorities of these leaders but also learn how to speak their language, so you can communicate the ROI of listening well over time. Employee engagement is a long-term process for a reason, and it's not something you can quickly do once and then move on. Don't overpromise the results you'll deliver. Instead, set clear expectations so leaders understand that you're playing the long game, with the success of the organization in mind.

When you discover key information, or feel like you've made a breakthrough, be sure to report your wins, but don't take all the credit. Instead, give credit to everyone who put forward ideas, connected the dots, and helped move the needle on important issues. This will strengthen your relationships with individuals and groups and help you engage their support on future objectives.

Forge Strategic Alliances

Long before I became a speaker, author, and consultant, I worked in organization development for a large company where I often felt like the Lone Ranger. I didn't have a team, but I did have a plan, and I worked that plan like my job depended on it—which it did. But, as I forged ahead with that plan and began to report back on my efforts, I heard members of the leadership team express feeling out of the loop. That was understandable because I hadn't included them in my plans or the progress I was making. I was simply working away by myself, and then relaying the actions I'd taken.

The lesson: Don't commit to organization development work alone. Instead, build key alliances and set clear expectations along the way, so you can create long-term, sustainable success. That starts with a shift away from Lone Ranger thinking. Instead, expand your organizational view to consider how you might involve others to develop initiatives that drive organizational effectiveness and improve performance.

If you're the only person dedicated to working on employee engagement, I'd recommend connecting with other people managers, as well as the leadership team and key stakeholders, sooner rather than later. You might even want to create an employee engagement council to form a direct line of communication between you and employees, facilitate idea sharing, and gain insights into the company culture. Including an executive sponsor in that council will ensure the senior leadership team knows what you're up to.

As an OD practitioner, you need to keep the corridors of communication open. So, take time to build strategic alliances that will help you plug the right people into conversations that are happening, identify key priorities, and make real progress that everyone can get on board with.

Tie Your Strategic Plan to the Bigger Picture

Because the pace of change can be slow, it's vital that you connect with the executive leadership team to make sure you understand the organization's multiyear strategic plan. Every employee engagement initiative should tie directly to that plan and reach the very top of the organization. The higher you can tie your initiatives to strategies and outcomes, the better.

Find out what the executive dashboard looks like. Which mission critical executive key performance indicators (KPIs) do leaders track to make decisions that drive productivity, grow revenue, and reduce risk? Which metrics do they pay attention to every day? What keeps them up at night? Then, ask yourself, "How does this affect me and the work that I do?"

When you can tie initiatives to the top line and what's most important to executive leaders and the people you report to—the people who push the green light on human capital or resources allocation—you set yourself up to have a greater degree of influence. My preference is to focus on three to five priorities at a time.

If one or two levels exist between you and the executive team (for example, you report to the head of HR), be sure to strengthen the relationships you have with those more senior to you. They will be vital for your understanding of the organization's multiyear plan; otherwise, your OD work will fall prey to competing priorities. It's hard to move your initiatives forward if they aren't seen as important.

Prioritizing your relationship building skills will serve you well in the long run too. A DISC assessment, for example, will help you better understand different communication styles and how to better interact with people. If you haven't already completed a DISC assessment, consider doing so—improving your ability to communicate will help you more quickly access to the information you need to do your job well (including that executive leadership team dashboard).

Line Up Some Quick Wins

While much of the work you do won't deliver quantifiable results immediately—that's simply the nature of employee engagement—try to find some quick, easy wins that create a sense of progress.

One financial services leader I worked with as a consultant listened to their employees and realized they needed a platform to allow for better communication and showing appreciation. Upon further investigation, they realized the software they were already using had a recognition component that was currently inactive. By activating that component, they would be able to publicly recognize one another for work well done. It was a quick win for everyone involved. In other words, they found a way to boost retention and productivity by making employee recognition part of the culture. Even if a bigger initiative is needed to address employee concerns over time, you can still find shorter-term fixes to show you care.

Another organization I worked with needed help retaining its clients, so we introduced partnership reviews that would provide a forum for addressing any problems from the previous quarter. Both sides could also reflect on successes, explore new ways to work together, and ask questions that would support decision making. While this example isn't directly related to employee engagement, you could introduce similar partnership reviews wherever key stakeholders are involved—whether that means checking in with individual employees or entire departments or teams. When it comes to employee engagement, it's easy for people to become disconnected internally if they feel unheard or like their opinions don't matter. When you create forums for them to share their thoughts and perspectives, they are likely to feel a greater sense of belonging and respect for the organization.

Measure Your Success

We've all heard the phrase, "What gets measured gets done." I might alter that to say, "What gets measured gets changed." Whichever adage you prefer, one thing's certain: If you don't take time to measure your success, it will be difficult, if not impossible, to demonstrate your progress. It's vital that you know what your starting point is, and what success looks like to the organization, so you can track and quantify the ways in which you've been able to move the needle.

This is the reality of having to prove your worth as an OD practitioner—especially because your work is considered an expense line, not a revenue line. But, if you can show the current level of employee engagement, and how that is negatively affecting the organization's bottom line, you're more likely to be successful when making the business case for your initiatives. Uncomfortable or not, it's incumbent on you to make the case for what you want to do because no one else will do it for you.

You also need to think of yourself as a change manager because you're creating and managing change at the same time. To track your success in the future, you must have a way to demonstrate what actually happened. So, spend time collecting data that will support your progress from the very start—whether that's through employee survey results, turnover rates, exit interview notes, L&D measurements, scorecards, or something else. Beyond the numbers, talk to people and listen to what they have to say so you can aggregate as much information as possible to build your case.

Think about what stories you hope to wrap around the data—for example, do you want to show that people are more secure and productive in their roles, have the energy and resources they need to succeed, or feel a greater sense of belonging than before? When you start with the end in mind, you can build up to revealing powerful insights and outcomes that remind everyone how critical your role actually is.

The Cycle of Active Listening

When you think about how to measure positive change as a result of your initiatives, the Cycle of Active Listening is a model you can use to guide your efforts. Listening never stops, and the ways in which you respond and take action must continue on a loop—hopefully with increasingly impressive results—if you want employees to feel heard, seen, and valued. When you know how to listen, employees will tell you everything you need to know to be successful and meet their needs.

The Cycle of Active Listening involves five stages: recognize the unsaid, seek to understand, decode, act, and close the loop.

1. Recognize the Unsaid

You can't reimagine a better workplace or move toward change as an OD practitioner until you can recognize the unsaid. When you interact with employees individually or in group settings, see if you can pick up on important cues signaling tensions that people aren't talking about out loud. Notice where people's words and actions don't match up, and show an openness to hearing the hard things.

A few years ago, I was explaining to the head of HR at a large organization why she needed data to understand what wasn't being said out loud by employees. Her team had been sending out yearly employee surveys but had never had the chance to do anything with them. However, after she made time to comb through the survey results, she had a huge aha moment. She could finally fix what needed fixing because she understood what employees had been saying all along.

Without taking the time to understand what is really happening in a situation, you may find yourself in a precarious position—lacking understanding in an area that has the potential to harm your organization. You might then end up forging ahead with the wrong initiative, project, or program. By taking time to review the available information, you'll be one step closer to understanding what needs to change and what your next steps should be.

2. Seek to Understand

When you begin to listen, it must be unidirectional. Your ears are open, you're receptive to receiving feedback, and you're requesting input from people. Resist the urge to share your own thoughts, perspectives, or opinions—simply request clarification when needed, and make it evident the other person has your full attention whether through your words or body language.

Only once they've finished sharing can you move into bidirectional communication. Paraphrase what you heard the other person say to ensure they feel understood. You might do this after employee surveys or during listening sessions or manager roundtables.

You might also ask deeper questions to gain a better understanding by gently probing to uncover the truth about what's really going on. You'll gain valuable insights about what team members actually want and need and capture key information—or even an undercurrent of emotions.

In the story I shared, after the head of HR recognized the unsaid, she realized that bidirectional listening was the key to understanding what employees wanted. The organization is now much more intentional about collecting quantitative and qualitative data each year, which has helped it get to the truth faster, build trust more rapidly, and improve the culture exponentially.

When you seek to understand, you'll gain the clarity you need to take the next step.

3. Decode

It's one thing to listen; it's another to reflect on what you've heard. When you've gathered as much data as possible, you can begin to analyze it so you can see a complete picture. A data-driven approach will reveal what disempowers your employees and identify the changes that will likely have the biggest positive impact. Decoding is the stage when reflection and analysis happen.

Remember, data isn't only numbers; it's any kind of input that provides the knowledge you need. When I went through a merger at an organization I used to work for, and employees began to lose their jobs, I noticed that communication silos were developing. So, I started to round up groups of people to talk about what was happening. I quickly discovered that they were hurting—and that's an understatement. As they began sharing and processing their emotions, I was able to see why these breakdowns were occurring. For example, someone shared that when he'd heard he might be losing his job, he brought it up with his manager. But his manager said he didn't know anything about it.

As you bring people together and ask open-ended questions, you're actively decoding. Afterward, you will continue analyzing the data by processing what you've learned and relaying any valuable insights back to key stakeholders—like HR or the executive leadership team. Your job is to aggregate the data and process it all to determine what the organization should focus on.

4. Act

At this stage in the Cycle of Active Listening it's time to take action—or, at the very least, decide how you want to act. This stage is when you capture hearts and minds at every level. By leveraging insights from prior steps, you can turn the data into an inclusive and collaborative strategic plan—one that's built with employees in mind.

People don't begin to feel heard until they notice people acting upon what they've told them. The aforementioned head of HR acted by creating an employee engagement culture team made up of cross-functional members from all levels of the organization. Together, they formulated next steps and presented their recommendations to the senior leadership team. When I visited the company to go over the feedback and my recommendations to act, I saw how aligned people were around the agreed-upon action steps—from frontline team members to supervisors to directors. It demonstrated how true it is that listening is a team sport.

During the listening sessions I facilitate, I like to have people list 10 action items that follow an open feedback time period, and then vote on their top three. Recently, during a diversity, equity, and inclusion (DEI) listening session with a group of employees, we selected three action recommendations for the group to take. One member of the group said, "Heather, this is exciting, but I want you to know we're putting a lot of trust in your hands that you'll give our voices and priorities to the leaders in our company. We know that these action steps will make things better, but we're putting our trust in you to communicate to them in a way they can understand." This was a humbling reminder for me that I held an immense responsibility to the employees—a responsibility you share as an OD practitioner.

You might want to do what my client did and put a subcommittee together to talk about how you'll work on your three action items. Remember, it's the connection between feedback and action that makes people truly feel heard—but it's not the last step.

5. Close the Loop

When you close the loop by sharing what you've heard and communicating next steps, employees will feel valued, heard, and included. They will give more and perform better.

A lot of companies fail to close the loop in this way, and it's a misstep that can create a lot of negative emotions. If done correctly, however, this is the stage that brings the Cycle of Active Listening full circle and validates the importance of your employees' voices, insights, and perspectives.

During the merger I mentioned earlier, the organization didn't recognize what was not being said or ask for feedback from team members. No one decoded the data because they never asked any questions; the action steps leaders took felt sporadic and uninformed. Not to mention, the lack of communication during the merger process left many people feeling fearful and mistrustful.

On the other hand, the head of HR who took the time to sit with me and recognize what wasn't being said followed the Cycle of Active Listening exactly. She strategically listened to employees and decoded what she heard using quantitative and qualitative insights. Then, she put a clearly communicated plan in place that would act upon what she'd heard in ways that made sense to everyone. The organization now starts this Cycle of Active Listening over and over throughout the year and whenever it needs to secure and process new feedback.

Communication is key in every single phase of the listening process, but this final stage explicitly reminds us to close the loop. You must take time to let employees know what will happen as a result of their feedback. And if you're unable to act upon certain feedback, be transparent and tell them why.

Summary

The number of people disengaging at work or choosing to quit is on the rise. As organization development professionals, it is our responsibility to step up and act by providing practical ways everyone in the workplace can create a better experience to improve productivity and satisfaction. From the C-suite to the frontline, we must implement new and relevant ways of ensuring everyone at work feels valued and heard. It starts with active listening.

When you commit to actively listening to employees, you might be surprised by what you uncover, and how that influences the employee engagement strategies you come up with as a result. You have more power than you think to create a culture of active listening in which employees feel engaged in meaningful work, supported to grow and contribute, and cared about by those higher up. Keep an eye out for opportunities to make changes and expand your impact.

Key Takeaways

Here are a few things to remind yourself as you work toward becoming an active listener:

- **Understand how important your mindset is to your success.** Do you see yourself as a strategist and not just a tactician? How will you own your growth and lead by example? Consider how you'll make consistent progress without overpromising. How will you secure the support of those higher up by tying your strategic plan to mission critical KPIs?

- **Keep the corridors of communication open by ditching Lone Ranger thinking.** How will you leverage strategic alliances with people leaders to identify opportunities for employee engagement together?

- **Remember, when you know how to listen, employees will tell you everything you need to know to be successful and meet their needs.** Making listening a core part of your employee engagement initiatives will not only make your job easier, but will also ensure employees feel heard, understood, valued—and like they want to stick around.

Change Management

HOLLY BURKETT

IN THIS CHAPTER

♦ Learn the fundamentals of change management
♦ Discover key tasks for implementing each phase of change management
♦ Identify critical success factors for implementing change
♦ Gain tips, tools, and resources for addressing barriers to change

In the wake of a global pandemic, shifting demographics, new models of working, and rapidly advancing technology, an explosive cocktail of disruption has become the new normal for organizations. Relentless, unpredictable, and unprecedented change is everywhere and coming at us faster than ever. With change as a constant, agility, adaptability, and change management have emerged as critical power skills.

Organizations need leaders who can maintain effectiveness despite constant uncertainty, act decisively without always having clear direction, and inspire trust through complexity, chaos, and confusion. Training professionals plays a key role in teaching leaders, teams, and individuals the essential elements of change management, including how to communicate, organize, delegate, and navigate change-related challenges. Change is central to talent development agendas designed to increase employee attraction, retention, engagement, and performance. And it is at the core of every organization development (OD) strategy meant to fuel innovation, generate revenue, and transform cultures. In short, today's L&D, talent development, or OD practitioner plays a vital role as change agent.

Becoming a successful change agent begins by first understanding the *what* and *why* of change management.

What Is Change Management?

Change management is the application of structured processes and tools to transition or transform an organization's goals, processes, or technologies. Ultimately, change management focuses on how to help people engage, adopt, and operationalize a change in their day-to-day work to achieve desired outcomes.

When defining change management, it is recognized as both a process and a competency (Prosci nd):

- **Change management as a process** is about helping organizations, teams, and individuals manage the transition from a current state to a desired state. It is the process of guiding organizational change to fruition, from the earliest stages of conception and preparation through implementation and, finally, to resolution. The process in between is dynamic and unfolds in phases.
- **Change management as a competency** is a strategic leadership skill for facilitating organizational change. For senior leaders, this means acting as an effective sponsor of change and demonstrating a commitment to the change through words and actions. For people managers, this is about effectively coaching direct reports through their change journeys. For change agents or practitioners, typical competencies include analytical skills, listening skills, emotional intelligence, detail orientation, process orientation, and OD knowledge and experience.

Why Is Change Management Important?

Why is successful change management so important? In a survey with nearly 3,000 executives, McKinsey found the failure rate of change efforts to be higher than 60 percent (Jouany and Martic 2020). On the other hand, highly resilient, change capable companies are much more likely to have outstanding business, organizational, and people results (Bersin 2020). Applying effective change management in both large- and small-scale efforts has been shown to:

- Ensure projects stay on schedule and on budget.
- Increase the likelihood of workforce engagement, allegiance, and resilience.

- Increase trust and confidence in leadership.
- Increase organizational, team, and individual performance.

What may be most surprising about the research is that poor change management correlates with better success than applying none at all (Prosci nd). In short, if we've learned anything about change over the years, it's that your approach to change is integral to business success regardless of your industry or geographical location.

Change Roles

In any change effort, a variety of roles are needed to defy the odds of change failure and ensure that an initiative meets its intended goals. The most common change management roles and responsibilities include sponsors, sustaining sponsors, change implementers, and change agents.

Change Sponsors

Sponsors are typically executives and senior leaders who authorize and approve the time, money, and other resources needed to make change happen. A sponsor has the ultimate responsibility for building commitment for change across all organizational levels, especially at the senior management (sustaining sponsors) level. To effectively drive change, sponsors direct and coordinate efforts with a coalition of change practitioners, change agents, project managers, and people managers.

Sponsorship can make or break a change effort. Active and visible participation from a primary sponsor is commonly cited as one of the key factors in change management success. Although sponsorship is critical, many executives and senior leaders struggle to fulfill these roles effectively. This is an area where OD practitioners can add great value as strategic change partners.

Sustaining Sponsors

Sustaining sponsors typically represent the coalition of senior leaders responsible for sponsoring change in their own functional areas, with top-level responsibility resting with an executive—the primary sponsor. Their key tasks are to demonstrate and solicit commitment to the change and to keep the sponsor informed of change progress.

Change Implementers

Implementers are responsible for applying the change across the organization and typically report to a sponsor or sustaining sponsor. Implementers may have decision-making authority and be responsible for implementing change as a change practitioner or project lead. If they don't have decision-making authority, they may serve primarily as a support person or a change management team member and be responsible for managing select change tasks or deadlines.

Change Agents

Change agents can be internal employees or managers—or external contractors, like consultants—who are responsible for assisting sponsors and implementers in promoting, championing, and facilitating a change effort. Their role is to inspire and influence others during a transition or transformation. Change agents usually wear many different hats and can act as business partners, educators, data gatherers, advisors, advocates, coaches, change network leaders, or meeting facilitators, to name a few.

It is difficult to draw up an exhaustive list of all the characteristics needed for effective change agents. However, the most frequently cited core qualities are shown in Figure 9-1.

Figure 9-1. Qualities of Effective Change Agents

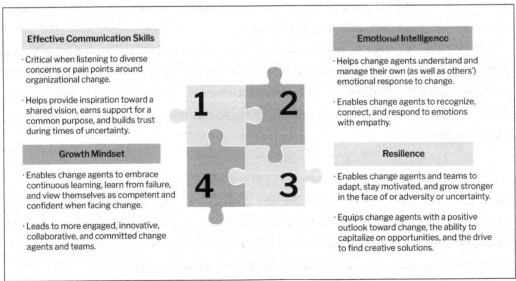

Effective Communication Skills

· Critical when listening to diverse concerns or pain points around organizational change.

· Helps provide inspiration toward a shared vision, earns support for a common purpose, and builds trust during times of uncertainty.

Emotional Intelligence

· Helps change agents understand and manage their own (as well as others') emotional response to change.

· Enables change agents to recognize, connect, and respond to emotions with empathy.

Growth Mindset

· Enables change agents to embrace continuous learning, learn from failure, and view themselves as competent and confident when facing change.

· Leads to more engaged, innovative, collaborative, and committed change agents and teams.

Resilience

· Enables change agents and teams to adapt, stay motivated, and grow stronger in the face of or adversity or uncertainty.

· Equips change agents with a positive outlook toward change, the ability to capitalize on opportunities, and the drive to find creative solutions.

Types of Change

No matter what role you play in a change effort, it's important to remember that not all change is created equal. While change typically focuses on improving performance on some level, the size and scope of change will produce varying degrees of impact to the people or processes involved.

Understanding the nature and type of change you're facing will help you decide which approach is the most appropriate for the situation. Common types of change include:

- **Adaptive changes.** These are small, gradual, iterative changes used to evolve organizational products, processes, workflows, and strategies over time. Examples of adaptive changes include hiring a new team member to address increased demand or implementing a new bonus structure to attract more qualified job candidates.

- **Transformational changes.** These changes are largely unpredictable and messy. They are characterized by scale (it affects all or most of the organization); by magnitude (it involves significant shifts in the status quo); by duration (the change initiative lasts for months if not years); or by strategic importance. Transformational changes are larger in scale and scope and often signify a dramatic and, occasionally sudden, shift in the status quo. Launching a new product or business division, deciding to expand internationally, or implementing a new hybrid work model are examples of transformational change.

In general, traditional step-by-step change management approaches work best with adaptive, development changes that have low to moderate organizational impact. Prevailing, one-size-fits-all change management approaches don't work well with complex, enterprise-wide transformational changes. Instead, large-scale efforts are best managed with an iterative process of staged or cascading changes.

Regardless of the type of change, a strong foundation in basic change-management skills—such as building stakeholder support and communicating vision and purpose—is critical. Unfortunately, these not-so-basic skills are often overlooked or assumed to be in place. By sharing knowledge and expertise about the nature and types of change, you can lay the groundwork for effective change management in your workplace and help ensure that change strategies are properly matched to the type of change demands at play.

Change Management Models

Change management models represent research-based, in-depth concepts, theories, and methodologies that describe various ways to view organizational change. They generally describe actions and steps that flow from one to another, with some overlap between. While steps are typically presented in sequential order, it's important to remember that change is rarely a linear process.

There are a wide range of change management models available to help you navigate the dos and don'ts of organizational change (Biech 2007). Although not comprehensive, Table 9-1 highlights six models that are influential to current practice.

Table 9-1. Common Change Management Models

Year	Model	Developer	Key Concepts
2003	Prosci's ADKAR Model	Jeff Hiatt	Five outcomes individuals need for successful change: (A) awareness, (D) desire, (K) knowledge, (A) ability, and (R) reinforcement
1999	Systemic Model	Peter Senge	Challenge top-down, large scale change. Start small, grow steadily, and expect challenges.
1995	Eight-Step Model	John Kotter	Eight-step linear process of change focused on creating urgency, a vision, and coalitions
1991	Transition Model	William Bridges	Transition consists of endings, a neutral zone, and beginnings.
1980s	McKinsey's 7-S Model, Organizational Design	McKinsey	Organizational effectiveness is improved through the interactions of seven key elements: structure, strategy, skill, system, shared values, style, and staff.
1951	Three-Step Model and Force-Field Analysis	Kurt Lewin	Unfreeze-change-refreeze. Change occurs when driving forces outweigh resisting forces.

Choosing and applying a consistent framework for change management is important. First it provides a common language for change and gives leaders and teams a road map for managing change and achieving results. In addition, it emphasizes the use of a disciplined, systemic process that goes beyond simple one-and-done activities or stand-alone training programs.

A Systems View

While there are pros and cons for each model, there is a common theme between each of the more credible and widely applied approaches: the principle of a systems view (Phillips and Holton 1997). A big picture, holistic view helps OD professionals see that:

- There are interrelationships among all parts of the whole.
- Parts and elements are dynamic and change constantly.
- A change in one element affects the others.
- Structural, cultural, and human elements must be properly aligned to ensure change success.

Structural Elements

Structural elements influence how the organization's internal systems, processes, and infrastructure will be leveraged to operationalize a change strategy. For example, *structure* represents the way business divisions and units are organized, and *systems* represents the processes and procedures that govern daily activities and decision making. For best results, structural processes should be adaptive and responsive to changing needs (Cummings and Worley 2016). OD practitioners can advise senior leaders about systems that are poorly aligned, too complicated, or too outdated.

Cultural Elements

Cultural elements represent organizational norms and values around communicating, decision making, including others, measuring success, and rewarding achievement. Cultural integration is a critical success factor with any transformational change effort. OD professionals can help facilitate cultural integration and support desired changes through mechanisms like employee networks, change academies, performance management systems, or communities of practice.

Human Elements

As the heart of successful change, human elements are often the most challenging to manage. An estimated 50 to 70 percent of all change initiatives fail to meet their objectives, and that failure is often due to an overemphasis on financial, structural, and strategic change issues at the expense of the human side of change. OD practitioners play a major role in helping senior leaders successfully manage the people side of change by ensuring that the right people are involved, engaged, and committed throughout each phase of the change process. Managing the people side of change also includes being sensitive to how employees are experiencing change.

Agile and Waterfall Change Methods

Agile and Waterfall are two well-known and popular project management methods that are prevalent in change management. Waterfall is a linear system of working that requires change teams to complete each project phase before moving on to the next. Agile encourages teams to work simultaneously on different project phases during iterative sprints. Table 9-2 highlights a comparison of the two.

Table 9-2. Comparison of Waterfall and Agile

Waterfall	Agile
Fixed timeline with start and finish mapped out from the beginning	Flexible schedule that adapts as the project progresses
Client or project owner is only involved for specific check-ins or deliverables	Includes clients in project development at every step
Each phase is fully completed before moving on to the next	Welcomes adapting to different directions
Provides concrete plans and outlines early requirements	Encourages productivity, efficiency, and experimentation
Can make it difficult to discover problems until a phase is completed, making it time consuming to go back and troubleshoot	Can result in lost work, redundancy, or miscommunication because deliverables are not a requirement to progress from a phase

In short, waterfall approaches are ideal for projects where expectations and end results are well defined at the beginning and the deliverables required to advance from each phase to the next are clear. Agile is more flexible and better suited for fast-moving projects with a lot of room to adapt and change course and where outcomes may be dependent on more feedback or testing. Common methodologies used in Agile include Scrum, SAFe and AgilePM.

Implications for Practice

The frequency of change generated by Agile approaches means that the traditional change management activities have to speed up to create mini waves of change. Subsequently, OD professionals are often challenged when trying to adapt and adjust their change management practices in a project that is using Agile. Conversely, there are also challenges for OD professionals when faced with organizations seeking to transition from traditional change management approaches to Agile approaches.

To effectively integrate change management in Agile projects or improve the adoption of Agile as a standardized change approach, OD professionals must ensure that the people side of change is properly addressed. Best practices include (Prosci Research 2021):

- Ensuring strong executive sponsorship
- Creating a change management plan
- Training on Agile
- Delivering coaching on Agile
- Communicating effectively
- Ensuring Agile experts are involved in the effort

Chapter 7 talks more about Agile and Lean methodologies.

Phases of Change Management

While no two change initiatives are alike, most successful ones follow the phases described in Figure 9-2.

Phase 1: Assess Readiness

The goal of phase 1 is to assess the initial readiness of the organization and its people to accommodate and internalize complex change. Like the diagnosis stage of organization development or the first phase of ADDIE (which you'd use to design a learning experience), assessment represents the fact-finding phase. It is a collaborative data collection process between you and organizational stakeholders in which relevant information about the change is gathered, analyzed, and reviewed.

Table 9-3 describes high level tasks and key questions for assessing readiness.

Figure 9-2. Phases of Change Management

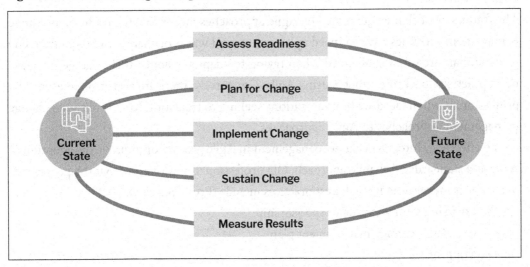

Table 9-3. Key Tasks and Questions for Assessing Readiness

Key Tasks	Key Questions
Establish the need for change	• What are we trying to achieve? • How does this change help drive strategic goals forward? • What is the gap between where we are and where we want to be? • What level of priority does this change have compared with other projects? • Is now the right time? What happens if we don't act?
Identify stakeholders	• Who is the target audience? • What jobs and roles will be most affected by the change? • Whose support do we need to ensure success? • Are senior leaders and management teams committed to this change?
Define the vision	• Is there a shared vision of a desired future state? • Are the right people involved? • What is the picture of success?
Determine success criteria	• How will success be measured? • What metrics or key performance indicators need to be moved? • What milestone targets are needed to track progress? • Who is responsible for collecting, analyzing, and reporting measures of progress?
Identify resource requirements	• What resources do we need to make this change successful? • Will information, tools, and resources be available for employees at the time and place of need? • How will we track access and use of available resources?
Assess potential risks or barriers	• What are the potential risks and barriers to change success? • What is the risk management plan for addressing barriers? • How many other changes are currently taking place? • Are we being sensitive to issues like change fatigue or burnout? • What lessons have we learned from other change efforts like this?

Sponsorship as a Readiness Issue

The active and visible participation of the leaders who authorize and fund a change initiative is a critical readiness factor. Unfortunately, many executives are not aware of the importance of their role and often do not understand what effective sponsorship looks like. Figure 9-3 shows key sponsorship roles and responsibilities.

Figure 9-3. Key Sponsorship Roles

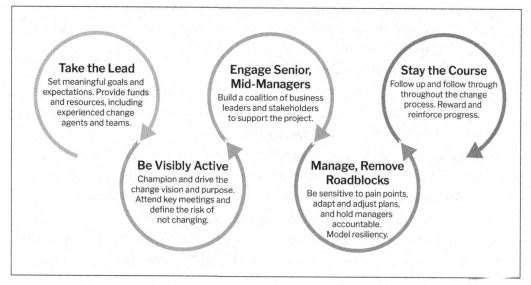

Take the Lead
Set meaningful goals and expectations. Provide funds and resources, including experienced change agents and teams.

Engage Senior, Mid-Managers
Build a coalition of business leaders and stakeholders to support the project.

Stay the Course
Follow up and follow through throughout the change process. Reward and reinforce progress.

Be Visibly Active
Champion and drive the change vision and purpose. Attend key meetings and define the risk of not changing.

Manage, Remove Roadblocks
Be sensitive to pain points, adapt and adjust plans, and hold managers accountable. Model resiliency.

Change Fatigue as a Readiness Issue

Change fatigue is one of the biggest barriers to change readiness. It occurs when people feel pressured to make too many transitions at once or when change initiatives have been poorly thought through, rolled out too fast, or put in place without adequate preparation. In today's organizations, individuals and teams constantly grapple with issues like change fatigue, Zoom fatigue, information overload, the accelerated pace of work, prolonged health and safety concerns, and lingering uncertainty about the future of the world, their work, and the workplace.

As change strategists, OD practitioners should recognize the impact of burnout and change fatigue upon employees' motivation and their overall capacity to perform. After all, the message of a perfectly designed and delivered change initiative will be lost if employees are too exhausted to hear or implement it (Burkett 2017).

To that end, some organizations reduce change turbulence with a vetting process, in which proposals for significant change are subjected to rigorous war room screenings by key stakeholders and then prioritized according to their importance to business strategy, financial impact, and probability of success.

Some indicators that your organization is ready for change include:

- The need for change has been fully defined and assigned a level of priority.
- Sponsors are prepared and able to fulfill their roles throughout the project.
- A coalition of supportive leaders is visibly committed to the change.
- Specific, measurable, and achievable targets for success have been identified.
- A risk management plan is in place.

Sample assessment tools include:

- **Business case.** A formal, structured document that tells the story of a change project from rationale to approach. Used to build support, gain credibility, and connect change efforts to business results.
- **Readiness assessment.** An analysis that evaluates whether an organization is prepared to initiate, follow through on, and maintain desired changes.
- **Stakeholder analysis.** Process used to identify key leaders, individuals, and groups that will have a stake in the impact of desired changes.
- **Change impact assessment.** Defines how proposed changes in skills, knowledge, culture, processes, or systems may affect target audiences as they transition from the current state to target state.
- **Risk management plan.** Describes factors that may cause a change project to fall short of desired results. Used to create pre-emptive responses and continually assess potential risks.

Phase 2: Plan for Change

A readiness assessment helps inform the planning process. The plan should broadly outline the reasons for change; define its schedule and scope; identify roles and responsibilities for change implementers, change teams, or change agents; and provide a detailed road map of the steps required to manage the change.

Table 9-4 describes high-level tasks and key questions for achieving planning objectives. Having a well-defined change plan makes it easier to communicate across the organization and monitor progress toward milestones and goals. One of the most powerful tools and outputs of this phase is your communication plan.

Table 9-4. Key Tasks and Questions for Planning

Key Tasks	Key Questions
Establish the project plan	• Who will oversee the project plan? • Who will be responsible for implementing the plan? • What actions are needed during each phase of this effort? What falls outside the project scope? • Who needs to sign off at each critical stage?
Establish a change implementation team	• What is the team's charter? • Who are the right people for the team? • How will roles and responsibilities be assigned? What accountability measures are needed? • How will the team help prepare and equip each level of the organization for change? • What kind of support does the change team have from sponsors, sustaining sponsors, and other management groups? • What kinds of rewards, recognition, or incentives are available for change team members?
Develop a training and performance support plan	• What formal or informal training is needed to help employees adopt new processes, behaviors, or tools? • What kind of on-the-job performance support is needed to reinforce change? • How do we ensure access to available resources? • Is coaching or mentoring appropriate? • How will training be tailored to different roles or functions? • Will managers support time to learn and train? • How and when will training results be measured?
Establish an evaluation plan	• Are the initial success measures still realistic and relevant? • What are the roles and responsibilities of stakeholders in collecting, analyzing, and reporting data? (What are they now, midterm, and long term?) • How will performance metrics be linked to recognition and rewards for change teams? • How will results data be used, in what format, and how often?

Develop a communication plan	• Who needs to know what, by when?
	• Who do we include in designing and delivering key messages?
	• What information needs to be tailored to various roles or functions?
	• How often will we communicate with specific groups?
	• What methods or media will we use for communicating?
	• How do we answer core concerns from employees, such as:
	   o What is happening and why?
	   o How will it affect me on my job?
	   o How can I get more information?

The What and Why of a Communication Plan

Change leaders cannot create participation and commitment to change by decree. A well-designed, well-executed communication plan is an effective way to share a change vision broadly throughout an organization and inspire employees' commitment toward a compelling future and new purpose.

For best results, plans should be tailored to two very distinct audiences. The first consists of employees and teams. These individuals need to understand the need for change as well as how it will affect their job responsibilities. The second audience includes key stakeholders, including members of the C-suite, mid- and frontline management, and even board members (Stobierski 2020).

Guidelines for developing effective communication plans include:

- Repetition is good, so communicate often and regularly.
- Use a variety of methods, including leadership briefs, town halls, stand ups, training, coaching, lunch & learns, job aids, check stuffers, ask-an-expert websites, change networks, games, puzzles, FAQ guides, wikis, and blogs.
- Keep it simple.
- Share responsibility for communicating across the organization.
- Have managers and direct supervisors send change messages because they're the most effective and preferred senders.
- Make sure plans emphasize two-way communication (listen).
- Use messages that capture both the head and heart.
- Post success stories, including testimonials from early adopters.

Sample planning tools include:

- **Change management (or project) plan.** A document defining the roles, tasks, responsibilities, and timelines associated with the change project. Used to manage and communicate change scope, schedule, and resource requirements. Note that project management and change management are becoming increasingly integrated, with both project and change management tasks and milestones often reflected in one plan.
- **RACI (responsible, accountable, consulted, and informed) matrix.** Used to describe the roles and responsibilities of various cross-functional teams or people in delivering a change project or operating a process.

- **Communication plan.** Details what information will be communicated to stakeholders and employees about the change, along with how, when, and who will provide information throughout the project.
- **Training plan.** Outlines the schedule, scope, and resources required to equip target audiences with the skills, knowledge, and tools needed to adopt and apply a desired change.
- **Evaluation plan.** Defines targeted change outcomes across organizational and individual levels and outlines how and when data will be collected (at various intervals) to determine if learning, performance, and business goals are being met.
- **Team charter.** Describes the purpose, direction, and duration of a change team, along with member roles and responsibilities and key deliverables. Developed early during a group session, the team charter ensures shared understanding and buy-in.
- **Change management software.** A variety of software programs (Wrike, the Change Compass, Whatfix) are available to track change progress. For information about the most common tools, visit thedigitalprojectmanager.com /tools/change-management-tools.

Phase 3: Implement Change

Implementation is about putting the change vision and plan into practice. This phase is especially critical because the costs are high if implementation goes wrong—costs include lost opportunity, wasted resources, and lowered morale. Consider how many times you've been involved in a change initiative that's been launched with great fanfare, only to fizzle out as another flavor of the month.

Proper assessment and planning can greatly improve the odds of change success. Remember, failing to plan is planning to fail! However, despite our best efforts, few change efforts go completely according to plan.

Anticipate Roadblocks and Barriers

OD professionals should help prepare sponsors and change teams for any number of potential roadblocks. Some of the more common barriers are:

- Ineffective leadership (especially sponsorship)
- Poor team communication

- Competing priorities
- Unrealistic expectations
- Flawed implementation
- Lack of buy-in or internal support
- Insufficient resources
- Change fatigue

Tool 9-1. "If This, Then That" provides high-level suggestions for helping sponsors, managers, and change agents work through these barriers.

Manage Expectations

Unrealistic expectations are a common barrier to change success. Sponsors and leaders need to give up the notion that employees can turn on a dime, quickly produce behavior results, and juggle all of their old and new responsibilities without missing a beat. One way OD professionals can level leaders' change expectations is by helping them prepare for a learning curve or slight performance dip after a change is introduced. For instance, any change that involves a reasonably large shift in daily work routines is likely to require an adjustment factor, no matter how motivated or skilled an employee may be (Herold and Fedor 2008).

Another effective way to level expectations is by helping leaders adopt a growth mindset, which means setbacks are viewed as a normal part of the change process and are used as learning opportunities. For example, Microsoft leveraged a growth mindset in its transformation to a more agile and adaptive organization in 2014. A growth mindset was the foundation of its culture change strategy, which included the use of education and training programs, conversation guides, town hall meetings, an empathy museum, and revamped talent management processes (Lutin 2020).

Reimagine Change Resistance

Organizations often attribute change failure to individuals' resistance, laziness, negativity, or lack of motivation. While these factors may be present, research has challenged these beliefs about the nature of change resistance. For example, much so-called resistance can be attributed to performance anxiety about learning readiness, as in, "Can I do what's expected of me?" (Herold and Fedor 2008).

Tool 9-1. Anticipating Change Roadblocks and Barriers

If This	Then That
Ineffective leadership	• Engage a credible sponsor and provide sponsorship support. • Build change capability among business units and strategic change partners. • Establish an executive steering committee to champion change. • Define roles and responsibilities before, during, and after implementation.
Poor team communication	• Define team purpose, roles, responsibilities, and ground rules. • Ensure teams represent a diverse and inclusive group of stakeholders. • Provide education, training, and coaching support to enhance team relations and collaboration. • Promote a growth mindset.
Competing priorities	• Use risk management and contingency planning processes. • Make necessary adjustments to schedule, scope, or resources. • Use a vetting process to prioritize competing demands. • Shift focus from projects that drain resources or fail to achieve intended results.
Unrealistic expectations	• Initiate goal setting to establish expectations at the start. • Ensure expectations are achievable, realistic, and relevant. • Identify opportunities to improve efficiencies or effectiveness. • Make change data accessible and available on demand. • Allow for "learning curves" and initial performance dips
Flawed implementation	• Create inclusive, collaborative implementation plans. • Apply a planned change process for consistency and credibility. • Ensure change leaders and teams have the proper skills and knowledge to manage change effectively. • Integrate project management approaches and partners. • Provide ongoing education, training, and performance support to increase employees' commitment to and adoption of the change. • Pilot change efforts to establish quick wins. • Avoid declaring victory too early (stay the course).
Lack of buy-in or internal support	• Openly and honestly address concerns or pain points. • Build partnerships and speak the language of the business. • Practice empathy. • Leverage change networks, change academies, or communities of practice to champion change. • Celebrate progress and communicate success stories. • Show how change efforts have helped solve real business issues.
Insufficient resources	• Define schedule, scope, and resource requirements early on. • Scale back as needed. • Customize implementation plans to address constraints in specific business units. • Consolidate steps, conserve resources, and leverage change teams.
Change fatigue	• Make change capacity a strategic readiness issue. • Cascade overlapping efforts to minimize impact and increase recovery thresholds. • Reward and reinforce "rest, recovery, and review" practices. • Provide performance support at the time and place of need. • Monitor fatigue and burnout with regular pulse checks, listening sessions, and town halls.

Change is more successful when individuals are confident that they can attain change goals, give and receive feedback, and meet performance expectations. Compared to on-site workers, fully remote workers tend to feel less confident and more uneasy about meeting change expectations (Lutin 2020). To minimize performance anxiety and increase commitment, OD professionals can provide more up-front training, work with change teams to remove environmental or on-the-job barriers, enhance incentives for performance improvement, and provide appropriate resource support at the time and place of need during change efforts.

Encouraging and rewarding risk taking and experimentation are also powerful ways change managers can reduce risks associated with performance anxiety or fear of failure. Garry Ridge, internationally acclaimed executive and former CEO of WD-40, encourages risk taking by framing mistakes as "learning moments" (Hoffman 2020).

Symptoms of change fatigue and burnout can also be confused with resistance. For instance, burnout is characterized by mental distance from one's job, brain fog, energy depletion, and apathy (Borysenko 2019). Burnout reflects an individual's *capacity* to accommodate change demands, not their desire, ability, or *capability* to change. Capacity is finite; people can only do so much, and there are only so many people (Burkett 2017).

Capacity becomes a strategic issue when senior leaders' demands require more capacity than there actually is or can be, or when senior leaders add major change on top of normal workload requirements without removing something from people's plates. In his book *How the Mighty Fall*, Jim Collins (2009) warned about the risk of frenetic, undisciplined change that goes beyond what leaders or companies can accommodate.

With burnout continuing to increase at alarming rates, OD professionals can add significant value by helping leaders understand that a well-integrated, well-planned change strategy is meaningless if an organization lacks the capacity to execute it. Encourage leaders to collaborate with change teams to monitor workloads, conduct periodic temperature checks, and remove on-the-job barriers. Employees across roles and levels must be encouraged—and even expected—to rest, recharge, and recover as a matter of personal effectiveness and well-being and as a way to maintain and sustain peak performance.

Implementation Guidelines

Building on what I've covered for phase 3, here are 10 guidelines you can follow to ensure your change implementation efforts succeed:

1. Apply a planned change process that includes milestones, timelines, and success measures.
2. Model the change through personal example and hands-on involvement.
3. Acknowledge challenges and roadblocks honestly.
4. Listen and encourage feedback.
5. Remove roadblocks and help teams overcome obstacles.
6. Look for quick wins.
7. Reinforce, reward, and celebrate change progress.
8. Stay the course, sustain momentum, and avoid shifting priorities.
9. Leverage change teams and networks throughout the change process.
10. Double down on mitigating change fatigue and burnout.

Sample implementation tools include:

- **Change management (or project) plan.** The planning road map is used to continually assess progress, ensure accountabilities, and modify or adjust the schedule, scope, and resource requirements as needed.
- **Heat map.** A one-page visual showing the impact of change on target audiences, groups, or functions. Identifies high-risk areas needing attention.
- **Risk management matrix.** A four-by-four chart that plots the severity of the impacts of a change against employees' receptiveness to the change.
- **Progress or status reports.** Provides the project sponsor, the steering committee, and other stakeholders with an ongoing assessment of how the change effort is being received.
- **Pulse surveys.** Short, focused surveys to gather employee feedback about a change strategy and pinpoint areas of progress or concern.
- **Agile tools or software.** Sample tools include Kanbanize, Jira, Trello, GitHub, and LeanKit.
- **Project management tools or software.** Sample tools include Gantt charts, Wrike, Monday.com, and Asana.

Phase 4: Sustain Change

The goal of this phase is to anchor the change in organizational processes, workflows, culture, and strategies. By embedding changes within the company's culture and practices, it becomes more difficult for backsliding to occur. OD practitioners can help organizations integrate change by providing coaching, building change capability, and taking the long view.

Provide Coaching Support

Many change initiatives flounder because leaders lack the skills to initiate and sustain change. For example, many leaders:

- Fail to acknowledge personal biases in change strategies.
- Jump too quickly from one change effort to the next.
- Underestimate the costs, challenges, and impact of change.
- Fail to assess the organization's capacity to change.
- Try to make too many changes at once.
- Neglect to cascade changes effectively.
- Declare victory too early.

To improve the odds of change success, OD professionals must provide managers with the tools and support they need to navigate both halves of the change equation: people *and* process.

From a coaching perspective, senior leaders tend to be the least proficient in the interaction skills required to lead change. Therefore they should spend more time and effort on improving the relationship building and interaction skills needed for effective change leadership (Mitchell, Ray, and van Ark 2014).

Companies like Biogen and Microsoft provide coaching support by having senior leaders serve as mentors and coaches to cohorts of managers, who learn how to lead during times of uncertainty, model a growth mindset, and grow more resilient teams. When leaders are coached to help employees translate the organization's mission and purpose to their individual work, the organization becomes 8.2 times more likely to be change adaptable (Bersin 2021).

Build Change Capability

Most organizations consider managing change to be an essential leadership competency, yet those behaviors and attributes are often ill defined. OD professionals and stakeholders can work together to identify the characteristics and competencies needed to drive change and create competitive advantage in their organization. While there is no one-size-fits-all profile for a leader—much less for a change-capable leader—it helps to have a shared frame of reference during conversations about building change-capable talent (Burkett 2017).

Because many organizations focus more on change *management* than change *leadership*, leveraging leadership development remains a key strategy for building change capability at the middle and senior leadership levels (McLean and Company 2022).

Keep in mind, however, that growing change capability is about more than standalone leadership development programs. For example, Prosci research suggests that developing a network of change-ready teams across the entire organization is strongly linked to change management success, yet many organizations don't have teams readily in place. Change networks, change academies, and communities of practice are common approaches for building change-ready teams across all levels.

Case Study: Leveraging Teams to Lead Change

The Situation

A large financial institution was implementing a new customer relationship management (CRM) system in its call center, with two members of the OD team assigned to assist key stakeholders in leading and managing the change effort. The technology was new to the 500 call center agents, and it was critical for them to adopt and use the system without disrupting customer service and existing service level agreements.

The Solution

To build buy-in and employee engagement, the OD project team partnered with stakeholders within each work stream to select informal leaders to serve as change agents. Change agents were responsible for filtering communication to their team peers; receiving feedback from their peers on the CRM implementation; and providing feedback to the change agent lead. Each agent underwent a one-day training orientation for the role. In addition, their job duties and related performance measures were updated to reflect the new responsibilities.

The Challenge

Key challenges around role clarity emerged during implementation. For example, change agents reported trouble distinguishing the difference between the role of the change agent and the role of each team's supervisor. Change agents also had difficulty removing themselves from the day-to-day operational management of their teams while performing their change agent duties.

The Results

From a change management point of view, change sponsors and stakeholders viewed the project as a success for several reasons:

- Capabilities were built in the organization for future changes.
- Potential leaders for career progression were identified through change agent participation.
- Strategic project objectives were met with the CRM implementation.
- Staff felt heard and included in the change because their issues were addressed by senior project staff.

Lessons Learned

The OD project team conducted an after action review with key stakeholders, team leaders, and change agents to identify lessons learned and continuous improvement opportunities. Key lessons included:
- Make better distinctions between the role of change agent and team leaders.
- Update change agent job descriptions and performance measures.
- Adjust change agents' daily workload so they can perform their change agent duties.
- Show staff their feedback is valued by giving them a voice and then acting on their input.

Take the Long View

An organization can build change capability by consistently applying proven, disciplined change management practices and by equipping individuals across all levels with the skill sets and mindsets needed to navigate change. It's important to remember, however, that growing change capability at the enterprise level goes beyond better change management by select individuals working with discrete projects. Building and sustaining change capability is best viewed as a long-term, developmental process where change practices and policies evolve from ad hoc, one-off approaches to consistent, integrated processes that are fully embedded in an organization's strategic priorities and core values (Bersin 2021).

Consider McKesson, a healthcare distribution company that delivers a third of all pharmaceuticals used in North America and employs more than 78,000 staff. McKesson grounds every change effort in their mission: "Improving healthcare in every setting—one product, one partner, one patient at a time." In addition, the organization's unwavering focus on purpose and global I.CARE Values was critical in guiding leaders, teams, and contingent workers through the change and transformation required for them to participate in the COVID-19 vaccination rollout (Bersin 2021).

Sample sustaining tools include:
- **Surveys or questionnaires.** Examples include periodic pulse surveys, satisfaction surveys, or follow-up impact questionnaires to determine how and where change is being integrated in standard workflows and processes.

- **Town halls or focus groups.** Formal or informal meetings between senior leaders, stakeholders, and employee groups, these groups to follow up on change progress, recognize achievements, report results, and uncover potentially risky areas of change impact.
- **Communities of practice (CoP).** A workplace community for those interested in learning more about managing change, those who already practice change management, and those who sponsor change, it fosters a common change language, promotes knowledge sharing, and grows change capability for both individuals and the organization.

Phase 5: Measure Results

An important ingredient for the success of any change effort is to plan for evaluation early and define the desired outcomes throughout each phase of the project. While some job performance measures can be gathered during implementation, business impact measures like increased revenue, improved leadership effectiveness, or increased retention are usually not evident until months after launch.

When reviewing change results, key questions include:

- Did users embrace desired changes and help drive business results?
- What is needed to ensure the change sticks?
- Who will assume ownership of sustaining the outcomes?
- Did the approach increase people's willingness to engage in more changes going forward?
- Will project results encourage strong sponsor support for the next big change?
- Have your investments in change management set the groundwork for strategic change management going forward, especially during turbulent times?

Remember, achieving change success is a team sport. It is unrealistic for the L&D and OD teams to define, track, deliver, and report results on their own. Use the early assessment and planning phases to partner with the project sponsor, project team, and change management team in identifying what the change impact should be, how it should look, and when it should happen. Here, it's also important to address the tendency some leaders have to create unrealistic expectations for immediate improvement or results.

When defining and tracking change outcomes, three focus areas are recommended (Figure 9-4; Prosci 2018):

- **Organizational performance.** Metrics here determine the extent to which the project achieved its desired outcomes.
- **Individual performance.** Use data collection tools like surveys, tests, assessments, observations, and performance evaluation to identify where employees are and how they're progressing in the change process.
- **Change management performance.** Metrics here are connected to the experiences and activities associated with the overall change management process and its process owners or change management teams.

Figure 9-4. Key Measurement Areas

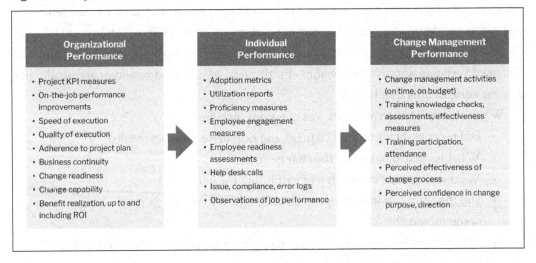

Finally, use these 10 critical success factors to help your change efforts achieve their intended results across all three levels of performance:

1. Establish success measures at the beginning.
2. Ensure success measures are specific, achievable, and relevant.
3. Share ownership for defining, collecting, analyzing, and reporting results.
4. Follow up and follow through.
5. Use results to show how change efforts have helped solve real problems.
6. Communicate results throughout the organization.
7. Give credit where credit is due, and avoid blame and shame.

8. Use results for evidence-based storytelling.
9. Honestly acknowledge what worked and what didn't.
10. Use results for continuous improvement.

Sample measurement tools include:

- **After action review (AAR).** A structured, post-project debrief process in which key stakeholders and the OD team can gather insights, review results, and capture lessons learned for future change efforts. Focused upon four questions:
  - What was our intended result?
  - What was our actual result?
  - What went well and why?
  - What can be improved and how?
- **Dashboard reports.** Used to see the trends in change requests or resolutions over time and across different groups, risk categories, and priority ratings, these reports are a way to present important KPIs in a single place so decisions can be based on the latest data-driven information.
- **Impact evaluation.** An analytic, disciplined process to determine the overall, aggregate outcomes of a change initiative based on the data identified and collected throughout the evaluation plan. The output is an impact evaluation report used for continuous improvement and action planning.

Summary

"Change is a threat when done to us, but an opportunity when done by us."
—Harvard Professor Rosabeth Moss Kanter

As we continue to adjust to new ways of working, living, and being, one thing's certain: Change and disruption are here to stay. The pressures for change are real, and the lackluster state of change management today shows that the world needs better change leaders. As OD professionals, we have a responsibility to heed the call by stepping up and embracing our role as change agents. This means we must continuously monitor our own aversion to change so we can best support the change strategies needed to drive performance, increase engagement, and improve employees' overall well-being.

While adapting to change is not always easy, we can build change capable skill sets and mindsets much like we'd build a new muscle—through repetition, training, coaching, and practice. Putting the guidelines of this chapter into practice will help you hone your own capability muscles and increase your effectiveness in managing both the people and process sides of change management.

How will you step up and deliver on the promise and opportunity of dynamic change? Remember, change begins with you!

Key Takeaways

Here are a few things to think about change management:

- **Change is a constant.** With change as the new normal, change agility, adaptability, and resilience have emerged as critical power skills for today's leaders, teams, and individuals.
- **OD practitioners play a vital role as change agents.** Leaders and teams are looking for positive support, motivation, and guidance during crisis or change. OD professionals are instrumental in shaping the conditions, capabilities, and confidence needed to help others navigate change.
- **A planned change approach is essential to success.** Applying a consistent, disciplined, and systemic change process provides direction, ensures better change outcomes, and increases the credibility of OD change agents.
- **Change fatigue must be addressed as a strategic readiness issue.** Change fatigue is a major barrier to change readiness. OD professionals must help leaders understand that a well-integrated, well-planned change strategy is meaningless if the organization lacks the energy and capacity to execute it.
- **Change communities lead to better change outcomes.** As teams become more scattered, change leaders must get intentional about building connections through inclusive change networks in which everyone has a voice, everyone can contribute, and everyone understands how their contributions connect with a shared vision and purpose.
- **Building change capability is a maturity process.** Growing organizational change capability is not a one-and-done event or simply the result of stand-alone change programs. Rather, it is a development process through which change practices are progressively transformed from ad hoc, undisciplined states to embedded, integrated practices capable of predictable, sustainable change results over time.

Workforce Design

PART 3

Workforce Design

Building a Global, Culturally Diverse Organization

NEAL R. GOODMAN

IN THIS CHAPTER

♦ Build a global pipeline of talent

♦ Tap into the potential of your international employees

♦ Capture the multicultural knowledge within your organization

♦ Create a globally inclusive DEI program

♦ Develop a global mindset and cultural competence across your organization

What does it mean to be a global and multicultural organization? While many large organizations believe they're global and multicultural, they're blinded by their own ethnocentric perceptions of the meaning of global and cultural diversity. The evolution of corporate structures to capture business globally has led to a constant quest to balance national economic interests and the need for differentiation at the local level. International expansion is an evolutionary process, and the functional areas and geographic regions that make up an international business may be at different stages of globalization.

The question for business leaders and OD practitioners is, how do we create an organization that maximizes a global mindset in a multicultural workforce and marketplace? Here are a few basic factors to consider:

- An organization's territory and scope must be determined by its customers' territory and scope of business.
- A primary cause of global business failure is myopia by organizational leadership.
- Globally inclusive systems need to be implemented.
- Local and regional autonomy must be considered.
- Diversity, equity, and inclusion initiatives must be tailored to universal and local circumstances.
- Systems must be created to store, promote, and share global experiences, expertise, and contacts.

If the CEO gave you the responsibility to build and sustain a global organization, what would you do? What organization development initiatives would sustain the organization in an ever-changing environment?

To build a sustainable global, multicultural organization, you need to address several areas:
- Implementing a global mindset and cultural intelligence
- Organizational initiatives to build a global pipeline of talent
- Applying diversity, equity, inclusion, and multiculturalism in the global organization
- Capturing and applying global and multicultural institutional knowledge

Implementing a Global Mindset and Cultural Intelligence

Enlightened self-interested corporations know that their next big innovation will not likely come from company headquarters and that potential disruptors likely won't be from obvious competitors in the same country. Increasingly, new markets are located across national boundaries, and products require adaptation to the preferences of local cultures. There are thousands of examples of business failures due to ignorance of cultural and diversity factors: Sneakers with country flags on them that are an insult in India and the Middle East or frozen pizza boxes that don't fit into European freezers.

What are organizations doing to meet the challenge?
- Corporations are becoming aware of their own myopia. They recognize that by selecting and developing leaders who are similar to existing leadership, they perpetuate groupthink and a very narrow view of the world. They are aware that their global leadership development programs are failing to bring in diverse talent.

- To create a more global talent pipeline, organizations are identifying candidates from developing countries and putting them through international assignments.
- Key performance indicators (KPIs) for existing employees are focusing on cultural competence and unconscious bias. Recent findings in neuroscience indicate that our brains are hard wired to making myopic decisions, which can cost a company in lost talent and innovation. To combat this, the entire leadership and management team must learn how to become more consciously in control of their unconscious minds.
- Senior leaders are being coached to be seen as role models and champions of inclusion.
- Innovative short-term international development programs are being created to push domestic high-potential employees overseas and pull international high-potential employees to the company's home office.
- Increasingly organizations are creating programs to attract employees and potential leaders with diverse backgrounds from underrepresented groups, including women, people from various racial and ethnic backgrounds, people with physical and neurological differences, the LGBGTQ community, and others.
- Project leaders are being made aware of their own blind spots in the selection of project team members, as well as cultural differences in collaboration styles.

However, most global initiatives fail because they lack systematic internal processes to create astute, flexible, and visionary employees who can hold multiple perspectives of the same situation simultaneously. This involves fostering a global business mindset, creativity, agility, and cultural intelligence.

A Global Business Mindset

People with a global business mindset have the intellectual appreciation of fundamental aspects for how societies and business practices are carried out around the globe.

Examples include:

- A keen appreciation of how historical factors within and between countries affect business relationships
- An understanding of how global demographic trends will influence the future of the organization

Creativity, Innovation, and Vision

Multicultural creativity refers to having the intuitive capacity to see issues from different, and sometimes competing, perspectives and create a solution that others could not see. From the leadership perspective, this means encouraging inclusion and participation of all colleagues, team members, and current and future business partners.

An example of multicultural creativity is the insight to design products or marketing strategies that balance with local tastes.

Cultural Intelligence

Cultural intelligence means understanding core cultural differences from around the globe and having the capacity to use this understanding to adapt to them. For example, a person's culture influences:

- Communication styles, including verbal, nonverbal, slang, speed and pacing, electronic communication, and direct and indirect communication preferences
- Global marketing tactics, such as sales techniques, decision making, quality, images used, and cultural factors in marketing
- How global relationships are managed, including recruitment norms, motivating global employees (rewards and recognition), superior-subordinate relationships, risk taking, and individualism versus group orientation
- Global business protocols, such as negotiation styles, decision making, how to build trust, forms of agreement, and socializing

Giving and receiving feedback for example is very different depending on the culture. In some countries you expect to receive direct feedback from peers, direct reports, and your leaders, whereas in other countries the manner, location, and context for giving and receiving feedback is very restricted and constrained.

For example: American talent development processes are developed so that the individual is the focus, which means they're assessed based on their performance independent of, and often in competition with, others. However, in most of Asia, talent development is more commonly based on a person's ability to be a contributing part of the collective. Rather than be trained as autonomous independent employees, the focus is on an integrated, interdependent organization.

Such cultural assumptions go to the heart of how we design reward and recognition policies. The differences between Western and Eastern approaches must be reconciled when creating global training programs.

Organizational Initiatives to Build a Global Pipeline of Talent

Every major organization is faced with the challenge of identifying and developing its current and future global leaders. Who are these people? What traits and attributes should they have? What experiences and training will ensure their success? These are the questions that OD practitioners can help organizations answer to compete successfully in the global economy.

Recruitment

A number of multinational organizations have developed a recruitment process in which they identify MBA students studying in leading universities from the key geographic areas where they need talent. These students are then recruited with the promise to put them through an accelerated development process to become future leaders. New recruits typically spend six to 12 months at the corporate or product headquarters where they learn about the organization's corporate culture and one or more of the specific functional areas for which they will be responsible.

Once the participants have completed the program and learned the core values, practices, and mission of the organization, the employees are then placed in a strategic position in their home countries.

Social Networking and Collaboration

A third approach is to leverage social networking and collaborative technologies to transcend boarders and silos. Organization development practitioners can take the lead in creating, coordinating, and monitoring global communities of interest within their companies. These communities can provide a culturally comparative perspective on new product development, marketing, training, and best practices in each location. This allows the organization to view the product from different perspectives, uncovering issues that would never have been seen from a monocultural perspective. OD departments would be wise to develop these types of global communities of interest and act on the resulting knowledge gained or they risk becoming superfluous.

International Assignments

An international stretch assignment is one of the most effective yet least used opportunities for global talent development. Most organizations only use international assignments as a requirement to achieve a functional need; however, when managed properly, these assignments can be a profound learning experience. OD departments must have a global perspective if they expect to create and implement such policies.

Even when organizations do include an international assignment as a prerequisite for global leadership positions, they don't always include a training plan to develop the skills employees need to become future leaders. In addition, the programs may not measure whether the participants have gained the necessary core competencies. As a result, employees may return from an international assignment with little cultural intelligence or multicultural skills.

To help retain international assignees who come back informed, skilled, and eager to take on a global leadership position, organizations can do the following before and after the assignment:

1. Interview the assignee and their sending manger to identify the manager's perceived expectations and the metrics for success. What should the assignees have learned, what skills needed to be developed, and what areas would be most valuable for improving the local organization upon the assignee's return? Create a plan with metrics agreed upon by the assignee and their manager that can be shared with the expat's manager in the host country.

2. Have the assignee and their family participate in an orientation program, coordinated by the group responsible for the move, that covers basic information the assignee needs to know about government compliance, housing, shopping, driving, and so forth.

3. Set up an in-depth cross-cultural immersion program in which the expat can learn about living and working in their new country. It could include topics such as making presentations, communication and management styles, and unspoken business rules.

4. Give the host country manager a cross-cultural briefing about the assignee's home culture so they can better understand possible unseen barriers that may influence how they manage the assignee.

5. Provide the assignee a host country coach who can support their needs. The coach can schedule an alignment meeting with the assignee and their host country manager to discuss goals, timelines, and measures of success. This meeting also provides space for reviewing and discussing the plans agreed to back in the home country, as well as any changes that need to be made. These changes should also be communicated to the home country manager through online meetings. This alignment meeting closes with everyone having a clear understanding of the assignment's goals and metrics for success.

6. Ask the coach to arrange an alignment meeting between the new assignee and their host country team members to cover any cross-cultural and organizational differences and discuss how they will work together so the assignee can meet their objectives and help the team.

7. Set up several coaching sessions between the coach and the assignee during the assignment, focusing on aligning expectations as well as specific challenges they're having, such as exposure to senior executives.

8. Hold a final session focusing on repatriation and how to leverage the full experience when the assignee returns home. Encourage the host and home country managers to participate in this meeting.

As a result of this initiative, assignees have a much better understanding of what they need to do, who they need to meet, what skills they need to develop, and who they should contact at the company headquarters to be considered for future promotions. These steps will help significantly improve the program and the assignees' ability to implement their knowledge upon their return home.

Applying the Hidden Potential of International Talent

International employees are among the most underused resources in today's global and multicultural organizations. Talent and OD leaders can play a significant role in maximizing the full potential of these important human resources.

As organizations compete for workers' talent, loyalty, and retention, they need to recognize that salary alone will not drive recruitment and retention. Unfortunately, many organizations do not know how to engage or retain their international employees and lose the benefit of their insights and the competitive advantage they bring. To differentiate themselves from their competitors, organizations need to develop strategies to sustain a global and multicultural advantage.

International employees face many challenges that affect their ability to fully contribute, such as culture shock or personal values and beliefs that conflict with the societal and workplace norms of their new culture (such as interactions between men and women). They may be afraid to speak up because they don't want to be judged by their accents or inappropriate use of an unfamiliar language. In addition, they may come from a workplace culture in which speaking up, asking questions, or seeking help may be seen as insubordination or a sign of weakness. In addition to these workplace stressors, they also have to deal with cultural differences in parenting, parent-teacher interactions, shopping, insurance, healthcare, and other daily tasks. If they don't have any resources to turn to, this can become overwhelming.

It's up to talent development and OD leaders to take action to dramatically improve international employee engagement so they can effectively contribute to the organization. Let's review some best practices that will enhance international employee engagement, success, and profitability.

Create an International Employee Resource Group

Employee resource groups (ERGs) usually fall under the umbrella of the diversity office and represent specific interests such as people from different cultures, parents, veterans, women, LGBTQ, and others including allies. OD leaders and L&D professionals can partner with the office of diversity to create an ERG for international employees. Employee resource groups provide a network that supports professional development, which in turn helps increase employee engagement and creates a workforce pipeline for the organization.

An international employee resource group (IERG) can add value to the organization's strategic goals by making a difference in policy improvement, professional development, networking opportunities, cultural competency training, social and cultural bonding, organizational inclusion, recruitment, social responsibility, increased volunteerism, and community support. In addition, the IERG could be used to connect new international hires with external resources in the community and may even act as a catalyst for open dialogue between employees who come from different cultures. It's also important to ensure that the IERG's executive sponsor has experienced what it's like to move to a new culture.

Record any new ideas and best practices generated by the IERG that contribute to the organization's success and present them to senior leaders in person.

Customize Onboarding for International Employees

Develop an onboarding process that focuses on challenges faced by international employees. For example, ask successful international employees to share their experiences. Or include a workshop on living and working in the new culture and workplace, and invite community representatives to attend. International employees may not be accustomed to joining volunteer organizations, taking advantage of community colleges or adult education, or using networking as a means for their professional and personal growth, so make sure they're aware of all opportunities available to them.

Develop a Buddy System

Assign new international employees with a buddy or mentor who is from the same culture or has had similar experiences. Expats who have returned home from an international assignment make great candidates because they typically want to continue connecting with and learning from people from other cultures. Remember that international employees may not take the initiative to ask for help, so make sure the mentors are calling or meeting with their mentees on a regular basis. One-on-one assistance can significantly improve worker confidence and help uncover hidden talents.

Create Opportunities for Socializing and Networking

Set up events focused on a particular topic of interest—such as education, religion, or food—and ask employees to share cultural insights and experiences on these topics. Social networking groups can also provide unanticipated opportunities for growth. IERGs can sponsor lunch & learn meetings in which employees can share insights about their home cultures. A dedicated website with frequently asked questions (FAQs) and resources can make a big difference for those who have linguistic challenges or are otherwise inhibited to seek help in person.

Offer L&D Programs

Host a cultural competency program for managers that's focused on working with international employees. This can be very powerful especially if they can hear stories from employees about incidents involving culture clashes or when they felt inhibited at work; for example, I have led many sessions in which employees have described how they were held back by their accents, their discomfort about taking credit for work, or speaking up at meetings. These training programs should examine the core cultural tendencies that affect manager-employee relationships, such as hierarchy (micromanagement versus empowerment), direct and indirect communication styles, processes of evaluation, performance reviews and feedback, and socializing during and after work.

Provide learning and development opportunities for international employees such as programs on speaking and presentation skills, financial planning, English language lessons, accent reduction, and health and nutrition.

Your international employees want to succeed and contribute to the organization. When you open the door for their full participation and inclusion, you will let in engaged and dedicated employees.

Applying Diversity, Equity, Inclusion, and Multiculturalism

The culturally diverse and geographically dispersed workplace and marketplace is our new reality; organizations that fail to adapt will perish. A proactive approach to diversity and inclusion at all levels of the organization is essential.

Unfortunately, while an increasing number of global companies are rolling out diversity initiatives, they're also seeing these programs fail at a relatively high rate. It's possible to successfully implement global diversity programs, but they must be done thoughtfully. Problems arise when companies try to geographically expand their original diversity initiatives—often based from an American point of view—without adjusting for cultural differences. In fact, diversity's very definition varies widely between countries, and the term *diversity* doesn't even exist in some languages.

So, what does a global company's OD department need to do when planning a global diversity initiative rollout? Here are just a few tips:

- Create a global diversity council with representation from all major countries in which you do business.
- Understand that while some diversity initiatives may make a lot of sense at home, they could lose their importance in other countries with different issues and experiences to consider.
- Learn the meaning of diversity in each culture.
- Read up on each country's current, recent, and historical issues to understand how those events have shaped their approach to diversity and inclusion.
- Make sure the OD team understands how each culture will likely receive the diversity programs they're creating.
- Research the key demographics and trends in each country and tailor the program to the needs of the people. Diversity consists of many different factors and weighing these dimensions can help you decide how to tailor the initiatives.
- Explore how diversity issues vary from culture to culture; for example, some nations may consider gender or class issues more important than race. Research what elements are most important for each region—and why.

What follows is a simplified snapshot of how different diversity topics are viewed around the world:

- **Nationality and ethnicity** remain a contentious point for some nations and have become more important points of discussion as immigration increases. For countries with relatively open national identities and citizenship, the focus is more on how to maximize the value of immigration. On the other hand, some countries focus more on how immigration can threaten their strong national identity. These feelings play a large role in how countries perceive inclusion and equity, and companies should carefully consider what that term means to their target audience before moving forward.
- **Gender and sexual orientation** are other important dimensions because gender roles and identity norms are changing and countries are trying to adapt and keep up. In addition, perceptions of gender roles vary greatly between countries, and historical and legal differences make the transition for a more inclusive workplace more of a struggle.
- **Age and generational** differences are other elements to consider. Younger generations tend to be more technologically inclined but may lack the wisdom and experience of their older counterparts.

- **Physical abilities** and the inclusion of people with disabilities are other important components to consider for inclusion.
- **Race** is often linked to nationality and ethnicity, and its perception varies widely around the world. Countries that are more racially homogenous, such as Japan and South Korea, focus more on national identity, while European countries often consider race alongside national identity. Other areas, such as Latin America, have begun to consider race, but overall it is a sensitive issue.
- **Social class** is often left out of US-based diversity initiatives; however, it is an important component in other regions of the world. In Latin America, for example, DEI executives have noted that it may actually be the most relevant component for their needs.

Although global diversity and inclusion initiatives start with good intentions, they will fail unless organizations design them with an understanding of each culture involved in the program. This knowledge and its application to DEI programs will help alleviate problems that arise when companies implement US-centric approaches, while also maximizing the effectiveness of those initiatives worldwide and garnering a positive response with business associates.

Capturing and Applying Global and Multicultural Institutional Knowledge

Organizations need to know what internal resources they have—and in most cases they don't. OD departments should conduct an organizational scan and create a database that identifies the current workforce's linguistic and cross-cultural skills. This should include language skills, cross-cultural experiences, and education. Those who have voluntarily studied in another country are more likely to already possess the intercultural curiosity to succeed.

From there, you can create a knowledge management process that captures employees' work-related global experience and training. Too often companies invest in the professional development of their workforce only to lose that investment after employees leave (or when they simply forget what they learned). A truly effective knowledge management system will improve an organization's ability take full advantage of the knowledge and experiences of its employees. The system collects that information and stores it for future reference by any group inside the organization. In addition, the system could connect people across departments through information retrieval, allowing for further discussion and the establishment of new networks.

In an international organization, a knowledge management system would store not only information from various training programs but also the experiences and names of company employees who have worked in certain regions and countries. This information could stimulate further discussion and internal networking among employees who share common experiences, thus bolstering the knowledge of the organization as a whole.

There are key functions of one such model that has been successfully deployed at leading global corporations:

- **Deliver** a core cross-cultural competency course for all employees that captures and categorizes each participant's global challenges, issues, personal goals, case studies, lessons learned, and email addresses to form an electronic community.
- **Establish** curriculum paths based on building specific core competencies. For example, a path focused on developing global leadership or paths on developing locally inclusive project management, customer service, and research and development.
- **Provide** the ability for each associate to create their electronic, competency road map and skills component. Systematically track individual progress toward competency goals.
- **Create** an international assignment series of initiatives in support of expatriates and repatriates.
- **Record** lessons learned throughout each international assignment.
- **Capture** international corporate issues that may trigger personal coaching based on individual circumstances.
- **Analyze** the information to interpret trends and identify process improvement opportunities.
- **Establish** a cross-cultural library of existing blended learning courseware that supports the road map concept.
- **Query** the collective knowledge derived from the case studies, lessons learned, and personal and business experiences maintained in the database.

Ultimately, the true value of knowledge management systems lies in their ability to limit the unnecessary repetition of tasks and improve efficiency and coordination within the entire organization.

The knowledge management system should develop a sense of community through shared employee information and create more awareness of the company's core competencies as a result of its employees' experiences. By improving the organization's internal awareness of itself, knowledge management systems allow organizations to find strengths that they never even knew they had.

A Case Study: Apple Global Retail Training Design By Brian James Flores

When I worked for Apple Retail as a training lead, there was a huge push to deliver services to small- to medium-sized businesses, supported by a nearby Apple retail locations. I had the opportunity to join the instructional design team responsible for designing training for retail employees to support these business partnerships with learning experiences. (For example, I facilitated a learning experience for a legal firm transitioning their staff from more than 20 years of using PCs to an office outfitted with iMacs and iPads.)

I was representing the central US region of Apple stores, and the ID team also recruited training leads from other regions in the US as well as a representative from every global market with an Apple retail store location. In total, 22 of us were chosen to share our perspectives to ensure quality and consistency of experience on a global scale. This was an example of Apple tapping its multiculturalism and cultural knowledge to not only create better training experiences for retail clients but also develop more culturally aware employees.

Here are some of the lessons we learned:

- **Translation isn't as simple as converting words and characters.** Many languages have multiple words with similar meanings. For example, our IDs used the word "power" in one module to convey presence while presenting to a customer. However, our German representative shared that the word used in the German translation symbolized military force and had a negative connotation. We were able to quickly swap it out for a word that would be more palatable to German ears.

- **Social constructs are not universal.** As part of the training design, the IDs leveraged the Apple idea of a "wow" moment when sharing a new feature of an Apple product with a customer. The representative from Switzerland let us know that there was no such thing as a wow moment in his country. He shared several examples of his attempts to share a wow moment with customers in his Apple store, only to be met with an unimpressed, "It's OK" in Swiss-German. It wasn't that he didn't try or didn't show something impressive; rather, the culture simply didn't do that.

- **Humor, pop culture references, and slang need to be localized.** We realized very quickly that puns, sarcasm, and innuendo were difficult concepts to grasp for most Asian cultures. Our two representatives from China (Mandarin and Cantonese) modified their training guides to completely eliminate the tongue-in-cheek humor that was included to add personality to the presentation. We also found that pop culture references should be used with intention, because people in different regions may not have exposure or access to connect the references. And lastly, through our discussions we realized that there may be a local way to say a phrase or to greet someone that you won't find in the guidebooks yet is used widely in local communities to create connection or immediate trust. The only way to discover (and subsequently use) those colloquialisms is to leverage the knowledge of the locals.

Ultimately, by bringing a team of 22 individuals representing different regions of the world together to aid in the creation of this learning experience, Apple helped ensure it created a consistent, high-quality, global training product with the value of diversity and representation at its core. And the bridge connecting culturally appropriate learning content to a company commitment toward diversity and representation is a beautiful example of how L&D and OD are inextricably linked.

Summary

The goal of this chapter is to provide guidance, strategy, and examples of the characteristics that define a sustainable, global multicultural organization. This includes implementing a new mindset with cultural intelligence, designing initiatives to build a global talent pipeline, applying DEI strategies, and leveraging global and multicultural institutional knowledge. While it takes the collective efforts of the organization as a whole to implement change of this scale, collaboration between OD and L&D professionals is often critical in the process.

It should not be surprising that OD and L&D efforts are so intertwined when creating a global and culturally diverse organization. When organizational change is needed, the OD practitioner evaluates the strategy from the broad perspective and incorporates the elements in this chapter toward a solution; meanwhile the L&D professional implements portions of the broad strategy in the form of learning experiences and tools to facilitate the change. Although there are distinct differences and separation between the two roles, they are increasingly reliant on one another and the line between them continues to blur.

Key Takeaways

Here are a few things to think about as you build a global, culturally diverse organization:

- **Building a global, culturally diverse organization starts with embracing a global mindset and strengthening the collective cultural intelligence of employees.** OD practitioners can form cultural committees comprising diverse staff to be part of education and training efforts that seek to build awareness of the core cultural differences that the organization faces.

- **Taking DEI initiatives global can be counterproductive unless done with a globally inclusive framework and mindset.** For example, topics such as race, nationality, and social class would be addressed differently depending on the country.

- **International assignments for leaders and key staff are an underused OD practice.** And when they are used, organizations often fail to get the most out of the knowledge from those returning from abroad. OD practitioners can rectify this by structuring the experience with what knowledge and skills the organization wants those going on international assignments to develop.

- **Tapping the hidden potential of international employees can unlock an important missing piece of the global talent puzzle and strengthen the organization's recruitment, culture building, and retention efforts.** OD practitioners can establish the cultural programs and practices covered in this chapter to lift up these employees, such as customized onboarding and buddy systems. This also includes L&D programs like management training to address potential culture clashes.

CHAPTER 11

Supporting Work in a Remote Environment

NEHA LAGOO RATNAKAR

IN THIS CHAPTER

♦ Discover the impact of remote work on organization development

♦ Understand what works and what doesn't in a remote setup based on current experience and research

♦ Learn what works and what doesn't across the employee life cycle from recruiting to separation

♦ Explore some ideas for measuring and evaluating the effectiveness of shifting to a remote-friendly workplace

Thanks to the COVID-19 pandemic, remote working is no longer just a possibility or a perk for a select few. Although millions of frontline workers had to continue working in person to keep essential systems running, many office workers were thrown into this (virtual) reality headfirst and had no choice but to make it work. Irrespective of their leadership style—autocratic or democratic, laissez-faire or micromanaging—leaders and managers suddenly had to cope with not seeing their employees face-to-face. The same goes for the employees who were forced into this situation without any prep time, training, or even the right equipment.

Some companies hit the ground running, while others staggered for a bit and fell down a few times, but most made it work. As L&D professionals, we found ourselves out of depth. Even though we had been experimenting with various learning modalities—including self-study, app-based, and digital micromodules, along with the more traditional forms—suddenly none of that mattered. People were living through the biggest ever experiment of just-in-time learning. Necessity made sure people quickly picked up new software and skills. Companies and service providers also responded swiftly to market needs.

While employees struggled with broadband upgrades and simple things like digital collaboration (*Zoom call:* "Can you hear me? You're on mute."), nobody had the brain space to learn other skills or knowledge. Yet L&D professionals were put under immediate pressure to transfer all in-person training to virtual. And beyond that, organizations also expected their L&D people to get involved in employee experience and well-being projects.

Once the pandemic came more under control and the world started trying to go back to normal, organizations faced the next big challenge: the great resignation. This led to a new set of priorities, including boosting employee retention efforts, hosting exit interviews, frantically rehiring former employees, and promoting internally. L&D professionals were once again tasked with contributing to a larger talent picture.

The pandemic, its challenges, and the situational gifts that came out of it have given many L&D professionals a head start into organization development. Now that companies are no longer forced to allow their employees to work from home, they are rethinking how and where their employees work. Remote work is no longer a short-term fix during a global pandemic; it's becoming a long-term decision for many companies.

With that new reality in mind, let's take a step back and make sure we have the right tools and understanding to make intentional decisions about remote work policies. This time, we can make these choices based on design, not a mandated default. As an L&D professional, you can make a better transition into OD instead of being pulled into a project because the company is grappling with a crisis.

The Impact of Remote Work on Organization Development

Remote work didn't just change the way we dress and how we commute. For many of us, it changed the very fabric of our work. When COVID-19 became a global pandemic, the processes, strategies, and tactics that had worked like magic for years in brick-and-mortar offices were made obsolete almost overnight. We had to reinvent how we managed recruitment, onboarding, development, and even separation without face-to-face interactions.

Reduced informal interactions—no more after-work drinks or water cooler chats about last night's games—consequently brought down employee engagement levels. But it also reduced the potential for micromanagement. In-person politics was not easy, neither was it possible to keep watch on clock-in and clock-out times. This finally forced many managers and companies to start evaluating people on their impact and alignment with business goals, rather than their ability to punch a time card. When the going got really tough, putting in the right effort was what companies and managers appreciated most.

Organizations were also handed a gift in terms of diversity and inclusion efforts. Companies that embraced remote work had a larger talent pool to choose from. Remote work also removed the human error element in terms of the equitable treatment of employees. Because everyone was working from their kitchen tables or bedroom nooks, they were forced to introduce their unique personalities and self to colleagues. Diverse candidates no longer had to increase awareness around their own identity.

On that positive note, let's dive into how you can make a difference as a new OD practitioner, as well as how you can design strategies for success in a market that's becoming hybrid or remote-first.

Recruiting

Hiring the right talent has always been a challenging job for HR teams, but remote work adds another layer of complications to the task. On one side, companies that embrace the remote-first approach have access to global talent. But, along with a global talent workforce comes global employee policies and expectations. It's possible for a person to go from job application all the way to onboarding without having to meet anyone in person. This increases the expectation from the hiring company to be more transparent and accessible in its processes.

For example, Johnson & Johnson has a custom-built platform called J&J Shine that provides transparency for applicants throughout the recruitment process. The design is user friendly and allows the applicant to have some control over tracking their progress in real time. At each stage, they can also access relevant articles, videos, and tips to set them up for success. Topics range from interviewing tips, company-related content, and even tips on negotiating an offer. As J&J Vice President of Talent Acquisition Sjoerd Gehring said, "Now you can track your recruiting status just like you can track a mail package" (Klahre 2017).

What works:
- Have an excellent brand presence online. This might be basic, but unfortunately not every company has gotten this correct.

- Use job portals more mindfully to make sure they clearly mention remote work as an option. Localized job ads will not help you reach out to the global talent pool.
- Make remote work a selection criteria. Try to find a match where the future employee is self-motivated and someone whom the hiring manager can trust. This can be a crucial early indicator of job success.
- Make sure your candidate communication is accessible for people with disabilities as well as non-native speakers.

What doesn't work:

- Not being transparent about your recruitment process.
- Not being accessible for people with disabilities.
- Antiquated job portals that expect users to capture unnecessary data and include a lengthy registration process.

Tools and resources:

- Simple job application platforms like LinkedIn, Greenhouse, and Lever
- Have someone with social media expertise join the recruiting team.
- Understand Web Content Accessibility Guidelines (WCAG 2.1 AA) to ensure your communication is accessible for everyone.
- Partner with an organization that helps your company's global footprint without having to worry about the payrolls and policies (Globalization Partners is one example).

Onboarding

If finding the right employee is difficult, retaining them is the next challenge and it all starts on their first day. According to a survey by Careerbuilder and Silkroad Technology, one in 10 employees have left a company because of a poor onboarding experience. Onboarding is much more than the first day orientation or filling out a few forms. To ensure employees are engaged from the start, your job as an internal OD expert will be crucial. If you just convert the in-person onboarding program to remote, you're missing a big opportunity to create an aha moment for the new staff.

What works:

- A well-designed buddy system can be the perfect addition to your onboarding process and can improve the employee experience from the very first day. The buddy is often selected from another department, and their job is help a new employee feel welcomed and get integrated faster. Since serendipitous introductions may not happen in remote workplaces, matching newcomers with a buddy is an important task for learning and OD professionals.

- One-on-one interactions with top leadership in the first week. Nothing beats being invited for a virtual coffee with the CEO or the head of a local business.
- Have a high-touch approach during the first 100 days of work.

What doesn't work:

- Death by PowerPoint, or old one-way downloads about company culture, policies, and the leadership team.

Tools and resources:

- Informal platforms like Slack can be used for keeping in touch and sharing ongoing activity in the company.
- The Facebook for Business platform gives people an interface they're used to in a controlled environment to build a network inside the company remotely.
- Gamified platforms can be used to create an engaging induction program. (Khojees is a good example.)

Workplace Setup

Many companies gravitate toward remote-first to reduce overhead costs like rent and energy consumption; however, unless they also significantly reduce the number of employees, just getting rid of the office building will not bring in a lot of savings. Your employees will still need equipment, conducive workspaces, and the flexibility to collaborate when needed. This might mean providing ergonomic chairs for some people, better headphones for others, or access to a co-working space for an in-person team meeting. The companies that get this right allow employees to decide what they need to be most productive and then provide the resources so employees can get those things.

What works:

- Grant each employee an individual budget to set up their home office. When possible, share discounts from office supply companies that sell ergonomic furniture or hardware.
- Offer added benefits, such as an allowance for managing responsibilities like childcare.
- Clearly articulate policies and guidelines around the duration of time an employee is allowed to work away from their home country.

- Make sure OD teams consult with the legal and finance teams to ensure compliance on all fronts.

What doesn't work:

- Expecting people to continue working from suboptimal conditions, like an ironing table (ahem three fingers pointing inward)
- Not updating outdated policies about removing company equipment from the office (Review these policies instead of responding on a case-by-case basis.)

Tools and resources:

- Marketplaces for employee discounts like Perkspot or Perkbox
- Provide employee discounts globally (like Uber or even health-related purchases).

Employee Well-Being

The ping pong and snooker tables are not fooling anyone anymore. Stepping out of a strategy meeting to play a quick game with the same team members doesn't really count as a break. Neither is going for a coffee around the corner with co-workers. Well-being is finally getting the attention it deserves; everyone has a right to decide how to prioritize their physical, mental, emotional, and spiritual well-being. You can use your experience in adult learning and performance to help organizations understand the importance of well-being practices and how they can start on the right foot when they embark on the remote work journey.

What works:

- Make mental health a priority; for example, offer special time off for winding down.
- Normalize transparency from senior leadership so employees feel comfortable leaving work early to watch their kid's ballet performance or see a therapist, or just because the weather is nice.
- Provide legal and financial support through employee assistance programs.
- Maintain confidentiality for any issues that might weigh heavily on your employees' minds or influence their well-being.
- Make sure employee support groups (ESGs) are funded and supported by the leadership.

What doesn't work:

- Health insurance plans that do not cover mental health or therapists
- Parental leave that is only allowed for mothers and is bare minimum for the local market (Use the best in the industry as your benchmark. Include parents of all genders, adoptive parents, and even child-loss leave to allow people to better manage the reproductive phase of their lives.)

Tools and resources:

- Global mental health platforms like Betterself and BetterUp can be leveraged for coaching, therapy, relationship counselling, and more.

Performance Management and Succession Planning

When companies decide to go remote, their core business or product doesn't change. What changes is the way they run the business. The same goes for performance management. Your key performance indicators (KPIs) might not change, but how these goals are reached definitely will. For example, how will the company continue to develop the business without taking clients on fancy dinners or reduce waste by negotiating better connectivity plans for employees? This is when putting on your OD hat will be useful.

Another important factor is succession planning. Just like companies have access to global talent, employees have access to global jobs. Hence it becomes imperative for OD practitioners to proactively guide companies to identify key positions and create a robust succession plan for each one.

What works:

- Consider evolved versions of objectives and key results (OKRs) or balanced scorecards. OKRs were developed by Google at least a decade ago. It's important to create custom versions that work for remote teams, for example keeping the OKRs front and center while collaborating online will provide clarity to employees irrespective of their location.
- Include purpose-related goals. People want to understand how their work relates to the organizational performance and affects society as a whole. If you make this connection clear to your employees, more people will feel inspired to contribute. For example, relating them to the United Nations Sustainability Goals will speak to people more globally and help attract and engage a diverse talent pool.

What doesn't work:

- Purely target-linked goals, or cookie cutter goals for the entire team (Instead, work with employees individually to set goals that are based on their abilities and interests, as well as company needs.)
- Only relying on annual performance evaluation cycles (Regular feedback and check-ins become even more crucial in a remote workforce because it is easy to assume the worst if you don't get any feedback. Share often. Make it an organizational practice to ensure all managers are doing it.)

Tools and resources:

- Workday back-office software
- ADP Workforce Now
- The book *Remote Work: Redesign Processes, Practices and Strategies to Engage a Remote Workforce* by Chris Dyer and Kim Shepherd is an excellent resource not just for succession planning and performance management for remote workforces but also beyond.

Learning and Development

L&D was your playing field—excellent classroom training sessions, on-the-job programs, university partnerships, and so on. But the pandemic threw a wrench in these plans. Luckily L&D professionals had spent the last half of the 2010s experimenting with different modalities like e-learning, app-based learning, and hybrid programs. This is your springboard opportunity. Adapting your educational offerings as the company goes remote will require you to understand how adults learn best—it's not sitting at home completing a static five-hour learning course. PepsiCo's PEP University is an excellent example of how a company was able to build a remote learning platform for employees around the world.

What works:

- Provide an individual budget employees can use for L&D opportunities.
- Offer bonuses or incentives related to learning new skills or upskilling.
- Give all employees access to self-paced learning programs, micromodules, coaching and mentoring relationships, stretch assignments to encourage learning on the job, and industry conferences so people can continue to collaborate and learn from each other.

What doesn't work:

- Using in-person training content as-is for remote learning sessions (Best practice urged against lecture-style training even when we were in person, so why would employees enjoy sitting at home watching the same slides and listening to an audio narration?)
- Most organizations add personnel development as a default goal for people managers. Although it is important to reiterate the importance of continued education, expecting managers to be completely responsible for their team's learning and development is taking it too far.

Tools and resources:

- LinkedIn Learning has a wide range of learning topics in an easy to absorb format. It and other massive open online course (MOOC) providers are here to stay; many colleges and universities provide educational content in an open-source environment.

Employee Engagement

Did your company depend on the quarterly picnic or an annual company celebration to check the employee engagement initiative box?

Stop right there. If your organization wants to become remote-worker friendly, this definitely cannot continue as-is. Every employee needs to have an engaging experience with the organization, not just those living in the same city as the CEO. This will require a mindset change, especially if you belong to a traditional organization. Your job as an OD practitioner will be to help company management understand that there are other ways to engage employees without breaking the bank.

What works:

- Make space for fun. Schedule regular open meetings where people can just come to chat and bond.
- Establish guidelines and best practices for collaboration and asynchronous communication. A common understanding of how best to work together in different time zones will ensure fairness and mitigate the risks of employee burnout.
- Create special interest groups for hobbies and internal networking.

- Create a generous time-off policy and encourage employees to take advantage of it. Advise your top leaders to make use of the policy to set the right example.

What doesn't work:

- Letting teams choose their own platforms (such as for chatting or project management), rather than mandating company-wide use of specific platforms
- Expecting employees to spend their own money to meet and collaborate with employees who live locally
- Not celebrating special occasions and wins because cutting a cake or opening a bottle of champagne in the office is not possible.

Tools and resources:

- Find a platform that allows the company or teams to create moments of interaction and fun. It could be as simple as Microsoft Teams group chat.

Knowledge Management

Documentation and knowledge management becomes even more important in remote workplaces. Proper documentation not only ensures the company's tacit knowledge base grows but also that there is transparency. Many remote-first companies build employee handbooks that document everything, be it big or small. For example, Gitlab maintains a handbook in the public domain that is sacrosanct and a must know for every employee. Documentation is important, especially when dealing with a global workforce, because it helps facilitate an asynchronous work environment.

What works:

- Have a clearly defined knowledge management strategy that all employees know about. Document anything that gets done more than once and save all institutional knowledge in a clear and obvious location.
- Assign one person to maintain the knowledge database.

What doesn't work:

- Being too inflexible about processes and not leaving space to learn from experience and best practices
- Being people dependent (When people leave an organization they take an enormous amount of tacit knowledge with them that may take years for the company to rebuild if it wasn't documented.)
- Relying on chat conversations to share important information

Tools and resources:

- Microsoft OneDrive and SharePoint—you likely already use Microsoft software like PowerPoint and Word, but when you add OneDrive and SharePoint to the mix, it creates a powerful tool for knowledge management allowing employees to have real-time access to information that results in efficient and error-free work.
- Scribe software allows you to turn any process into a step-by-step guide. This can help in creating standard operating procedures (SOPs) and building training material for new hires.

Separation

Separation is inevitable, but outgoing employees won't always have nice things to say about your organization. So, this is your last chance to make sure former employees become brand ambassadors for life. At the very least you want to ensure they're not departing on bitter terms. Just like onboarding remotely, this can be tricky to navigate without any in-person interaction. Maintaining a high-touch approach and simplifying the closing processes can make a huge difference in ensuring an employee's last few days are effortless.

What works:

- Work with legal, IT, facilities, and so forth to create a clear exit process. Make sure all bases are covered and company property gets handed over without much hassle.
- Conduct well-structured and unbiased exit interviews. I recently left a position in a remote setting, and the HR representative conducting the interview shared her screen so I could see her notes. This ensured transparency and allowed me to clarify if the notes did not reflect my position. Small steps like these in the context of your organization can make a big difference.

What doesn't work:

- Long notice periods. (There is no point in keeping a person employed for longer than necessary for a smooth handover. If the employee is disengaged already, the company doesn't need to continue paying them.)
- Automatically adding former employees to your salesforce account. (Do not assume they will be interested in becoming your client. Follow protocol and General Data Protection Regulations (GDPRs), even if your company doesn't need to comply legally.)

Tools and resources:

- Use LinkedIn and emails (with consent) to keep former employees informed about what is happening in the company.

Measuring and Evaluating the Effectiveness of Remote Work Policies

The old adage "What gets measured gets done" still stands true in the new remote reality. The conventional productivity measures of time in and time out are no longer relevant for a typical white-collar job. The same goes for typical metrics, like the number of lines of code written by tech workers or the number of customer queries resolved by support staff. Even though these metrics showed an upward trend in the beginning of the pandemic, they were not sustainable. Microsoft Global Work Trend Index found out that as the boundaries between home and work continued to blur, burnout and exhaustion levels increased.

Whether the company goes completely remote or chooses a hybrid model, the OD team will still be expected to help establish appropriate performance management criteria and outcome and output metrics. As an OD practitioner, your task will be to explore how impact and effort can be quantified for each line of business instead of focusing on output.

Some metrics to measure include:

- Engagement levels using pulse surveys and annual or semiannual surveys
- Social proof through anonymous ratings on Glassdoor, social media platforms, and so on
- The number of people taking wellness days and not just sickness days
- Launching 360-degree evaluations of managers to understand which styles are working
- Teams using their learning and team building budgets
- Customer satisfaction surveys

Of course, overall business performance and growth will be the litmus test. As L&D and OD professionals, we need to ensure our initiatives align with business goals and create business impact, not just a feel-good atmosphere.

Case Study: Becoming Flexible-First to Keep Employees First

CSG International is a provider of software and services that help companies around the world monetize and digitally enable the customer experience. The company employs about 6,000 people globally and is headquartered in Englewood, Colorado.

During the COVID-19 pandemic all CSG staff were forced to work remotely. A year later, the company observed that not only were productivity and delivery to customers as expected, but employees were happier with the flexible work arrangement. In fact, a November 2021 employee engagement survey showed that 91 percent of employees liked the flexible-first approach CSG had put in place. The OD team took up the goal to maintain employee morale while meeting the business goals.

CSG leadership and HR decided to make the flexible-first approach permanent, which would give people the power of choice to better manage their lives. For example, Bangalore India is home to CSG's main hub, but 60 percent of the workforce is located outside the city. Since 2020, the company has also hired 300 new people in a location-agnostic manner. In addition to expanding access to talent across India, this also reduces the load on Bangalore, which is an already crowded metropolitan area.

CSG has two requirements for every country in which is it based; There must be an office to act as the country's home base, and every employee must have a permit to work in that country to ensure tax compliance. Other than that, CSG has embraced a flexible-first approach across the board.

The company has also implemented new practices to ensure employee needs are met; for example:

- Hotdesking. Because CSG was able to reduce its office spaces, infrastructure costs went down as well. CSG uses a hotdesking platform to ensure people have access to optimum workspaces whenever they decide to come into the office.
- Friday lunch. Each hub and head office hosts Friday lunches for any employee who wants to network and socialize in person. These lunches are sponsored by CSG, which gives an extra incentive to people to join.

While becoming a flexible-first organization had many benefits, CSG also faced some challenges when rolling out the policy. For example, the cost of living and taxes are different from state to state even within the same country. Hence final pay and benefits may look different. But to maintain equity, CSG ensured that the base pay in the country of employment stayed the same and people received relevant allowances and benefits based on their location.

Since going flexible-first, CSG has:

- Seen engagement scores continue an upward trend—up by 2 percent in 2021
- Been recognized as a best place to work in 2022
- Had employees report better work-life integration; more time spent near their family and friends; and share that they feel mentally, physically, and emotionally supported

Here are a couple quotes from employees about the remote work policy:

- "Just want to take a moment to thank CSG for their flexible-first mindset. Thanks to this, I've been able to enjoy time off all over the world, disconnect from technology, and strengthen relationships in person with those I hadn't seen in years due to COVID-19 and other factors."
- "A year back I joined CSG virtually and never got a chance to meet my team in person. As CSG is a flexible workplace and most of the team put WFH (work from home) as their first preference, I thought I would never meet any of my co-workers in person. However, after a lot of surveys, planning, and approvals, it was decided to have a fun week at the office. I was pretty excited to meet the faces behind those voices. The week was filled with fun and joy, and I got to know many of my team members and enjoyed every moment at the office."

Summary

Remote work is here to stay. Whether your company is making a complete transition to remote or adopting more flexible work arrangements, this change is inevitable. OD and talent development can do more than simply change along with it—they can be a catalyst in that change. The guidelines and resources covered in this chapter will empower you to be a change maker in your organization.

Key Takeaways

Here are a few reminders of how to support work in a remote environment:

- **Remote working and hybrid work models are still in a nascent stage.** Keep an eye out for changing trends and internal pulse surveys to make sure your organization stays on top of its game.
- **Be an advocate for people.** While tools and platforms make our lives easier, there is no substitute to one-on-one interactions to ensure people are getting intended benefits out of them.
- **Track the success of the transition to remote working** and remember that this is not a panacea for all organizational problems.
- **Your experience with adult behavior and learning can translate very well** to helping companies make the transition to remote first while catapulting you on your OD journey.

CHAPTER 12

The Skills Revolution: Transitioning to a Skills-Based Organization

BRANDON CARSON AND SEAN MURPHY

IN THIS CHAPTER

- ♦ Find solutions to workforce challenges
- ♦ Learn how skills-based solutions can answer the call
- ♦ Start to understand the change management necessary to successfully transition to a skills-based organization

Introduction: Our Capability Crisis

The core strategic advantage of every company sits with its workforce. Technological disruptions were bringing about dramatic shifts to work and workplace conditions prior to the COVID-19 pandemic. And then that global crisis accelerated those shifts, causing fundamental and systemic change to the labor market, leading many organizations to rethink their workforce strategy, especially as it applies to capabilities. The increasing global complexity during the pandemic rapidly evolved from the VUCA (volatile, uncertain, complex, and ambiguous) world we were navigating to what is now referred to as the BANI world (Cascio 2021):

- **Brittle:** Many of our business systems are now extremely fragile due to the rapid transition to the cloud over the last two decades. As we moved to more interconnected systems, we increased system fragility to the point where viruses (and other security challenges) can suddenly appear with disastrous and cascading results. This lack of systemic resilience means that one system failure can have significant impact beyond just the walls of one company.
- **Anxious:** Our complex and complicated business world can bring about stress when decisions must be made quickly—bringing about the feeling that every choice matters. This anxiety can result in paralysis due to a fear of making the wrong decision and may lead to an epidemic of mental issues triggered by anxiety.
- **Nonlinear:** Many decisions are made without the ability to fully understand their cause and effect, leading to disproportionate or disastrous results. Even small decisions can have significant and consequential impact. COVID-19 showed us that it's often impossible to predict outcomes when we fail to determine the nonlinearity of the decision's impact.
- **Incomprehensible:** Change is happening so quickly that the fire hoses of information coming our way can make it problematic to separate the signal (meaningful information) from the noise (variations of information that distract from useful information). This can result in information overload that potentially leads to misunderstanding and incomprehensibility.

More than 114 million people worldwide lost their jobs in 2020 and many others faced new work conditions, leading them to reassess their priorities (Richter 2021). As businesses and the workforce navigate this BANI world, it's become apparent that to remain competitive, organizations need to build a more diverse talent pool, increase career mobility, and advance more equitable growth and development opportunities for all employees. It is necessary to re-evaluate job architectures, including required credentials, for roles across the enterprise to achieve a comprehensive reconstruction of talent processes that accommodate the new business world.

As people face an onslaught of change in the ways of working, how work gets done, and what customers and businesses expect of them in this new world of work, it is critical for companies to provide opportunities for them to continually update their skills and abilities. The deficiency in needed skills also highlights the fact that there are simply not enough people with the right skills (SHRM 2019). This precipice is dangerously steep. To remain competitive, businesses must assertively build the capabilities needed in their internal talent marketplaces while simultaneously identifying external talent to fill the gaps.

A key challenge is how to correctly identify the critical skills needed and then broaden the talent pool through intentional and strategic skilling efforts. Countless HR and L&D functions are embarking on a reinvention of their training strategies, realizing that a dynamic enterprise skills graph is a necessary element of a more adaptive and flexible business environment. This is the essential component in diminishing the greatest threat facing companies today: the talent capability deficit.

While it's paramount for those most directly aligned with company talent systems to understand the state of their current workforce, as well as where it needs to go, it will take company-wide change management to activate real system change. This chapter will dive into the possible solutions that will help senior executives all the way to frontline recruiters and trainers better understand the skills movement and how organizations can start to prioritize their journey—it is not an overnight transition.

Why Move to a Skills-Based Talent Solution?

In today's business world, data drives much of what we do. With data, we make more informed decisions about where to establish a new location, how much inventory to carry, how many employees are needed for a specific shift, and many other use cases. Data often provides a personalized experience for customers, delivering on-demand experiences and recommendations. Considering how important data is to businesses and their customers, one would expect data to be a central player in talent solutions. However, the reality is that both businesses and workers lack the data they need to optimize decision making in employment, upskilling, and mobility.

Today's talent systems are designed primarily around a single credential—the college degree. While obtaining a degree is one path for gaining knowledge, skills, and abilities (KSAs), it is no longer the only option. The hiring data in front of us is stark: 74 percent of new jobs created between 2008 and 2017 were in occupations with employers that required a four-year college degree. However, 60 percent of the US adult workforce does not have a college degree (Blair et al. 2020). This is a key reason almost any chief learning officer (CLO) you talk to is working on a skills strategy.

Simply stated, too many job description requirements are mismatched to the workforce's capabilities. This is the primary driver behind the move to skills-based hiring.

Hiring requirements that center on degrees exclude many quality applicants from the talent pool, especially people from various racial and ethnic backgrounds. Based on research from Opportunity@Work (2019), the requirement of a degree automatically excludes 76 percent of African Americans, 83 percent of Latinos, and 81 percent of rural Americans from attaining quality employment. And this is despite the fact that many of these individuals have gained high-demand KSAs through other mechanisms, such as on-the-job work experience, boot camps, or microcredentials.

Moving to a data-driven, skills-based system will enable workers to be successful through multiple pathways and ultimately strengthen organizations' talent systems. Skills should be treated as the language that crosses all forms of learning and employment. It will open businesses to new talent pools, provide a deeper level of data for workforce planning, and recognize learning as a necessary lifelong strategy delivered through different modalities. This transition does not mean that degrees go away or become any less valuable. Many paths will continue to require degrees; they'll just become one of many routes through which skills are obtained.

The business strategy for many companies now revolves around quickly inventorying current skills, identifying the needed critical skills, exposing gaps in the identified skills, and formulating plans to close them. Key to this plan is a total reimagining of traditional hiring and training strategies, pivoting to an intentional focus on how to future-proof the workforce and unlock value by matching workers to optimal roles and reconfiguring work systems and environments to accommodate continuous learning and performance support. It is a journey that requires large-scale change management across the entire talent ecosystem, including hiring managers, recruiters, HR staff, workers, and the technology systems needed to attract, acquire, advance, and retain talent.

Although transformational advances brought by the digital age have been a continuing catalyst for the rapid shifts in business innovation, several factors are currently intersecting to create a perfect storm of talent challenges:

- **Significant global demographic shifts.** According to PBS (2020), the US is seeing three trends that will continue to reshape the workforce. Our population will continue to grow and is expected to add another 20 million by the 2030 census. We will continue to get older in the next decade, with the number of individuals above 65 matching the number of those below 18. And we will certainly become more diverse. These trends, along with the increased percentage of migration to urban living, are also being seen around the world (UN 2020). We need to rethink how we train and retrain talent to ensure the ever-changing skills required to meet the needs of our economy are successfully transferred to the workforce.

- **Tightening labor markets.** Unemployment has been in decline for several years. Prior to the pandemic in 2020, we had seen one of the lowest levels of unemployment in years. As the world recovers, we are seeing a return to these historic lows. We are also seeing an increase in the labor participation rate, but not fast enough to meet the record number of job openings. While these trends are presenting a talent supply challenge, we also know that we have a significant talent matching problem.

- **Rapid technological advancement.** The future of work has arrived, and it is now. The skills needed yesterday are not the same as those needed today, nor are they the same as those needed tomorrow. While soft skills (essential skills) are as important as ever, workers now need a combination of essential and hard skills, with digital literacy arguably the most important due to the rapid advancement of technology in every facet of our economy.

These challenges will not dissipate in the short term. The pandemic accelerated the scramble that businesses find themselves in as they formulate new business models and devise new ways of working to remain competitive in the hyper-dynamic digital age. Professionals responsible for talent, and especially developing talent, have an important role in meeting the challenge. They are front and center in the fight to accelerate the building of future talent systems that will meet employers' needs today and in the future. This will require data-driven decisions, new models of learning, and a willingness to evolve in a world that is constantly changing.

Transitioning to a Skills-Based Organization

While the postpandemic world of work has already seen many positive changes—such as increased access to remote work, new jobs, and streamlined workflows—businesses are now uncovering significant skills deficiencies across the enterprise. In fact, the total number of skills required for a single job is increasing by 10 percent year over year, while 33 percent of the required skills from an average job post in 2017 are no longer needed (Gartner 2020). For example, frontline retail workers must now have the digital skills to use devices that support product search and many other services that further support the customer experience; L&D practitioners need to be able to build content for remote workers. While not every role is evolving at the same rate, roles are still changing faster than the workforce can adapt.

A successful transition to becoming a skills-based organization includes these outcomes:

- Reducing the time it takes to successfully skill the workforce in critical areas of need
- Unblocking any technical hurdles to offer a clear path for career advancement and mobility
- Removing systemic friction in hiring, development, advancement, and retention
- Activating a healthy pipeline of accessible talent across the enterprise

A skills-based strategy is not just about documenting and cataloging skills; instead, it recognizes that skills are fluid and change over time. The right strategy also recognizes that experiences and attributes are critically important for people to realize optimal capability. As you embark on the transition to skills-based practices, include affordances for individual experiences and attributes as core enablers of capability across the enterprise.

While some businesses may choose to focus on hiring new workers with the skills needed to stay competitive today, all employers need to be diligent about reskilling and upskilling their workforces in this hyper-competitive labor economy. According to the World Economic Forum, there is a growing gap between the digital tools that companies are integrating into the workplace and the skills the workforce has to successfully operate them (Kande and Sonmez 2020). With more than 2 million new jobs projected to be created by 2025 due to the integration of artificial intelligence (AI) technologies, investment in skilling must be an imperative for every company. Many businesses are now formulating strategies that focus on the systems, processes, and people that comprise the talent ecosystem and surgically identifying what needs to change, what needs to be strengthened, and what is working. These strategies can be enhanced using data-driven decisions, something a skills-based system enables, and deliberate engagement of workers in inclusive learning and development system design.

Four fundamental components are necessary for a skills-based organization to operationalize credentialing and build a more equitable, dynamic talent pool:

- Build a common skills language.
- Identify what skills you have and need.
- Validate skills through learning and experience.
- Assure system integration and tracking.

The following information will provide guidance on what to consider as you design the strategies your company needs.

Unify Around a Common Language

Skills-based approaches to talent acquisition and development often require input from multiple business functions across the organization. Recognizing and integrating a common language for these approaches across the enterprise is the essential first step in developing a scalable, enterprise skills architecture. This allows you to create a consistent approach to skills and credentials regardless of the business function. Having a more effective skills-based ecosystem helps stakeholders and the workforce communicate more effectively, make better decisions, and accelerate career growth and mobility. A common language can scale both internally and externally and advance the creation of standardized credentialing instruments.

Additionally, we recommend you partner across the enterprise to construct a governance model that integrates the disparate work streams and documented best practices to ensure the common understanding of the enterprise skills architecture is representative of all necessary inputs. In effect, the skills architecture creates a skills data language that crosses all forms of learning, development, and employee experience. If implemented correctly, as well as being friendly to the human eye, this language can be machine readable by different internal and possibly external technology systems.

A streamlined, common language for your skills architecture will rapidly advance your transition to a skills-based organization and reduce redundancy, confusion, and inefficiency. Consider these guiding principles as an underlying foundation to your common architecture:

- **New talent culture.** Changing talent practices to unlock a skills system and focus on reskilling and upskilling will need an executive sponsor, buy-in from company leadership, and resources, as well as an understanding that this effort will not be an overnight transition.
- **Create in a vacuum.** Too often when we make changes—whether in technology, operations, or talent systems—we do not engage the right partners. Making the

transition to a skills-based system, especially when unifying around a common language, will require engagement from across the company.

- **Tough conversations.** We've all dealt with managers who tell us that they will know the right fit when they see it, which often leaves talent systems to chance. Managers, and professionals involved in leading talent across the enterprise, must be prepared to align behind the skills model to ensure it is threaded through all systems.

- **Change management.** Implementing a common skills architecture is not a sprint. It is a journey and it needs a flexible plan that can evolve over time. There must also be an understanding that while many current practices will need to change in the future, they may need to be kept in place to continue meeting the current needs of the company.

Identify the Skills You Have

Every company is involved in hiring, training, and activating the upward mobility of its workforce, which requires an understanding of talent from a macro and micro level. From a macro level, companies need to understand what talent is needed, what talent they have, and what options are available for retraining and reskilling talent. From a micro level, companies need to evaluate what each individual can do, what they need to grow, and how to best leverage resources to see improvement or further build on their talents. At either level, companies need to compare data and maximize inputs and outputs.

When implementing a skills-based system, companies should first evaluate their internal systems to help determine the path forward. We recommend evaluating your needs for a skills taxonomy, where the common language can be used across the skills system, which business partners are needed to implement the conversion, and whether the current HR technology can maximize the use of a skills system. Often the most natural partners are those who support job descriptions and announcements, build or select training, evaluate performance, and are responsible for workforce planning. For bigger companies, this will require a task force, whereas smaller companies may be able to appoint a lead implementer, but in all cases, this must be a company-wide initiative.

To determine what is needed in a skills taxonomy or library, it is important to evaluate whether to build a skills language that is specific to the company or industry or if it is more appropriate to buy it. Skills taxonomies can be purchased from providers (such as IBM, Workday, or Lightcast) that may also offer additional services to help make the transition easier. Understanding the transition's conversion goals will assist in not only determining the right taxonomy but also what additional services will be most useful in widespread understanding of your current skill demands.

Once you have a system or heat map that identifies the necessary skills, ensure the company's skills architecture is appropriately prioritized to expose the most critical skills. Consider these guiding principles as an underlying foundation to your skills architecture:

- **Quality over quantity.** Segment the work of identifying the skills you need into actionable components that prioritize quality over quantity of output. In a complex work environment, it's easy to become overwhelmed by the number of skills and their complexity. We recommend beginning with the enterprise's most critical roles and deconstructing and recredentialing them to identify the best process you can scale.

- **Keep scale in mind.** While you should continually analyze the impact of the skills transition on the workforce, we recommend you initially focus on the systemic components that address the top of the talent funnel to speed the adoption of skills-based practices at scale.

- **Reduce workforce friction.** Focus on educating stakeholders through in-depth collaboration, partnership, and documentation instead of relying solely on organic knowledge transfer. It's important to understand that a shift of this nature is paradigmatic and requires advocacy and championship at multiple levels of the organization.

- **Take a digital-first approach.** We recommend formulating a clear publishing path for skills and credentials, and your tools and technology should assist in making this process as easy and intuitive as possible.

- **Prioritize culture, diversity, equity, and inclusion.** Focus on developing relationships with stakeholders and employees who are willing to support and collaborate on the transition to skills-based approaches. Remember that mutual interests are the most sustainable way to maintain long-term success. A key objective in transitioning to a skills-based model is to broaden the talent pool and provide access and opportunity to more employees.

Implement a Skills Validation Process

As of 2023, there are limited universally available tools or strategies for the validation of skills. In time, best practices will continue to be recognized, which will ultimately drive mass adoption of these practices. There are actions that can be started today, including evaluating training strategies to ensure they include skills-based practices. This should encompass planning around the validation of skills in internal and external training and through job performance evaluation processes. Each skill's level of importance should inform the level of validation required—some skills can be self-assessed by a worker, but others will require assessments, manager reviews, or even an independent reviewer. For example, a restaurant may launch a new table side service requiring staff to make a dessert in front of the customer. If this new service is critical to the customer experience, it may need more validation than simply trusting the employee to learn it on their own or through a video. Leadership will need to decide if simply watching someone make the dessert is enough, or if the employee will need to demonstrate their abilities in front of a manager or customers.

Answering this question will also support understanding the processes needed for scaling. Depending on the importance of a skill and the size of the company, some validation techniques will not be scalable or could be cost prohibitive.

Once a skill is obtained, assessed, and validated, it will be important to determine how to share it across systems to support the recognition of the validated skill. Many companies are using technology tools like open digital badges, which can be presented through a recognizable image while also incorporating machine readable metadata. This important data must be protected, evaluated for possible bias, and translated across HR technology platforms, but it also needs to be human readable, transparent, and accessible.

Consider these guiding principles as an underlying foundation for skills validation:

- **Governance.** Setting up a structure that lays out the priority of which skills will be viewed and ultimately validated needs to be a core role of learning and development practitioners. The model should present clear processes people in the field and across the company can use to define, design, and offer retraining and upskilling, as well as to clearly define the validation techniques needed to support awareness of skills currently held by the workforce.
- **Level of importance.** Not all skills need the same level of attention. When it comes to validation, employers must evaluate how important the skills are to the individual, their team, and to the enterprise, and determine what level of

validation to require. Some businesses may prioritize future skills versus current needs, but either way it will be important to develop a baseline, all of which needs a validation process.

- **Internal versus external.** Many employees who join the company will bring with them skills they've earned through prior learning and experience; however, not all will come with validated skills. It will be important to determine the value of third-party, prior employer, or training provider validation when evaluating an employee. If employees don't come with validated skills, is self-validation enough or is something more needed? In addition, how much of the company's validation processes will be externally accessible, either for external learning purposes or use by other employers.

Include System Integration and Tracking

While some steps are relatively straightforward, such as converting job descriptions to skills-based descriptions, steps like this will only be maximized if there is full system integration of skills. The use of a skills-based approach across the talent life cycle will need to incorporate multiple factors:

- Update policies and practices to codify how you manage systems and provide guidance to the enterprise. To ensure compliance with this new system, policies and practices will need to be updated with continued implementation as well as future use.
- Revamped hiring and promotion processes are needed to ensure skills are not seen as just another layer of data but a core part of talent operations. Everything from job descriptions to interview questions to employee and manager reviews to training will need to incorporate skills.
- Encourage and incentivize lifelong learning, with the understanding that multiple paths and modalities should be considered. According to the Pew Research Center, employees were most likely to leave their jobs in 2021 due to low compensation and lack of advancement opportunities (Parker and Horowitz 2022). Using skills to develop personalized career paths that enable advancement, while presenting a track that leads to increased compensation, could demonstrate how continuous learning drives future success and show workers that their current employer is investing in them.

- Evaluate supporting technology platforms to determine how skills will be leveraged to aggregate information, such as workforce planning and evaluation, as well as how learning new or future skills is presented. Many companies are not just relying on managers to train and assess, they are leveraging AI-supported tools, such as virtual reality. In addition, the accumulation of validated learning will need to be visible to workers, their managers, and external partners, such as training providers.

The integration, especially with technology tools and platforms, must be designed and evaluated from the perspective of business needs, but it also must include a clear picture of the user experience. If workers do not understand the change in direction, or are unable to leverage it to meet their needs, full system adoption is unlikely and it won't be fully maximized.

Summary

Moving to a skills-based system is a proactive strategy that broadens your talent pool, offers more opportunity and growth to your diverse workforce, and reduces the inherent bias of a degree-based recruiting and hiring strategy. A skills-based hiring and development system will provide the level of data needed to make better decisions, either as a business or as a worker. Instead of simply relying on the proxy of a degree, development will be continuous, verifiable, and comparable to multiple types of learning and experiences. It will enable companies to not only calculate how many employees they need for a specific shift or role, but ensure they have the right mix of talent with the skills needed to best support the customer. It provides workers with a transparent view into the opportunities that align with their interests, current skills, and those skills that will keep them relevant into the future. Most importantly, a skills-based system will further ensure talent is being matched with the right opportunity at the right time, while doing so efficiently, limiting bias, and building pipelines for the future.

Key Takeaways

Here are a few things to remember about the skills revolution:

- Moving to a skills-based system must be considered a journey, not a sprint.
- Create a shared language to enable alignment and engage HR partners with people across all parts of the organization—from technology to the C-suite to workers.

- In addition to new technology, these solutions will require changes in policies and other aspects of the business.
- To see the true benefits of shifting to a skills-based system, there will need to be changes to all aspects of the business, from recruiting and hiring to learning and development to annual reviews and development planning.
- It's important to understand how the skills revolution will enable workforce optimization and strengthen planning, as well as how the data created will support better career pathway development that supports retention and advancement.

PART 4

Leadership Preparedness

CHAPTER 13

Relationship Building

PAUL FALCONE

IN THIS CHAPTER

♦ Support relationship building among your clients and stakeholders to connect with and impact organization development

♦ Measure your relationship building efforts

♦ Prepare for resistance from operational manager-clients

What Is Relationship Building?

The most critical soft skill in hiring and professional development lies in the ability to build healthy and constructive relationships in the workplace. Trust, accountability, authenticity, and innovation are the key attributes of high performers and the foundation of successful teams and organizations. Relationship building in the leadership realm typically focuses on helping organizational leaders strengthen connections with their teams—achieving higher performance, creating a higher level of employee engagement, coaching others to success, motivating staff without money, and garnering trust and respect from those they lead by modeling those very behaviors themselves.

Relationship building starts during the interview and onboarding process, continues through opportunities for performance management and leadership development, and even thrives during times of constructive confrontation. How do you help create opportunity to incorporate relationship building into your organization's corporate fabric? How do you help frontline operational leaders and senior executives make space for human connection to serve as the glue that binds your employees to your company and influence your organizational culture? Most important, how do you move from training and educating workers to having a greater impact on the organization as a whole? So much depends on the structure you build, the tools you provide, and the questions managers ask their teams.

What occurs in the L&D realm influences organizational culture and translates into employees having a greater impact on the bottom line. That's your critical starting point. This chapter's focus is on how to leverage your organization's talent to drive stronger results through human connection. Relationship building is key to OD success because of its potential for bottom-line impact.

Let's set some important assumptions before we build out the structure to transition successfully from an L&D professional to an OD internal consultant:

- Relationship building is a fun, creative topic that's enjoyed by many and will cement your reputation as a people and talent developer and leadership turnaround expert.
- The greatest impact of the training-to-OD conversion stems from driving higher-level organizational results, in this case, through the people that do the work. Building relationships, whether in person or remote, is a core step for OD champions to move the organization's needle forward.
- Moving from training and educating workers to having a greater impact on the organization as a whole is measurable and manageable.

In this chapter, we'll explore relationship building within the overall talent management context and cover six key stages of the journey and transition:

1. Enhance the interviewing experience.
2. Extend onboarding to 30-, 60-, and 90-day intervals.
3. Introduce quarterly individual development plans (IDPs) to drive real performance.
4. Introduce the leader-as-coach model to spike employee engagement and confidence.
5. Make it safe for leaders to engage in constructive confrontation.
6. Measure success and, when necessary, course correct.

Together, these simple touch points will help catapult your clients' and stakeholders' abilities to lead effectively, build stronger relationships based on trust and open communication, and create a culture focused on selfless leadership that helps employees do their best work every day with peace of mind.

1. Enhance the Interviewing Experience

You've likely trained managers in the various aspects of interviewing, including telephone screens, behavior-based questions, documentation techniques, and candidate evaluations. But how can you translate those specific tools and practices into something that builds relationships and human connection throughout the organization? Simple: Add additional questions to the interviewing process that build trust with candidates right from the very first meeting—that reach candidates' hearts as well as their minds.

For example, operational leaders should construct relationship-building questions that break the ice and make it safe for candidates to think out loud. Again, this goes beyond mere skills training because it influences transparency and communication, which are hallmarks of a culture built upon trust. Continue developing similar selfless questions throughout the interview that help candidates see that the interview is a two-way street—it's not only import-ant that the candidate fits the company's needs but that the company fits their needs as well.

Some icebreaker questions you can ask during the interview include:

- Tell me about your job search up to now. What's motivating you to look for another opportunity, and what have your experiences been as a candidate in the open market?
- Before we launch too deeply into your career experience and background, as well as what we're looking for in our next hire, tell me what criteria you're using in selecting your next role or company. What's really important to you at this point in your career?
- What's one thing about your career that's guaranteed to make you smile?
- If you've hired people in previous roles, what do you look for when interviewing candidates in terms of their background, experience, and overall style? What do you like or dislike about hiring candidates from the other side of the desk?

Example career and professional development interview queries include:

- Walk me through your career progression, leading up to how you landed your current role at your present company.
- What would be your next career move if you remained with your current employer? How long would it take you to get there?

- Based on your understanding of the role so far, why would this position make sense at this point in your career in terms of career development? In other words, how would it move your resume and LinkedIn profile forward?
- If you were to accept this position, how would you explain it to a prospective employer five years from now in terms of serving as a link in your career progression?
- Based on what your most respected critic would say, what's the greatest asset you'll bring to our company, and what areas for career development and professional improvement are you focusing on at this point?

2. Extend Onboarding to 30-, 60-, and 90-Day Intervals

Developing the organization's capability in relationship building continues well beyond the first day of new-hire orientation. Schedule dates on your calendar to follow up with new hires, who should come fully prepared to discuss their onboarding experiences, mini successes, technical or people challenges along the way, and anything else they might want to address. Include questions to really get them talking.

Questions to ask during the 30 day check-in include:

- What do you like about the position and the company so far? What's been going well? What are the highlights of your experiences so far?
- Tell me what you don't understand about your role or about our organization now that you've had a month to roll up your sleeves and get your hands dirty.
- Have you faced any surprises since joining us?
- What one thing stands out to you most in terms of capturing your first full month with us?
- Is there anything I can do to help you at this point and provide additional support, structure, or direction?

At the 60-day check-in ask:

- Do you have enough, too much, or too little time to do your work?
- Do you have access to the appropriate tools and resources? Have you been trained sufficiently in all aspects of your job so you can perform at a high level?
- How do you see your position relating to our organization's mission, vision, and values?

- Compare the organization and your role to how we described it when you initially interviewed with us. Have you experienced any surprises, disappointments, or other aha moments that you're comfortable sharing?
- How has your relationship with your peers developed over the last two months? Have you been made to feel welcome, and do you think you've made others feel welcome in partnering with you?
- Don't be shy: Tell me about some of your accomplishments thus far.

During the 90-day check-in ask:

- Are you ready to begin discussing quarterly and annual goals, or would you feel more comfortable doing so in 90 days from now?
- Do you see any major pivots coming in terms of your approach to your work or your peers?
- Is any additional training or education required to help you meet your expected performance standards?
- Do you see any stretch opportunities or areas where you'd like to assume additional responsibilities or gain broader exposure?
- How will you plan to strengthen your capabilities in the areas of leadership, communication, and team building?
- What are you working on and interested in learning more about at this point in your career development?

Note that at day 90, operational managers and senior leaders can introduce a pivot that will help new hires develop a strong achievement mentality. This can involve encouraging employees to take control of recurring meetings and stepping back into more of a *mentor* or *coach* role. Using terms like mentor and coach helps to redefine working relationships and enforce a mutually beneficial culture in which everyone is on the same side. Open communication builds trust, and trust begets discretional energy—the extra effort that workers put in because they want to, not because they have to.

The Upside

Day 90 is your launching pad. This revised approach to onboarding helps new hires rise to the occasion by taking the lead in their own career development and codifying their achievements. You're not holding anyone by the hand, but pointing them to greater levels of accountability, especially in terms of codifying and quantifying their achievements for their quarterly or annual self-reviews in addition to their own bios and LinkedIn profiles.

Insights Through Pain

I've experienced resistance to these types of extended onboarding commitments from people who challenge the amount of time it takes and the opportunity costs of having people off the floor. In fact, while you may not be able to mandate this practice in your organization, you can make a very compelling argument for why doing so is in their best interests:

- Meetings typically only last 20 to 30 minutes and create a sheltered onboarding experience for new hires, who come to rely on their supervisor as the buddy and mentor to help get their questions answered, make additional connections, and ensure their training skills are where they need to be.
- Depend on new hires to identify the most helpful teammates and leaders, supporting your high-potential and succession planning efforts.
- Transition to a quarterly feedback program that allows the new hire to create the agenda and schedule time on your calendar to take the lead in ensuring that their performance and productivity are on track (enabling an achievement mindset).
- Provide an opportunity to celebrate successes, course correct, and minimize any drama that might come from that feeling of flying blind in terms of what new hires are up to do at any given time.
- Separate operational day-to-day discussions from career and professional development consultations, which meet one of the primary needs of millennial and Gen Z workers.

Opportunity costs for being off the floor for a half-hour once a month or once a quarter pale in comparison to the benefits that result from strong one-on-one relationships that combine the individual's best career and professional interests with the organization's benefits of getting a motivated and accomplishment-focused workforce.

Your Tools

Encourage operational leaders and senior executives to make space for employees to express themselves. After all, all motivation is internal. Managers are not responsible for motivating their employees, but they *are* responsible for creating a work environment in which their employees can motivate themselves. This creates an opportunity for everyone—especially millennials and Gen Z, who rank career and professional development among their top motivators and work values—to find new ways of reinventing themselves, building technical muscle, gaining broader organizational exposure, and developing an achievement mentality. Simply making time to ask someone how they're transitioning into the organization and how you can help builds trust and gratitude.

3. Introduce Quarterly Individual Development Plans (IDPs)

As you can see, transitioning from an L&D to an OD mindset can stem from selecting new questions to help frontline operational managers motivate their staff members. In addition, OD-level impact derives from engaging employees to do their best work every day and codify their achievements. It's a game changer in the highest sense and requires a simple adjustment to your fundamental thought as an L&D specialist about who you are and what your ultimate role is. The wisdom simply lies in providing content that helps managers understand how to lead more effectively by customizing the material to make the ideas their own.

This OD perspective continues into the quarterly feedback sessions, which are scheduled and managed by the employees themselves. If the purpose of organization development is to drive organizational effectiveness, solve problems, and improve organizational performance, then building your organization's people muscle via inclusion and relationship development between a supervisor and direct report is likely the quickest and most direct way to drive real change. The questioning strategy of managers may focus on key developmental and achievement areas by opening with queries like these:

- What are you working on and interested in learning more about at this point in your career?
- On a scale of one to 10, 10 being best, how well are your personal and professional interests connecting to the work you're doing day in and day out?
- On a scale of one to 10, how would you grade your overall contributions to the team and the organization in terms of being able to do your best work every day?
- What three adjectives would your most respected critic use to define or describe you as a leader or team contributor?

- How can I help you expand your professional network, build stronger technical muscle, or gain greater organizational exposure?
- What would you change or amend in terms of your target goals or timelines to ensure you're remaining on track?
- What can I do to help you meet your goals or otherwise assist you with your own career and professional development?
- *(For supervisors and above)* If the whole organization followed your lead, would you be happy with where you took it?
- *(For supervisors and above)* Would you want to work for you?

The Upside

An OD perspective sees human capital talent as the ultimate profit lever. Develop a rhythm of quarterly reporting that drives real results, whether you manage exempt professional or hourly employees. Sure, the nature of the questions may change, depending on the sophistication of your team members, but developing awareness of achievements and accomplishments hones muscle, increases accountability, and delivers results in all cases. It all stems from the trust employees have in their immediate superiors. As Marcus Buckingham (2016) pointed out in his bestseller *First, Break All the Rules*, people join companies but leave managers. Build the muscle of your frontline management teams to become outstanding leaders who make employees want to stick with your company. That's a wise investment in your OD efforts that can have an immediate impact, one leader and one department at a time.

Insights Through Pain

Rolling out a program based on mentoring, selfless leadership, and coaching questions— if your organization has never done it before—can make employees suspicious. For example, some may wonder why the tone of the more personal relationship with their supervisor feels more structured or deliberate. Some may be hesitant to make themselves vulnerable if their current relationship with their boss has been arm's length (or worse). Likewise, it can leave operational managers questioning whether their workload has just doubled—at least initially and until they see how it works. Share your OD wisdom by pointing out that this won't require any additional effort on the manager-client's part;

Each leader is simply making space for employees to put their best foot forward in terms of their contributions to the organization and their commitments to their own professional growth and career development.

True, some employees may not want to participate and take an attitude with their managers of, "You're my boss. You tell me what to do and assess my performance. That's your job." In such cases, don't fret. No need to discipline anyone who refuses to schedule time with their manager each quarter. (Sometimes, workers have simply been there for so long that they can do their jobs in their sleep; at other times, they may suffer from entitlement mentalities and see their manager's efforts as another "HR du jour" project that will soon fade away.) When it comes time for an employee's annual performance review, however, recommend that manager-clients make a simple note in the narrative section, such as "Rico was invited to meet with me quarterly over the past year to review his accomplishments and discuss amendments to his goals as well as career and professional development. He opted not to accept my invitation at any of those quarterly intervals." Enough said.

Your Tools

Again, remember that revising your questions represents a new system that aligns performance, rewards, and culture. Your efforts to capture quarterly performance feedback and hold career and professional development discussions using adult education and motivation techniques affect people strategy, change management, and organizational behavior. Such initiatives represent high payoff activities with a quick return on investment, so long as your manager-clients can build such relationships upon trust and goodwill.

Further, from a pure OD perspective, the question remains, how do you drive stronger, more measurable performance and productivity? How do you measure the results of greater trust and heightened relationships between managers and staff? The answers are as unique as your manager-clients themselves, and the only way to capture and quantify results is to ask (coach) your operational leaders and senior executives about how to best measure changes in behavior and performance in their respective departments. Increased revenue, decreased expenses, saved time, greater customer satisfaction, and successful project rollouts that are under budget and on time are all reasonable measurement points. "Turn around leadership" is a special skill and game changer for managers and executives to master. Discuss expectations upfront for what success might look like so you can capture and measure it together in the future.

4. Introduce the Leader-As-Coach Model to Spike Employee Engagement

Listening is key to creating a coaching culture in your organization. Specifically, develop the habit (and teach it to others) of listening with your heart and eyes, in addition to your ears. Encourage your manager-clients to allow their employees to interpret their questions out loud, work through them together, and reflect and respond. Foundational, strategic questions like these help employees find their own way and ponder mistakes. Further, it may initially seem challenging to demonstrate to operational leaders how to give a little less advice and ask more questions, especially since it may mean it takes a bit longer to arrive at the ultimate goal: employee understanding. But if operational managers' goals truly are to serve as mentors and coaches to their team members, then listening more effectively should become a key focus area for their own personal and professional development.

Further, operational managers and senior leaders need to get used to uncomfortable silence. If they're truly serious about becoming better coaches and mentors, they'll need to withhold more than they divulge. Remember that this is their journey, and your role is to support them in finding their best path. For example, if they want to present an idea to their employees, they shouldn't necessarily offer it up immediately. Instead, they can simply ask, "And what else?" They may find that the staff member comes up with the same solution they were about to offer, although the employee will have come to the solution on their own. Managers will quickly learn that their employees' responses are often close to what they were originally going to suggest, and a few simple qualifying questions will help them refine those responses.

In a similar manner, when someone responds, "I don't know," managers can attempt to redirect and rephrase the question. I've jokingly asked my own staff over the years, "I know you don't know, *but if you did know,* what would your answer be?" Employees will realize that while you're making light of the immediate situation, you're serious about leading them to their own answer rather than giving it to them—even if a wild guess is the only available option. Teach them how to fish—don't just give them a fish. Such are the makings of great talent development leaders—a noble OD goal in any organizational playbook.

The essence of coaching lies in unlocking others' potential. Managers and leaders should focus their employees on building their strengths and codifying their achievements. The stronger their achievement mindset and the accomplishments they garner, the better for the leader's department and the organization overall. Remember that the greatest leaders are not those with the most followers; they are the ones who create the most leaders in turn. A true OD tenet lies in building and sustaining a new desired state for the entire organization. Each step you take to strengthen relationships and build an inclusive culture will go a long way in driving the change that develops an ownership mentality among workers across the organization.

The Upside

Coaching rests upon trust. It builds relationships and creates inclusive cultures. It helps people believe that they're special and capable of coming up with their own solutions to even the toughest challenges. Coaching builds accountability and fosters a desire to pay things forward in a selfless and empathetic way.

Insights Through Pain

When trust in a manager doesn't exist, moving to a leader-as-coach style may be thwarted by those being mentored. Without goodwill, employees won't want to make themselves vulnerable (again, in a healthy and trusting sense) in front of their leaders. If your manager-clients sense that the level of trust on the team isn't where they need it to be to establish and sustain a coaching culture, delay the initiative. Focus instead on helping that manager strengthen relationships at the new hire, onboarding, and quarterly IDP windows. Wait to discuss creating a coaching culture until the time feels more appropriate.

Nothing has to be done immediately. Everything presented in this chapter can be rolled out tomorrow or a year from now. Manager-clients should make this part of their own goal setting initiatives and career and professional development aspirations with their boss' support and guidance. But managers have to start *somewhere* to have real organizational impact over time. They shouldn't delay rolling out this type of program (or part of it) until everything is perfect. They may never get there if they hold themselves to any sort of perfection standard.

Your Tools

Your manager-clients' tools lie in their questions—as long as they are ongoing, systematic, and long-range in nature and drive organizational effectiveness, solve problems, and improve team performance. Likewise, remind your clients that *beingness* trumps *doingness*. In other words, who they are is much more important than what they do at any given time. This piece of workplace wisdom can be easily understood by thinking of the favorite boss paradigm. When someone describes the best boss they've ever had, they usually describe that relationship and experience as follows:

- She always made me feel welcome and like my opinion mattered.
- He challenged me to do things I didn't think I was capable of.
- She seemed to have more confidence in me than I had in myself at the time.
- No matter what emergencies we faced, she always calmed things down and helped us think through an alternative clearly and without drama.

In almost all cases, employees describe their best bosses' *beingness*—that is, who they were, what they stood for and believed in, their character, and the genuine care they showed for others. Yet, how many times do we hear the question, "What are you *doing?*" to curb turnover, hire more people, increase employee or team performance, and the like? We're asking the wrong sponsoring question of ourselves. Always come from beingness; always filter your definition of yourself in terms of who you're being at any given time. The *doingness* will simply follow from your beingness. Unfortunately, society tends to get these concepts backward, including, in my experience, in many workplaces.

5. Make It Safe for Leaders to Engage in Constructive Confrontation

Building relationships through human connection is a noble goal with concrete results: more engaged employees, higher levels of employee satisfaction, pride in achievement, and trust in leadership. It encompasses so many aspects of the OD promise: improving an organization's capability through the alignment of strategy, structure, people, rewards, metrics, and management processes. And it creates a healthy culture in which innovation and creativity can thrive, and people don't have to worry about being caught making mistakes, feeling micromanaged or over controlled, or being held to a standard of perfection.

Yet, your manager-clients will likely have questions similar to these:

- What if an employee or set of workers won't play along?
- How do you hold people accountable who appear to resist your best efforts, no matter how noble or selfless your intentions?
- How do you effectively deal with employees who may be suffering from an entitlement mentality or victim syndrome?

No human behavioral program can be built solely with carrots; a stick may be needed from time to time to hold others accountable. In fact, just one case of sweeping a problem employee under the rug can damage your program and reputation because it will spark perceptions of favoritism or weak leadership, which hold operational managers and their teams back. This is the thornier side of building relationships between managers and employees, between employees and their peers, and in the organization at large that OD practitioners face.

When working with stalwart holdouts, it's OK for managers to move into leadership defense mode to protect the company, their teams, and themselves from those who refuse to participate in the turnaround of a unit, department, or division. A manager's tools in such cases will consist of verbal conversations that attempt to reset expectations as well as progressive disciplinary documentation to place the individual on notice that their behavior and conduct must change or else they could face further disciplinary action, up to and including dismissal of employment. Here's how managers can map out their next steps in an environment where others cannot or will not get on board with their new direction.

Holding Tough Conversations to Establish a Record of Expectations

There are certain key rules in communicating challenging news to employees (Falcone 2019). First, managers should come from the angle of observation but avoid appearing to render any form of judgment. In other words, coming from the "what's so" is fine, but avoid coming from the "so what," which tends to sound judgmental and subjective.

Second, managers should hold workers accountable for their own perception management. *Perception*, like feelings, isn't right or wrong; it just is. No one can tell you that you have no right to your feelings, just like they cannot tell you that you have no right to your perceptions. By holding employees accountable for the perception they create in others, managers not only have an opportunity to salvage a flagging performer but also to help them address a roadblock that could otherwise hold them back for the rest of their career.

Third, come from awareness rather than anger. *Anger* is purely external. If someone is mad at someone else, they'll typically assume zero responsibility for the problem at hand and deflect all blame outwardly at the other person. *Awareness*, in comparison, drives internal reflection. Managers can help staff members build their own emotional self-awareness and emotional intelligence by helping them look inward and assume partial responsibility if something goes wrong.

For example, shouting at a direct report in a staff meeting is a form of public shaming, and pulling rank diminishes an individual's worth. If this happens, ask to meet privately, one-on-one after the meeting. Tell them something like "I'm not sure why you felt it was appropriate for you to use that tone and language in front of the rest of the staff. Truth be told, I felt embarrassed by your actions. And I wouldn't ever do that to you in front of the team. I respect you too much to do that. Can you understand my concern?"

When done correctly, such leadership approaches typically invoke a response like "Oh, I'm sorry, Keisha. I never meant to make you feel that way, especially in front of everyone else on the team. I'm sorry about that and I apologize."

As soon as we assume partial responsibility for something gone wrong, healing can begin, and the problem likely won't resurface.

Similarly, you might want to open or close your conversation by stating, "The most important decisions about our careers are made when we're not in the room. Let me help you influence what's being said about you when you're not present so you can influence those conversations. Often, it's a matter of something simply missing awareness. What's important is that you hold yourself accountable for your own perception management—regardless of your intention, it's the impact of your message on others that counts." Such guidance allows your client-managers to feel more comfortable engaging in difficult conversations rather than looking the other way or sweeping things under the rug.

Document Corrective Action in the Form of Progressive Discipline

When documenting progressive disciplinary actions, managers should always attempt to hear out the employee before issuing the warning. Whenever possible, include the employee's feedback in your documentation, showing that the manager-client did not rush to judgment and heard both sides of the story before moving to disciplinary measures. ("When we asked you about . . . , you stated . . .") Next, managers should include who-what-where-when-why-how descriptors in their documentation, remembering that they're writing this not only for the employee but also for a potential jury one year from now, should things escalate into a wrongful termination or discrimination suit. Will their documentation stand up on its own if blown up on a video screen and displayed to a jury without further commentary?

Likewise, operational leaders should invite the employee (using your organization's written template) to share their insights into what happened and offer suggestions for improving the situation. Few employees take the time to write rebuttals, which can play favorably to the employer's advantage in litigation. Logically, if the employee didn't rebut the findings at the time, it would be very difficult to challenge them after a lawsuit has been filed. Finally, operational leaders should include strong consequential language, such as "Failure to demonstrate immediate and sustained improvement may result in further disciplinary action, up to and including termination of employment."

In cases of final written warnings, you might want to include language like "This is your last chance. Your position is now in immediate jeopardy of being lost." Such are the makings of workplace due process that will minimize claims of wrongful termination and other legal challenges.

The Upside

Building relationships depends on communication in both forms—verbal and written—to hold others accountable. It also creates a record that protects your company should a case of wrongful termination or discrimination proceed to trial. Written communication, even in this confrontational sense, remains an aspect of relationship building. For example, a manager-client might verbally state, "I wouldn't be doing you a service as your supervisor if I didn't bring to your attention and make you aware of [X]." And in cases of documented discipline, manager-clients extend their feedback to a new level—corrective action notification—in communicating their concerns and expectations more specifically in writing. This may feel like a negative side of relationship building, but it's also necessary because it allows the individual to see what needs to be done to retain their job.

Insights Through Pain

Beware of senior executives who avoid progressive discipline and instead argue to simply eliminate the position (that is, lay off the worker) or otherwise terminate them because they are employed at will. While that path of least resistance may seem like the easiest way to sweep the problem under the rug, it will also expose your organization to legal vulnerability.

Likewise, if operational managers and senior leaders don't leverage feedback or constructive confrontation in real time, it's not just legal exposure that should concern you; it's the hit to your culture and reputation. No one wants to work for an organization that doesn't give people a fair chance to improve before pulling the plug and terminating them. When co-workers see this happen to their peers, they lose faith in the organization's honesty and transparency, begin to worry about making mistakes, and avoid taking healthy risks. Worst of all, management loses trust. And without trust, respect and camaraderie suffer irreparable damage.

So even if a senior executive tells you "We don't like to issue progressive discipline and preserve our right to terminate employees at will," simply respond that such a strategy may help your employee relations practice but will kill your recruitment and retention practices. Word will surely get out that your organization removes people without giving them the chance to rehabilitate and reinvent themselves. Would you want to work for an organization with that type of reputation? Probably not. Your job as an OD practitioner is to move the needle forward in terms of trust, communication, and transparency. Don't be afraid to push back when errant client-managers look to avoid necessary confrontation.

Your Tools

Progressive disciplinary documentation typically falls under the realm of employee relations, not L&D or OD. But again, leadership sometimes requires a stick—not just a carrot. And as an OD practitioner, you have to have both levers available at all times. Know when to advise manager-clients to meet with their HR business partner or employee relations representative. Understand how to guide them to the appropriate resources within the HR department or elsewhere. You can't be the best resource for every situation that comes up in the workplace, but relationship building rests on your ability to become a trusted resource to your partners, someone who gives sound and dependable advice in *all* situations, not just those situations that pertain to organization development.

6. Measure Success and, When Necessary, Course Correct

The court of public opinion will likely provide feedback regarding the results of your efforts and your perceived return on investment. No, this can't always be captured in hard dollars and cents. We know intuitively that happy employees, fully engaged in their work and thriving under strong leadership, tend to perform at a higher level than those who feel boxed in, burned out, or afraid of making mistakes. But depending on the systems you have in place, you should see changes in your human capital metrics over time. Here are some measurement-related questions you can consider:

- What trends and patterns are you seeing and hearing about in climate surveys or focus groups, especially in terms of leadership communication, team building, and culture?
- What primary reasons for leaving the organization are employees identifying in their exit interviews?
- Is your average tenure trending upward or downward?
- How is your organization's net promoter score trending? Are changes being implemented based on employee feedback and recommendations?
- Do your employees score the organization higher along the lines of diversity, equity, inclusion, and belonging (DEIB)?
- Can you identify upticks in the number of high-potential or cross-trained employees?
- What trends are you finding in terms of your company's internal fill rate? What percentage of positions are filled internally versus with outside candidates?
- What patterns can you identify in regrettable turnover, in which key employees leave for greener pastures?
- What about your boomerang ratio? How many people who have left the organization are rehired within a year of their resignation?

It's reasonable to see changes in trends and patterns within six to 18 months. And while overall organizational metrics and statistics may have trended positively, there are often departments or units that can't seem to meet the heightened expectations of this enhanced leadership initiative and as a result begin to unwind (which in turn brings down the overall average scoring trends). That's okay, though. Your metrics will point out very quickly which groups are suffering from excessive turnover, negatively trending performance, workers' compensation, leaves of absence, or even lawsuits. That can become the focus of your next quarterly initiative—constantly strengthening areas where managers or teams may be experiencing challenges.

The Upside

What gets measured gets managed. So much of effective leadership rests upon trust, respect, and general likeability. But we all know that numbers constitute the language of business. As an OD practitioner, being able to point to changes in patterns and trends over time that are concrete and numeric in nature make for a much stronger case of organizational and cultural change. Being able to demonstrate your abilities as a turnaround expert—whether of operational results or people performance—provides irrefutable proof of your contributions as an OD expert and facilitator of progressive change. But each division, department, unit, team, or individual leader will also take work on your part. Each constituent or cohort can become a true believer of your abilities once they can see the results on paper. Yes, feeling better about their leadership style or their relationship with their team makes client-managers happy. But showing them concrete results in terms of metrics or analytics makes them soar. And they have you to thank for it.

Insights Through Pain

My experience in most organizations where I've worked—in entertainment, healthcare, biotech, or financial services—is that many organizational leaders won't or can't understand what we as OD practitioners do. They know their business line. And that's about where their understanding of true leadership ends. It takes some convincing in many if not most cases to demonstrate your strategic value, so don't give up or get discouraged. Just because they don't initially understand what you do or the value you bring doesn't mean they can't benefit from it. But you'll need to show them the way, model the behaviors you want to see in others, and above all, make yourself a trusted resource.

Your value lies in leveraging talent to perform at a higher level for the organization, in this case by facilitating stronger communication and building greater trust through relationships. It may feel like you're bringing fire to the cavemen, but rest assured that they'll understand your real value once they see, feel, and hear the feedback from their team. Add key operational metrics that affect their bottom line, and you'll have a friend and advocate for life. Such are the makings of an outstanding OD practitioner.

Your Tools

There are many books on the ROI of human capital, so ask your HR partners and leaders which ones they recommend. This doesn't have to be overly complicated. You only need to identify around six key drivers of organization performance. Let's use internal promotion rate (IPR) as an example. The IPR tells you what percentage of hires are made from internal transfers or promotions versus outside hires. Easy enough. Now cut that list in two and look only at internal promotions (and not lateral transfers). Where are internal promotions happening most, and where do they cut off or choke?

In my experience, it's not uncommon to find that internal promotions happen at the non-exempt level (for example, from cook 1 to cook 2 to lead cook). But how does your organization fare when backfilling cook supervisor positions? How about dietary managers? Or directors of dietary and hospitality? That's where you can really see the strength of your internal pipeline. Now look at those same stats—whether filled internally or externally—through the lens of female or diverse candidates. Where do the promotions stop feeding a diversity progression track?

Interesting, isn't it? In fact, it's fairly easy to identify once you map it out on paper. Yet so many companies fail to look at this simple funnel metric and instead promote haphazardly—or at least without purpose or intention. Use human capital metrics to raise awareness of issues that may be right in front of a client-manager's eyes, and build action plans to strengthen those gaps.

OD is a practice of both evolution and revolution, depending on how quickly you can get to a desired outcome. As an OD practitioner, you're the organization's eyes and ears and in many ways, conscience. And nothing builds stronger relations of trust and respect with clients than when they begin to see you as a welcome solution to issues that they may have missed to that point in their career. You're making them better leaders and strengthening their organization, and for that they'll always be grateful.

A Mini Case Study

A blood banking center was having challenges meeting the volume demands and goals set by management. The center manager argued that the organization had to pay higher donation fees to entice potential donors to apply. Management felt the donor center leadership team wasn't doing enough to create marketing opportunities to raise awareness about their services and life-saving capabilities—regardless of the amount offered per donation. This presented the L&D manager responsible for this center with a dilemma. If employees are trained in the basics of their roles, this must be a morale or cultural issue. The OD solution: Look to a human capital approach to find new ways of driving donor volume.

From an OD standpoint, simple questions to the management team quickly ferreted out the problems:

- Only a small percentage of staff were triple trained to work as donor processors, plasma processors, and phlebotomists.

- The donor center had no high-potential employees lined up to assume broader leadership responsibilities.
- It took an average of 120 days to fill an open position, relative to 40 days at other centers.
- There was high tenure in this group but no progressive discipline had occurred over the past year, indicating that employees were not being held to high performance standards.

Once these operational and leadership shortcomings were identified, the L&D manager looked closer at the state of the center's relationships. A lack of an aligned people strategy, weak communication, and little opportunity for recognition left this donor center flailing. Relationships among and across the center were self-admittedly weak, and there was little evidence of connection between management and the rest of the staff. The overriding piece of feedback was that "No one ever says thank you around here, no matter how hard you work, but make one mistake, and they're all over you!" Further, "We rarely hold staff or all-hands meetings, we never know what's going on outside our immediate areas, and management doesn't seem to care."

Yes, this would be a nightmare for most, but it's an OD practitioner's dream! The L&D manager then set out on a five-step process to address the issue:

- Poll the team to establish the baseline.
- Keep local management (and corporate leadership) informed about their initial findings.
- Partner with local management to ask the employees for ideas and suggestions on improving the situation.
- Focus on the action plan to ensure feedback they received from the team was acted on.
- Shepherd the leadership team through the action plan while focusing on the three big concepts of leadership, communication, and team building.

Discussions between management and staff naturally led to hiring and onboarding considerations. For example, why couldn't they create a buddy program where more senior team members took new hires under their wings? After all, it makes for a more sheltered transition for new hires if they have someone they can rely on while also giving senior workers an opportunity to build their leadership skills. And that would also help qualify the center for the high-potential program because new hires would be better trained and motivated. In fact, they could advertise this in their recruitment literature and generate internal competition to see who's best at growing talent.

In addition, employees were coached about the benefits of obtaining triple certification as donor processors, plasma processors, and phlebotomists, including how the dollars added up with each new area of cross-training. The center manager selected two individuals for potential consideration in the center's high-potential program, encouraging them to enroll in leadership training and additional certification areas. The center manager likewise built a program to meet quarterly with each direct report, focusing on their career ambitions and how to build their skills to assume greater responsibilities or a promotion to a regional-level job.

In short, a new life was breathed into a tired group. Donor volume increased significantly within four months as employees' suggestions to build a donor ambassador program got traction and expanded (which increased the center's donor return rate). Engagement soared, as did turnover. After all, some employees were simply more comfortable with the old way of doing things. They eventually self-selected out and resigned, unhappy with "the changes being made around here these days." For those who didn't voluntarily resign, tough conversations and progressive disciplinary initiatives held everyone accountable to the renewed high standards. Trust in leadership took some time to increase but eventually did. Healthy competition for the high-potential program re-energized seasoned employees who were simply going through the motions. And one quiet, low-profile individual volunteered a "probably silly" idea that led to a team lunch on the last Friday of that month, where people prepared and brought in their favorite dishes.

This is how it works. There are no airy-fairy, pie-in-the-sky wish lists. It takes time, patience, and hard work, but turnarounds like this are definitely possible.

Summary

Transitioning from an L&D mindset to an OD mindset, replete with organization-changing results, can be informal (in terms of reinventing your L&D role) or formal (by transferring out of L&D and into OD). This is where the rubber meets the road in the corporate workplace. Trust, respect, and accountability go a long way in building the bonds of retention. Discussing "How can you become someone's favorite boss?" or "How can I become one of the best bosses you've ever had?" may sound naive at first, but actually poses meaningful questions for employees who are often starved of recognition or otherwise treading water career-wise.

Relationship building is all about the questions you ask, your selflessness in making another's cares and concerns your own, and a willingness to make space for others to motivate themselves. After all, in its purest form, organization development's goal is to drive planned and systematic change of processes and structures to generate stronger organizational productivity. The coaching questioning strategies introduced during different touch points in the employee life cycle are designed to strengthen your organization's talent management program and culture.

When all is said and done, a focus on relationship building and inclusion will cement in others' minds your creative and refreshing approach to change and agility. The most critical soft skill in hiring and professional development lies in your ability to build healthy and constructive relationships with team members. Trust, accountability, authenticity, and innovation are the key attributes of high performers and the foundation of successful teams and organizations. OD practitioners can drive, measure, and demonstrate improvements in those areas, building on the natural skills and talents they already possess from their L&D roles. Your next step lies in making relationship building and human connection an annual goal that you can roll out quarterly in bite-sized chunks, beginning with interviewing and onboarding, progressing through quarterly IDP meetings, and culminating in annual performance reviews. What an exciting transition awaits!

Key Takeaways

Here are a few things to remember about relationship building and inclusion:

- **Strengthening personal relationships** between management and staff and between staff members themselves is a critical part of OD initiatives that may initially be missing among participants.
- **Leadership, communication, and trust** are the three big attributes that organizational leaders should be asked about, especially in terms of what they believe will strengthen relationships and build greater trust and respect.
- **The best feedback will often come from those working in the trenches,** so create the space for the doers to provide input and suggestions. Just ensure that you're willing to act on and implement some of those ideas so their feedback doesn't go unheeded.

- **Ask the right questions to coach your manager-clients** so they can see any gaps in their leadership styles and proffer appropriate solutions. As in all coaching situations, remember to try to get them to figure out the answers, rather than telling them what to do. Then step out of the way and let them execute.
- **Managers will typically lead more effectively if they have stronger relationships with their team members.** Trust and respect will flourish when open communication and transparency are at hand. You now have many of the questioning tools needed to coach your manager-clients and senior operational executives to become stronger leaders, capable of creating more agile teams that can positively impact organizational culture and performance.

A Holistic Approach to Developing a Leader's Soft Skills

CATHERINE ALLEN

IN THIS CHAPTER

♦ Explore OD principles and practices to support a more holistic and integrated approach to developing core soft skills for leaders and emerging leaders

♦ Identify the core soft skills required to lead and some of the human and organizational dynamics and challenges at play in soft skill development

♦ Look at the shifts in mindset and approach organizations must make to more reliably build soft skills for leaders and all employees

A growing strategic issue for many organizations is how to foster more effective soft skill development and practice among current and emerging leaders. Soft skills—the short-hand term coined by the US military for all our interpersonal and people skills—have always been a differentiating factor in effective leadership. But smart technology along with the volatile, uncertain, complex, and ambiguous (VUCA) world we live and work in today is revealing just how critical soft skills are for working and leading effectively at any level. It seems the whole world is looking to learn more about soft skills; a Google search on the term "soft skills" returns about 4 billion results.

If you ask C-suite executives what challenges their leaders face today, they'll likely describe some of the following:

- Resolving issues with their peers
- Taking initiative instead of waiting to be told what to do
- Sharing the bigger picture with their staff
- Building diverse and inclusive teams that work collaboratively within and across business units
- Responding to their customer's changing needs
- Learning and adapting quickly
- Driving change
- Enabling creativity and problem solving
- Keeping the workforce motivated and engaged, especially following a shift to a hybrid or fully remote working environment
- Giving effective feedback and developing and scaling leaders

Answering these challenges requires the effective use of not just a leader's cognitive intelligence abilities (IQ), but also their emotional and social intelligence abilities (EQ and SQ). We all know that solid technical skills can be easily derailed if a person has poor people skills. And soft skills are what really enable organizational effectiveness.

Now that executive leaders fully appreciate that strong soft skills are key to the ability to lead effectively in today's VUCA business environment, they're asking HR and L&D to help leaders effectively employ those soft skills. But becoming more capable in the way we think, relate, and learn is not just a developmental challenge for individuals and teams but for organizations as well. The L&D industry is leveraging exciting new technology-based learning solutions to support the full range of skill development needs. However, despite these advances, the reality is that in an organizational environment, effective and sustainable soft skill development requires a far more holistic and systemic approach than the traditional content and delivery focus many training programs have for technical, job-specific skills. It calls for a fundamental shift in the way organizations orient their mindset, strategy, culture, and daily practices to support the way people need to learn and grow their skills and abilities. To lead and support this shift, HR and L&D professionals will need to leverage organization development (OD) concepts and skills.

This chapter explores how to use OD principles and practices to support a more holistic and integrated approach to developing core soft skills for leaders and emerging leaders. It identifies the core soft skills required to lead in today's world of work and examines some of the human and organizational dynamics and challenges at play in soft skill development. Finally, it will look at the shifts in mindset and approach organizations will need to make to more reliably build soft skills for leaders and all employees.

Why Soft Skills Are Evolving

Before we explore ways to better develop a leader's soft skills, let's first define what we mean by soft skills and address the evolution of the term and how we think about it. The US Army invented the term *soft skills* in the late 1960s as a contrast to the term *hard skills*. Their intention was to distinguish between the skills needed to operate anything tangible (like tanks, aircraft, and early computers) and the more intangible and often vague human character traits (such as integrity, self-discipline, strategic thinking, and fostering teamwork) that seemed to be present in leaders who successfully led their groups of soldiers (Wright 2018). Over the decades, these terms have become well-entrenched shorthand.

Although soft skills may be a convenient term, many believe it is out of date, confusing, inaccurate, and gender-biased (Villiers 2020). Until recently, soft skills were viewed as less important than hard skills, somewhat vague and "squishy," and awkward to even talk about in workplace settings. We've all come to appreciate that there is nothing soft (from a business relevance standpoint) or easy about how to teach, apply, or master these skills effectively and consistently in the workplace.

In addition to the term, another challenge is the sheer number of cognitive, emotional, and socially derived soft skills leaders are expected to employ. Leadership competency models were created to provide a structured framework for defining and developing the range of knowledge, skills, and abilities (KSAs) as well as the mindsets and behaviors associated with effective leadership. But aspiring and even experienced leaders often find the range of soft skills in these competency models overwhelming and intimidating to learn and apply effectively and consistently. Nevertheless, leadership capability and competency models will always be necessary for defining the range of KSAs leaders need to tap into as their roles increase in complexity and responsibility. Today there is more focus on building strengths, linking competencies to performance outcomes, and improving competencies that will make the most difference for leaders.

Perhaps the biggest influence on the way we think about the relevance of soft skills at work is the impact of smart technologies. As smart technologies continue to disrupt and replace many of the jobs humans do—even the knowledge-based jobs once thought to be immune to automation—people will need skills that either complement technology or constitute what machines can't do well (Hess and Ludwig 2017). These include soft skills like critical thinking, complex problem solving, creativity, flexibility, resilience, as well as the emotional and social skills to communicate and collaborate effectively with teams. Business and individual career success will continue to depend on the ability to continuously learn, grow, and adapt quickly.

But we need to think more broadly than just the soft skills leaders need. We need to account for the human skills all adults need to work and collaborate successfully in the 21st century. This suggests that organizations will need to agree on a set of core people capabilities so the entire workforce can be successful inside and outside their jobs. Companies are moving in this direction because they see the business imperative of developing strong people capabilities much earlier in every employee's career.

Core People Capabilities

The idea of a core people capabilities model could help bring the need for core or foundational soft and hard skills together in a way that is more accurate and approachable for both employers and employees. Such a model could organize core skills into three overarching buckets (Offterdinger and Allen 2021):

- **Mind skills** are embedded in the brain's cognitive function and are closely associated with learning, problem solving, and decision making.
- **People skills** reflect interpersonal and behavioral skills and abilities, such as the ability to know oneself and communicate and relate to others effectively on a personal and professional level.
- **Technical skills** are the abilities and knowledge needed to perform tasks within a field or specific discipline.

Table 14-1 provides an example of a core capabilities model that groups the skills an organization determines are essential for all employees to develop and practice in their jobs. (Tool 14-1 at the end of the chapter provides a more detailed version.)

Table 14-1. Core Capabilities Model

Mind Skills	People Skills	Technical Skills
• Executive function skills • Growth mindset • Adaptability • Critical thinking • Curiosity • Creative thinking • Decision making	• Emotional intelligence • Authenticity • Kindness • Balance • Communication skills • Giving and receiving feedback • Teamwork • Resolving conflict • Leveraging differences • Integrity	• Domain skills • Digital readiness • Multidisciplinary skills

There are many ways to approach a core capabilities model, but what's important is that companies be explicit in naming the human cognitive and behavioral skills that the organization needs its employees to develop and practice to perform well in their jobs and throughout their careers. When employees understand what specific skills their employers value, why those skills are relevant to the company's success, and that the skills are expected to be practiced in their jobs and will be incentivized, they will have greater clarity and motivation to learn and grow those skills.

Applying an OD Lens to Soft Skill Development

To understand why soft skills development needs a more holistic and integrated approach, it's important to break down the underlying human and organizational dynamics at play. This is best seen through an OD lens because it combines the disciplines of human psychology, organizational behavior, and adult development with management sciences around culture, strategy, leadership, process improvement, and change management to help people and systems function better within an organization. Whether you associate yourself with an HR, L&D, or OD field, a more holistic way of thinking is necessary to factor in and support the human and organizational dynamics that need to connect and align when developing human abilities at work.

Let's apply the OD lens to assess the realities, challenges, and barriers to soft skills development from two viewpoints:

- The human behavior lens (psychology, neuroscience, and adult development)
- The organizational lens (culture, strategy, systems, processes, and practices)

The Human Behavior Lens

The fields of cognitive, behavioral, and developmental psychology, as well as neuroscience and sociology, have made major breakthroughs in our understanding of how humans learn and develop. Let's review some key insights about how people learn and develop soft skills in an organizational environment, as well as what can get in their way. This is by no means an exhaustive list; rather, they're some of the most important factors to keep in mind.

Over Time, With Practice, and in Relationship With Other People

A training program can introduce soft skill concepts, but it cannot develop them in the leaders. Take, for example, active listening. Arguably the most important of the communication skills, good listening is core to understanding other people's perspectives, taking directions, collaborating, and resolving differences. In a training environment (whether in person or online), we can learn about active listening and even practice it through role-play exercises.

This is important, but becoming a better listener only happens when we practice that skill with people on a regular basis over time. Obviously, the whole point of soft skill training is to apply what we learn back in our jobs. But the reality is that it can feel awkward to talk about interpersonal skills like active listening, empathy, and compassion in a meeting with team members. And while we are all constantly using soft skills in our jobs to one degree or another, most company cultures haven't normalized talking openly about using them or intentionally supporting efforts to apply specific soft skills learned in training.

Horizontally and Vertically

One of the biggest advancements in the leadership development field is the emergence of the terms horizontal and vertical development. *Horizontal development* refers to the adding of more knowledge, skills, and competencies—growing what we know, which can be assessed through competency measurement tools like 360-degree feedback. It's an important foundation or starting point. *Vertical development* refers to advancement in a person's cognitive ability. The outcome of vertical stage development is the ability to increasingly think in more complex, systemic, and interdependent ways (Petrie 2014). In other words, as we develop and expand how we think, we can be more aware and effective in the way we employ our skills. Horizontal and vertical development helps us understand the interplay between our outer game (how others experience the way we use our cognitive knowledge, behavioral skills, and expertise) and our inner game (how our beliefs, assumptions, meaning making, and mindset inform our choices and behavior).

Today, we understand that developing a leader's soft skills needs to be a blend of horizontal learning and vertical development. To support horizontal learning, we're using tools like leadership competency models, 360-degree assessments, and content driven experiences like in-person training classes, programs designed around workshops, informal learning with peers, and a range of tech-enabled learning methods to find out more about the behaviors that make up our outer game. With vertical development, we are examining the inner world of how we think, how our life experiences influence our beliefs and assumptions, why we get stuck in the same patterns of thought, and how to become more conscious in how we use our cognitive, emotional, and social skills competently in our leadership roles. Individual and peer coaching, mentoring, and stretch assignments that push us out of our comfort zone all help us grow and expand our minds' capacity to think in more complex ways so we're more self-aware, adaptable, resilient, and collaborative. As leadership development experts, Robert Anderson and Bill Adams (2016), say in their book, *Mastering Leadership*, "The maturity of the inner game is always mediating and managing the outer game."

Ego, Fear, and Complacency

The fields of psychology and neuroscience help us understand perhaps the biggest human barriers to continuous learning and applying soft skills at work—our ever-present egos, fears, and tendency toward complacency. According to Edward Hess (2014), a professor at the Darden School of Business, we tend to defend, deny, and deflect what we think may cause us to lose face or look uninformed or not particularly smart. We seek to avoid the embarrassment of failure. And we also tend to become complacent after learning something, retreating to autopilot mode and resisting new challenges and ideas.

Harvard developmental psychologists, Robert Kegan and Lisa Lahey (2016) liken managing the inner workings of our egos and fears at work to having a second job. They observe that globally, "most people are spending time and energy covering up their weaknesses, managing other people's impressions of them, showing themselves to their best advantage, playing politics, and hiding their inadequacies, uncertainties, and limitations."

This dynamic of protecting ourselves is often at play when we are trying to learn and employ soft skills in organizational environments. This is why psychological safety is now considered to be a core human need and enabler to learn, grow, and work successfully with others. Coined by Amy Edmondson (1999), professor of leadership and management at Harvard Business School, *psychological safety* refers to an individual's level of confidence that they will not be embarrassed, rejected, or punished for speaking up. In teams, it's a climate of interpersonal trust and mutual respect that enables individuals to feel comfortable being themselves and able—even obligated—to be candid. As Edmondson notes, making it safe for people to fearlessly speak up, share information, and challenge one another will always be something organizations continually strive toward rather than achieving once and for all. None the less, she says that more and more leaders recognize that psychological safety is mission critical when knowledge is a crucial source of value. When it comes to fostering soft skill development, it is paramount to institutionalize principles and practices that make learning and growth psychologically safe in any kind of organizational team or group setting.

The Organizational Lens

Since Peter Senge popularized the concept of a learning organization in his 1990 book *The Fifth Discipline*, companies have pursued the idea of people intentionally and continuously learning to identify and solve problems quickly and drive management improvement and innovation with varying degrees of success. What successful companies, especially those that out-innovate their competitors, seem to have in common is a strong culture of learning. In fact, HR and L&D industry analyst and researcher Josh Bersin and his team produced compelling research findings more than a decade ago that found a strong learning culture is the single biggest driver of business impact (Bersin 2010). Companies such as Cisco, Bridgewater Associates, Apple, Pixar, American Express, SAP, Google, Citi, Starbucks, GE, Corning, and Honda credit their learning culture as key to their ability to innovate, survive, and thrive through market disruptions. These companies are all led by people who enable a culture that encourages asking hard questions, challenging one another, taking smart risks, valuing mistakes and failures as opportunities to learn and change, and rewarding employees who take initiative to learn new knowledge and skills. These companies also clearly show how their learning orientation supports the business strategy. Leaders at the top empower the leadership across the company to communicate why a learning culture is so important. And they invest in getting the right management practices in place to remove behavioral roadblocks around collaboration, creativity, and problem solving at the lowest levels. In short, they understand that an environment that is good for learning is also good for business performance.

Now, one might argue that these are big companies with the necessary deep pockets to invest the time and financial resources to design, foster, and sustain a learning culture. But in truth, it's not size or resources that power a learning culture. The biggest enabler of a learning culture is the mindset and commitment of the leadership at the top combined with the alignment of senior leaders around a learning culture throughout the organization. There are many small and medium-sized companies that have also built a strong learning culture that correlates to positive performance and business outcomes. As Peter Senge says, in addition to the right mindset, leaders build strong learning cultures in their organizations through *focus, commitment,* and *practice* (O'Neil 1995).

There is no question that the learning organization and today's focus on creating a culture of learning and development have taken root in companies of all sizes. But as HR and L&D practitioners know all too well, creating a strong, sustainable learning culture is a lot easier said than done. When you apply an OD lens, you can see how the challenges and barriers to soft skill development can show up at least initially, and often persistently, through the organization's culture, strategy, systems, processes, and practices. You might recognize these examples from my own lived experiences working to create people development strategies:

- **Value and relevance.** "We aren't really clear what soft skills our employer values beyond good communication skills and teamwork, or how they relate directly to our jobs and business outcomes."
- **Training and development is time consuming.** "We're oriented to think that training and development is a separate kind of activity from the day-to-day work. We are too busy and don't have time to participate in development activities whether they are online or in-person. It's extra work that is separate from our job."
- **Awkward to talk about.** "We don't really talk about how we use soft skills in day-to-day work or team meetings. It just feels awkward to discuss. We mainly talk about soft skills or touch-feely stuff at retreats and training classes."
- **IDPs are more career-focused than skill-focused.** "Most of what I talk about with my manager is how I'm performing in my job and how to get to the next level. I don't have specific soft skills to work on."

- **Recognizing and incentivizing strong soft skills.** "Rewards are too exclusively focused on technical and financial performance (such as finite results) and don't reward broader leadership capabilities. We need to expand incentives to include the intangible leadership skills and capabilities. We should incorporate KPIs for measuring nontechnical leadership competencies."
- **Leaders aren't walking the talk.** "It's discouraging that leaders in my company aren't consistently talking about or modeling the soft skill concepts I learned about in my leadership development program in their own behavior."
- **L&D isn't a part of business strategy conversations.** "We're [an L&D leader] buried two levels down in the HR function and don't participate in business strategy discussions on what skills and capabilities are being developed and for what strategic reason."
- **How soft skill development translates to business outcomes.** "How do we know that our investments in developing leadership skills, especially soft skills, correlate to meeting our business goals?"

Organizational Mindset Shifts

Before we can look at specific strategies to enable more holistic and effective soft skill development for leaders and employees, it's important to acknowledge three fundamental shifts companies will need to take when thinking about the role of learning and development. These shifts will be foundational for holistic strategies to succeed:

- Looking at L&D as core to a company's business strategy, purpose, and contribution
- Normalizing the language and practices of L&D as part of daily work culture
- Embracing L&D as an individual and collective expectation and responsibility of all employees

HR and L&D practitioners have a key role in supporting these fundamental mindset shifts in their organizations.

L&D Is Core to Strategy, Purpose, and Contribution

Given how central learning agility and adaptability will be to a company's ability to compete and succeed, corporate L&D can no longer be viewed as an appendage to the business, but rather it should be embedded as a core element of the company's business strategy. Business strategy experts suggest that CEOs should develop new company-wide strategies that recognize learning as the internal engine of organizational change and optimal performance and as fundamental to the success of the entire business (Dyer et al. 2020).

An even more fundamental shift is to embrace the development of human capability as a core value and an expanded purpose of the company. If we all agree that developing people capabilities is a lifelong requirement of working adults and the organizations that employ them, then perhaps it's time to expand the organization's purpose to also include contributing to people's development and potential. When we elevate developing people to the level of an organization's core purpose—why it exists in the first place—then it is easier for employers and employees to embrace the implications that come with creating and sustaining a conscious and vibrant development culture. It also rationalizes and invites a broader role for the L&D function in the organization. And, it bridges the relationship between the work adults perform every day and their developmental journey to learn and grow the full capabilities they need to be successful at work, at home, and in society.

It is also time to recognize the important contribution to society that organizations can make when they invest in and consciously nurture the development of their employee's full capabilities. As my co-author, Ed Offterdinger, and I note in our book, *Conscious, Capable and Ready to Contribute: How Employee Development Can Become the Highest Form of Social Contribution* (2021), we believe that developing people and equipping them with the human capabilities to succeed and thrive is not only key to business success, it also makes the most positive difference in our world. This is the ultimate contribution an organization can make to society. We envision a world in which the conscious practice of people development will become a recognized and incentivized form of social contribution for 21st-century organizations.

L&D Normalized in Daily Work Culture

We've been talking for some time about the importance of finding ways for companies to embed relevant learning and skills development in their employee's everyday flow of work. According to the 70-20-10 framework, we learn 70 percent of our knowledge and skills from experiences and assignments, 20 percent from relationships, and 10 percent from coursework and training. So, if companies want their employees to increase their use of specific soft skills, companies need to make sure that leaders talk about the value of those skills, the relevance to the business, and the expectation that the skills will be practiced with fellow team members and customers. That's part of the 10 percent of learning about a soft skill. The 90 percent comes from seeing and experiencing others using those soft skills and practicing them ourselves. For example, we learn what humility and vulnerability looks and feels like in a work situation when someone models it for us. Making it feel normal and comfortable to talk about how we are learning and growing our soft skills in workday conversations will also be important for the third major shift—our individual and collective responsibilities.

Individual and Collective Responsibilities for L&D

Two important leadership development trends are the transfer of greater developmental ownership to the individual and a greater focus on collective rather than individual development. These two trends may at first seem paradoxical, but they are vitally important paradigm shifts in the way we approach L&D. Leadership development researcher, Nick Petrie (2014) notes that people develop faster when they believe they're responsible for their own progress. And we see this a lot more with younger employees who tend to seek out and expect feedback and opportunities to learn and grow for the sake of their career. This trend also recognizes that peers are powerful teachers and that leadership capacity has to be nurtured throughout an organization because everyone needs to lead effectively in their roles.

While intrinsic motivation is certainly an important driver for individual development, organizations must balance this with their need to drive a cultural mindset that L&D is an individual and collective *expectation* and *responsibility* of the job. This means that organizations may have to shift from offering L&D opportunities as individual career development perks to clearly articulating the value and expectation of all employees from the moment they enter the company until they leave. Employees have to be able to rely on one another to stay actively engaged and mutually supportive in the organization's daily rhythms and routines that support conscious learning and growth.

Shifts for the L&D Professional

Now that we've covered a bit of soft skill terminology and the human and organizational dynamics around developing soft skills, let's turn to the L&D professional and look at ways that role can shift to support more holistic OD approaches for helping employees develop their leadership skills.

There will always be a content development and delivery component to an L&D professional's role, but it is becoming an increasingly secondary focus. The primary focus should be to enable a healthy and safe leadership and learning culture by shaping executive conversations to look more strategically at what core people capabilities are required to drive strategic business goals and outcomes and how development fits into the business strategy. User-friendly informational resources on core skills will be important to have readily accessible for managers and employees to reference. However, much of the rich content for learning and developing skills will be found in daily work situations and conversations. Your job will shift to supporting business unit leaders, managers, and teams as they shift their mindsets and behaviors to a learning and development paradigm that builds confidence, creativity, psychological safety, and a dynamic capacity to be leader-led and more focused on learning skills with and from peers in real-time work situations and conversations.

As an L&D practitioner, you will be helping leaders embrace an expanded view of L&D, the purpose of people and leadership development, and their role in leading it. Company leaders will need to see how you can leverage learning and development messages and practices to support employees through each stage in the employee life cycle. Perhaps most importantly, you will need to help leaders lean into creating a healthy, safe learning environment—one that emphasizes the respect, empathy, care, and compassion everyone needs to succeed in the messy, often uncomfortable, but ultimately fulfilling sandbox of intentional learning and growth.

To support these big organizational shifts, tap into an OD practitioner's mindset and toolbox of skills and practices. Your role will be that of a consultant and business partner, similar to an HR business partner, and you'll likely find yourself collaborating with functional leaders and teams on defined and phased projects to implement pieces of the L&D and business integration strategy. You might also find yourself working with external subject matter experts as part of the support team approach. And you'll surely use such OD skills as project design and management, data collection, data analysis and measurement, strategy and change management, and facilitating lots of conversations! Frequently used soft skills include relationship building, communicating (listening, speaking, and writing), critical and systems thinking, and collaborative and creative problem solving.

Building Blocks for Leadership Culture and Development Integration

Perhaps it goes without saying, but it's really true that the best place to start when building a holistic and integrated development culture is leadership development. All the elements that make up a strong leadership culture also serve to foster a stronger L&D environment throughout the organization. And the result will foster better soft skill development and use.

So, what does an organization need to create a strong culture of leadership and continuous learning and development? I suggest that there are five elements:

- Understanding the role of leadership
- Aligning business and people development strategies
- Identifying core leadership capabilities
- Defining principles to guide leadership and development culture
- Embedding development messages and practices throughout the employee life cycle

Let's explore how these elements support leader soft skill development through a case study outlining the experience of one of my client companies. This case study demonstrates how I helped company leaders engage the five elements by employing OD principles and skills while also showcasing the collaborative nature of this work between the internal HR, L&D, and executive leader teams and the external team of leadership development coaches and OD consultants.

The client—a medium-sized, US-based global software company employing more than 3,000 people—was a recognized industry leader of its products and through its values-driven approach to its people and customers. It had a strong commitment to learning and development with a dedicated L&D team and mature, award-winning leadership programs that supported leaders in all stages of development. However, the CEO recognized that he and his executive team needed to enhance their leadership capability to scale their people and the business to the next level of growth. Even with strong company fundamentals, year over year financial performance, and a clear growth strategy in place, the CEO understood that company leadership could not get the business to the next level without placing a greater focus on individual and team development at the senior levels.

Understanding the Role of Leadership

The first task was for the executive team to understand what it would take to scale the leadership capacity and capability in the company. They needed to understand that scale would start with themselves—they had to *own* their development journey as leaders. Whether or not they had experienced leadership development in their career, they had to get reacquainted with their current developmental needs. So, my team introduced an industry-leading, competency-based 360-degree assessment instrument that could also serve as a framework to help leaders align around a common competency language and leadership practice. The CEO tested out the assessment with his executive coach, working through the framework for six months. This experience convinced him of the framework's ability to help increase his awareness and choices of leadership behaviors. He then asked each member of the executive team to take the 360-degree assessment and spend the next year working with an executive coach.

The executive team also met for a series of conversations facilitated by the external coaching team. During these sessions, they shared what they had learned so far about their leadership strengths as well as the specific areas for growth they had identified to become better leaders. This developed their comfort and skill of what Bob Anderson and Bill Adams (2019) call "learning out loud." In addition, these sessions brought the executive team much closer together, building stronger trust and relationships among the members.

This experience helped them engage the second principle—*modeling* the development journey. In this case, leaders modeled their learning by sharing their development gaps with their direct reports. Each leader had to consciously practice the emotional intelligence skill of being vulnerable by sharing more of their own life story and how it had influenced their leadership journey. Leaders worked with their coaches to prepare for this step. As each executive team member became more comfortable learning out loud with their business unit leadership teams, they discovered how important owning and modeling their leadership development journey was for strengthening the relationship dynamics with their own teams. For several executives, it led to a measurable positive shift in team morale and performance.

Once they understood what it felt like to *own* and *model* leadership development, the executive team began to explore the meaning of the third principle—*driving* the leadership culture and development agenda. Many senior leaders were familiar with the importance of owning and modeling the leadership culture, but far fewer fully appreciated how critical their role was in defining the leadership culture (and how it is grounded in the company's core values), as well as driving the organization's leadership development agenda. While this company had a leadership culture, it hadn't taken the time to define and articulate it. A well-defined and articulated leadership culture is the anchor for effective leadership and leadership development.

With my facilitation assistance, the executive team began to define the leadership culture they needed to foster before they could scale the leadership mindset and behaviors necessary for growing the company in a healthy and sustainable way. I partnered with the company's HR and L&D teams to undertake a leadership culture assessment using the 360-degree leadership assessment framework as a guide. Armed with qualitative interview data and quantitative survey data, my team helped the executive team to explore the current leadership culture and define the type of culture that could guide a more conscious approach to leadership. This opened up conversations about what was required of the executive leaders to drive the leadership culture and development agenda they envisioned.

At this point, the executive team could fully understand and embrace the first and most important principle in a leader-led development culture: The senior-most leaders in a company must practice the idea of *Own+Model+Drive* in the leadership culture and development agenda. This means they must own and be responsible for setting the tone and expectations that shape the leadership culture's mindset and behaviors. By drive, I mean ensuring that the company's rationale, expectations, and approach to developing people are understood and embraced by everyone in the company. Driving the culture and development agenda is the job of the CEO and each member of the executive leadership team. The *Own+Model+Drive* concept not only resonated with senior leaders, but it became a mantra that was easy for them to remember and use for themselves and with their teams.

Leveraging the Other Elements

The other four elements I mentioned don't need to be done in a linear fashion. This company already had a fairly well-aligned business and people strategy but needed a more integrated development approach for senior-level leaders. Rather than just delegating the job to the HR and L&D teams, the executive team took a collaborative approach. They kicked off the initiative by holding a strategic off-site meeting with the company's senior leaders, which allowed them to talk candidly about their leadership challenges and development needs. Together, they identified an action plan to refine and define a clear capabilities and competency framework for senior leaders, embed use of competencies in day-to-day leadership efforts, support leaders in executing the competencies, strengthen peer-to-peer and experiential learning opportunities, and clarify performance, rewards, and incentives to better balance technical and functional financial performance with rewarding broader leadership capabilities.

During the next two years, executive and senior leaders, supported by the HR and L&D teams and external consultants, held a series of meetings in which they carefully discussed the framework of leadership principles, capabilities, and incentives. The result was a playbook clearly defining values-based leadership and principles that would give clear guidance on how to embody the company's values in the way they lead. It also outlined principles to clarify and support their learning culture and defined the relevance of their leadership capabilities

Figure 14-1. Conscious Development Employee Life Cycle Model

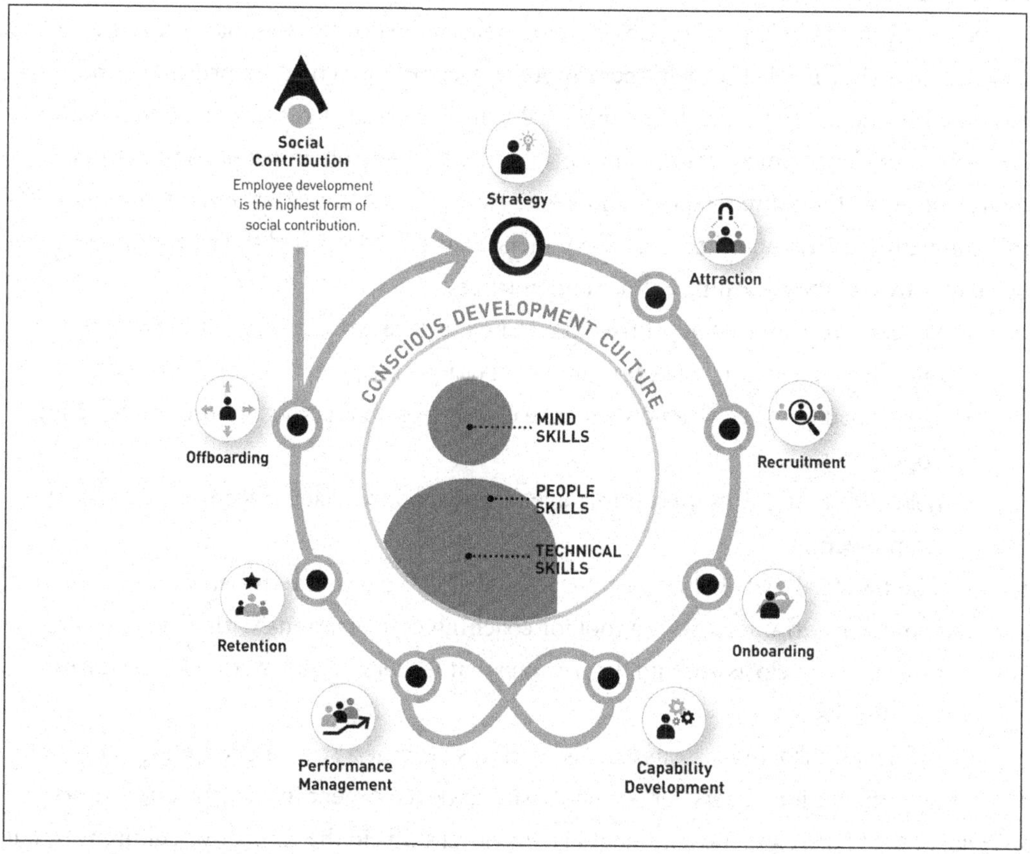

Offterdinger and Allen (2021).

and competencies model to the business. The playbook also better defined and connected leadership competencies and behaviors to the company's business key performance indicators (KPIs) and rewards and incentives.

Creating a development strategy with a foundation of clearly articulated principles, capabilities, and competencies, allowed the leaders to better leverage the employee life cycle to embed leadership culture and development messages and practices. Figure 14-1 presents a holistic view of the employee life cycle model, which the team leveraged to foster a conscious development culture for success and contribution. This, in turn, inspired the talent acquisition team to look at how they could integrate values-based leadership principles into their interview and selection process for hiring senior-level candidates. They ended up with a more rigorous and collaborative interview process and interview tools that significantly reduced bias and risk in hiring candidates for senior-level leadership positions.

When it came to better integrating development in the flow of everyday work, the leaders had the tools they needed to help them more consciously practice the principles and capabilities with one another and their functional teams. Each leader had to embrace and own not only their development journey but play a more direct role in supporting the development journey of their direct reports and peers. Here are just some of the activities and shifts this company's leaders and their teams experienced as they deepened their commitment and behaviors around their learning culture and practices:

- Leaders were given a lot of freedom to be creative and experiment in ways to integrate leadership development conversations into meetings and routines.
- Teams had to adjust to a new practice of using team meetings to process learning opportunities.
- Leaders had to get more comfortable talking explicitly about leadership skills in team meetings.
- The L&D partners helped business unit teams learn to use the leadership competency framework as a tool for coaching conversations with direct reports, as well as to help assess and determine what leadership moves to take to address business issues.
- Informally sharing lessons learned and tips became a source of ongoing support to help the senior leaders get better at leading development in their business units.

One of the biggest and most influential behavioral shifts in the company's culture was that leaders got more comfortable openly and directly challenging one another's perspectives and discussing hard-to-face business issues in group settings. In a company that valued caring for people and being nice to one another, this was a very noticeable and sometimes uncomfortable behavior change. But leaders found that they could work through issues faster because, with more trust between them, they could be direct, honest, and open about one another's ideas and perspectives.

This company is still very much in the process of transforming the way it thinks about and approaches leadership development as a more holistic, leader-led, and collaborative experience. It truly is a journey that requires focus, commitment, practice, and patience from its leaders. The company is fortunate to have a CEO who is open and committed to moving the leadership teams in this direction. It also has HR and L&D teams that are open and willing to step into the role of support partner to assist senior leaders in shifting their mindsets and behaviors to integrate development principles and practices into the culture and daily flow of the business.

Summary

It is an exciting time to be in the L&D and OD professions. L&D professionals are continuing to take on a more strategic and consultative role to support leaders as they transition their companies toward a more holistic and integrated approach to people development. OD approaches and practices are essential tools that enable L&D professionals to help their organizations build leadership and people capabilities for success and contribution.

Key Takeaways

Here are a few things to remember about taking a holistic approach to developing soft skills:

- **In an organizational environment, effective and sustainable leader soft skill development requires a far more holistic and systemic approach** than the traditional content and delivery focus of many leadership training programs.
- **Companies need a common way to identify which soft skills are important for enabling the business.** You can use a core capabilities model to work with leaders to group skills into mind, people, and technical categories, as shared in this chapter.
- **Companies might be unsure of how to develop soft skills in an organizational environment. You can help them see that soft skills are grown over time,** with practice and with other people. Soft skills development

also needs to happen horizontally (through adding more skills) and vertically (through advancing their thinking). And don't forget that ego, fear, and complacency can get in the way of learning and performing soft skills.

- **Help leaders understand the role of leadership within the organization.** Then you can help them align business and people development strategies, identify core people capabilities, define principles to guide development culture, and embed development messages and practices in the employee life cycle.

- **The role of L&D professionals, whether internal or external, needs to shift from the traditional focus of content delivery to an OD focus** on enabling a leader-led development culture. This means becoming a trusted support partner to business leaders to help them own, model, and drive the integration of a development mindset and practices into the company's systems and regular workplace rhythms and routines.

Tool 14-1. Core Capabilities Model

Mind Skills

- **Executive function skills:** The brain-based skills enabling focus, organizing and planning, and understanding different points of view
- **Growth mindset:** Belief that most basic abilities can be learned through dedication and hard work
- **Adaptability:** Capacity to reflect dynamically amid a constantly shifting work landscape
- **Critical thinking:** The objective analysis and evaluation of an issue in order to form a judgment
- **Curiosity:** Desire to learn, know, and understand; fueled by inquisitiveness
- **Creative thinking:** The process of generating new and imaginative ideas and solutions; happens best in psychologically safe environments, which enable inspiration or innovation
- **Decision making:** Ability to make quality decisions in a timely manner, taking into consideration uncertainty and the possibility of not having complete information

People Skills

- **Emotional intelligence:** Ability to manage one's emotions in the workplace, home, and community through self-awareness, self-control, self-motivation, empathy, and compassion
- **Authenticity:** Ability to be true to oneself and relate to others in a genuine, courageous, and high-integrity manner
- **Kindness:** Ability to be gentle or considerate of others; the act of goodwill

- **Balance:** Ability to manage commitments and make trade-offs to keep a healthy balance between business and family, activity and reflection, work and leisure; tendency to be self-renewing and handle the stress of life without losing a sense of self

Communication Skills

- **Active listening:** Fully concentrating on what is being said rather than just passively hearing the message of the speaker; listening with all senses
- **Effective speech:** The ability to verbally advocate, inquire, illustrate, and frame one's thoughts and ideas
- **Effective writing:** The ability to use written words to convey information clearly and persuasively
- **Giving and receiving feedback:** The ability to receive and hear a person's feedback with the intent to improve and achieve
- **Teamwork:** The ability to work cooperatively or collaboratively as part of a group of people acting together as a team or in the interests of a common cause or goal
- **Influencing:** Ability to persuade others and cause desirable and measurable actions and outcomes
- **Resolving conflict:** The ability to reconcile opposing views in a manner that promotes and protects the interests of all concerned parties
- **Leveraging differences:** Ability to appreciate and incorporate diversity of thought, experience, and culture in a way that engages and encourages better collaboration with one another
- **Integrity:** Ability to adhere to a set of values and principles that one espouses; follows through on commitments and leads by example

Technical Skills

- **Domain skills:** Specialized knowledge or ability needed to perform a specific task or function
- **Digital readiness:** The knowledge, skills, and ability to use technology to effectively perform one's job
- **Multidisciplinary skills:** The appreciation for and ability to engage different disciplines and perspectives to solve problems and create new solutions

Building High-Performance Teams

DAVID C. FORMAN

IN THIS CHAPTER

♦ Describe how the world of work continues to adapt and adjust to the economic and social requirements of the times

♦ Discuss the rise of resilient, agile, high-performance teams in the context of a turbulent, interdependent, and uncertain world

♦ Recognize that L&D and OD professionals have vital roles in developing high-performance teams by improving the workplace so the workforce can flourish

"The greatest danger in times of turbulence is not the turbulence. It is to act with yesterday's logic." —Peter Drucker

The world of work is increasingly a team sport. Why? Because many of the current organizational and economic structures that exist today are remnants of previous eras and not designed to take us into the future. Consider three challenges that we all face. First, the pace of change is unrelenting. Stability is an artifact of the past, and turbulence is the new norm. Organizations that are agile and adapt quickly survive and possibly thrive; those that don't, won't. Second, the world is a smaller place; we are not just connected, but interdependent. What happens in one part of the world can no longer be isolated and restricted. The COVID-19 pandemic is a tragic example of how this interdependence affects everyone. And third, given this chaos and upheaval, the future is uncertain. It is not apparent whether the norms, practices, and institutions we value now will exist in several years, let alone the next decade.

In the late 19th to mid-20th century other forces were changing more dramatically. New sources of energy, mechanic automation, and the production line, for example, fundamentally reshaped the world of work. In the mid-19th century more than 70 percent of the US workforce toiled on farms and ranches. A century later, that percentage was in single digits.

The keys to success during this first industrial revolution were economies of scale, effective asset utilization, efficiency, and strict adherence to a defined production process. People, like machines, were a cog in the process. Companies were hierarchical, driven by top-down leadership that wanted to control practices and the workforce.

The large, multilayered organizations (or bureaucracies) that arose during this era have gotten a bad rap, but they served an important purpose. In periods of stability, expansion, and economic growth, the development and wealth they stimulated were unprecedented. They must, however, be viewed as an example of how organizations must adapt to the times—the policies are neither good nor bad but a reflection of the current requirements. And as the economy shifted to value services and information (not just goods and products), these organizations became part of the problem, not the solution.

Gary Hamel and Michele Zanini (2020) have analyzed the initial decades of the 21st century and make a strong case for more agile, adaptive, and resilient organizations. They see bureaucracies and ossified organizations as being incapable of acting with the needed speed and dexterity. A truly resilient organization, they argue, is characterized by:

- Rushing out to meet the future
- Changing before it has to
- Continually redefining customer experiences
- Capturing more than its fair share of opportunities
- Never experiencing an unanticipated earnings shock
- Growing faster than rivals
- Having an advantage in attracting talent

These characteristics set a high bar for future organizations. Increasingly the way ahead is being demonstrated by smaller communities and teams that, when properly constructed, can demonstrate these resilient qualities. In his book, *The Future of Management*, Gary Hamel (2012) recognized this reality when he wrote, "Communities outperform bureaucracies every day of the week." This insight has not been a secret, but businesses can sometimes be slow to react.

When the ADP Research Institute studied work patterns in 19 different countries, it found that 82 percent of work was done in teams. This percentage has doubtlessly grown because of the pandemic and the proliferation of virtual meetings. Teams, therefore, are fully present in today's workplace but often not recognized or appreciated. According to Buckingham and Goodall (2019), "Companies almost universally miss the importance of teams, as evidenced by the fact that most companies don't even know how many teams they have at any one moment and who is on them, let alone which are the best ones—we are functionally blind to teams."

It is time to take the blinders off. First let's discuss the role of the learning and development (L&D) and organization development (OD) functions in furthering these teams, and then we'll look at what the research and leading practices say about the secrets to high-performing teams.

The Role of L&D and OD in Developing High-Performance Teams

As an organizational tool, teams are clearly in the OD realm, but team members must possess the skills and abilities to make successful contributions. This latter requirement is the contribution that L&D makes to team performance. Another way to highlight the different perspectives is that L&D is focused on the *workforce* while OD is centered on the *workplace*. Some background about the history and purpose of both L&D and OD helps explain these differences.

The central purpose of L&D is to improve the knowledge, skills, and performance of people. For decades, L&D was synonymous with formal training, and the dominant teaching method was the trainer in front of the class (or the sage on the stage). As economic requirements shifted, the role of L&D evolved. Formal training became less important, and development relied more on learning from others and engaging in new, challenging experiences. For employees themselves, L&D also became more meaningful as it provided opportunities to gain new experiences (not just knowledge) that were valued in the marketplace. L&D has therefore evolved from a training support function to a strategic capability. But the core aspects of L&D have remained constant: Its focus is on the individual, and its job is to improve a person's knowledge, skills, and performance.

Organization development, as the name implies, is focused on the organization—namely on building strategic alignment, culture, values, high-performance workplaces, resilient organizational structures, and organizational learning; navigating change; and driving business outcomes. Introduced in 1946 by Kurt Lewin, the discipline of organization development was mainly focused on larger organizations that were characteristic of the time. It wasn't until the late 20th century that work teams started to be recognized as major drivers of productivity.

L&D and OD have the greatest impact when they are synchronized and symbiotic. The workforce and workplace are inextricably linked and one without the other is useless. Increasingly, the best results are achieved by "improving the workplace so the workforce can flourish" (Forman 2015). Even the best talent will fade in an alien organizational context, just like a beautiful flower will wither in a barren garden.

Dave Ulrich (2017) published research in *Victory Through Organization* that spoke to this very issue. He found that focusing on improving organizational capabilities and strengthening how people worked together led to a return that was four times greater than just developing individual talent. Improving individual talent is important, but it's no longer sufficient on its own. Greater performance and return can be achieved by improving the workplace so the workforce can realize its potential.

Characteristics of High-Performing Teams

> "Not finance. Not strategy. Not technology. It is teamwork that remains the ultimate competitive advantage, both because it is so powerful and rare." —Patrick Lencioni (2002)

There is a fluidity, harmony, and magic to successful teams that goes way beyond the sum of their parts. We have all been on teams—whether in sports, orchestras, dramatic productions, or community activities—and when they work well, it is memorable. Unfortunately, most teams do not work well. So, what's the secret? Is there a right equation that fits all situations? No. But there are several elements that every great team has. Let's look at them now.

Principles of Effective Teams

Remember when we used to pick teams on the playground? We all lined up, the captains quickly chose members, and off we went to play the game of the day. We were on a team, but we weren't a team. A team is much more than a collection of individuals. What makes a true team is the strength and meaning of the connections, the ability to work together, and the desire to reach a common goal.

Great teams exemplify three principles. If you have these principles, there is an opportunity to achieve success. If you don't, you won't. It's just that simple.

- **Trust.** All great teams have team members that trust one another. If not, the team can quickly dissolve into competing factions or, worse yet, silent acquiescence. Most measures of trust include indicators such as communicating honestly, keeping the best interest of others in mind, respecting the contributions of each person, following through on commitments, and openly admitting mistakes. An interesting fact is that when trusting relationships exist, our bodies produce more of the hormone oxytocin, which triggers a reciprocal act (Zak 2017). In other words, trust begets more trust.

- **Collaboration.** It is not enough for team members to be connected; they must function together effectively. Open and honest communications must occur, and the team must become a smooth, functioning unit that builds on the work and accomplishments of its members equally. Teammates must work together, share perspectives, and learn from one another.

- **Commitment.** Teams exist for a purpose: A problem needs to be solved, new products released, bureaucratic barriers eased, supply chains smoothed out, a competition to be won, costs reduced, or new opportunities explored. In effective teams, team members are committed to this purpose and, even more significantly, are committed to holding one another accountable for results. The power of colleagues committing to one another is arguably the strongest motivator. Accountability is a characteristic of all high-performing organizations.

In *The Fearless Organization*, Amy Edmondson (2018) explains that psychological safety creates a safe zone of contribution in communities and teams, in which people can be heard equally, feel respected, take risks, and be honest with one another. Sharing and collaboration takes place in this trust-enriched environment. Two measures of psychological safety are conversational turn taking (so no one person dominates) and high social sensitivity (recognizing verbal and nonverbal cues). Psychological safety is an important foundation for the three principles of team trust, collaboration, and commitment.

Skills of High-Performing Teams

Organizations can build on these three principles and psychological safety to foster high-performance teams. Their experiences and lessons vary based on their challenges, competitive environments, and context, but the common skills are apparent.

Google

When Google studied the characteristics of its high-performing teams, it dubbed the study Project Aristotle in honor of his statement that "the whole is greater than the sum of its parts." In the study, Google analyzed 180 teams and conducted hundreds of double-blind interviews. Many people, including Google's leaders, thought that this study would reveal that the key to a successful team was for it to have as many smart people as possible. However, it turned out that the search for these qualities was illusive. It wasn't until the research team came across the work of Amy Edmondson that the data began to reveal itself. Psychological safety was the key.

Project Aristotle also revealed what was not connected to team performance: The performance level of individuals did not matter, nor did team size, extroversion of team members, co-location, tenure, or team size. It was much less about who was on the team than how the team operated. Specifically, Google found that its high-performing teams exhibited the following characteristics:

- **Psychological safety.** A shared belief that the team is safe for personal risk taking.
- **Dependability.** When teammates say they'll do something, they do it.
- **Structure and clarity.** The team's plans and goals are clearly understood.
- **Meaning.** The work is personally meaningful to team members.
- **Impact.** The work matters.

Haier

Haier is a world leader in household appliances. Based in Qingdao, China, it has more than 84,000 employees, revenues greater than $38 billion, and competes against such world-class companies as LG, Whirlpool, and Electrolux. The margins in a very competitive, mature marketplace (such as household appliances) are usually extremely small, but Haier has grown by more than 22 percent a year for a decade. How can this be true? We have already discussed how big companies are slow to adapt and adjust.

The answer is to make big, small. Haier has divided itself into more than 4,000 micro-enterprises (MEs) composed of 10 to 15 employees each. The MEs are further divided into subgroups—market-facing legacy teams, incubator teams that form startups, and node MEs that sell services and components to other MEs. While MEs are free to form and dissolve with little central direction, they must conform to the following core principles:

- Turn every employee into an entrepreneur.
- Create zero distance between the employees and customers. Everyone reports to the customer, and customers are involved throughout the team's activities.
- Establish platforms to expand ecosystems to include services, customization, and new revenue streams.
- Adopt aggressive leading targets, such as external market goals that are four to 10 times the industry average.
- Stay market-driven, adaptable, agile, interdisciplinary, self-governing, and highly accountable.

Cisco

Cisco also undertook an analysis of its best teams, tapping Marcus Buckingham and Ashley Goodall to consult. They built on the foundation of the Gallup engagement and employee experience surveys, noting that "at Cisco, the best teams harness individual excellence of each team member, unlock the collective excellence of the team, and do so in an environment of safety and trust" (Buckingham and Goodale 2019).

In their research, Buckingham and Goodall were able to identify the employee experience that existed on high-performing teams, as rated by team members. Eight items emerged that can be grouped into two categories—the best of me and the best of we. Both are necessary for people to flourish and teams to excel (Table 15-1).

Table 15-1. Items that Characterize High-Performing Teams

The Best of Me	The Best of We
• At work, I clearly understand what is expected of me. • I have a chance to use my strengths every day at work. • I know I will be recognized for excellent work. • In my work, I am always challenged to grow.	• I am really enthusiastic about the mission of my company. • In my team, I am surrounded by people who share my values. • My teammates have my back. • I have great confidence in my company's future.

Team Meta Skills

The previous discussion highlighted the principles and skills that are important for teams to be successful in different contexts. There is, however, another set of skills that is important to possess in times of accelerating change, growing connectedness, and uncertain futures. These higher-level, meta skills influence the team's ability to learn new knowledge and skills quickly and apply them in a turbulent world. If teams don't adapt quickly, they will end up addressing yesterday's issues. Teams must look to the horizon if they are to be proactive, adaptive, and responsive.

In *Fearless Talent Choices* (2020), I outline seven learning skills for the future. These meta skills are vital to not just survive but thrive in a time that has decimated predictability:

- **Gritty learning mindset.** Embrace learning as an ongoing responsibility. Enjoy the activity of learning.
- **Learning velocity.** Get up to speed quickly.
- **Curiosity.** Ask good questions; challenge conventions.
- **Anticipating change.** Think about what might happen and get out in front of change.
- **Resilience.** Get back in the game quickly after being disappointed.
- **Influencing others.** Attune to the needs of others and influence them to change.
- **Systems thinking.** See the bigger picture and how all the pieces fit together.

L&D and OD Initiatives for Improving Team Skills

The principles, skills, and meta skills that are characteristic of high-performing teams can all be further developed and practiced. Team members need to be skilled in psychological safety, building trust, effective team dynamics, patterns of collaboration, and achieving business outcomes, as well as the meta skills that prepare teams for uncertain futures.

The best way to sharpen these skills is not through formal, structured classroom or asynchronous training. Rather, it is best provided by developmental activities that present challenging new experiences, coaching, colleague interactions, immersion techniques, and accountability to teammates. It is not about telling people what to do; it is about enabling them to experience the needs and consequences themselves. This is especially true when so many of the needed skills are not technical in nature but pertain more to relationships, meaning, context, mindsets, and psychological strength.

Here are several practical examples of L&D developmental initiatives:

- Have team members come up with two possible future scenarios that could influence the business and three skills that need to be improved to be able to address these scenarios now.
- Split team members into groups of three, and have them anticipate problems that may arise on the team (or with a new strategy or approach) and identify how to overcome them.
- Have team members discuss the most and least trusting teams they have been on and try to discern the reasons.
- Join with other teams to analyze how one team's work dovetails with another.

A Real-World Example

One of the most dramatic examples of a team that was hugely affected by a developmental initiative was not from the world of work but from sport. Volleyball was first played in Holyoke, Massachusetts, in 1896, just eight miles from where basketball was similarly invented. Because it was simpler and easier to implement than basketball, volleyball immediately spread globally, becoming hugely popular in Eastern Europe, the Far East, and South America. In the US, however, it took more than 50 years for the sport to take hold, and that was largely on the beaches of Southern California or in YMCAs in the Midwest.

Through the 1970s, the US had never won a major international competition in this sport that it had created. The reason? Other countries had better systems, resources, commitment, and teams. The individual volleyball talent in the US was as good as or better than the rest of the world, but it was inconsistent and teamwork broke down under duress. This pattern continued until a group of people decided to make changes in preparation for the 1984 Olympics in Los Angeles, California (Murray 2022).

US volleyball's problems were characteristic of many teams: too many cliques, big egos, not enough communication and transparency, lack of trust, wavering commitment, varied goals, and sporadic teamwork. The coaches recognized these issues and continued to talk about them, but the team wasn't embracing their message. The players thought things were good enough and didn't want to rock the boat.

So, the coaches decided to rock the boat for them. The best volleyball players in the United States and their coaches were sent to the remote wilderness of Utah in the dead of winter to spend two weeks in an Outward Bound program. This highly meaningful shared experience took the team out of its comfort zone and put stars, subs, and coaches on equal footing. Through rope lifts, rock climbing, and blind navigational exercises with maps and compasses, teammates were put into situations in which they had to trust and learn from one another. Not to mention learning how to keep warm in 15-degree temperatures and reduced oxygen at 10,000 feet above sea level. Over the two weeks, barriers came down providing platforms for open and honest sharing of opinions and views. The team learned to trust one another and work together.

The result? A whole new style of play emerged to fit the players' strengths, a gold medal was won, and the sport of volleyball was never quite the same.

This case, of course, is a bit unusual, but it does illustrate the key principles of great teams, the importance of psychological, collaborative, and relationship strengths—not just physical skills—in achieving a team's potential, and the importance of choosing the right type of L&D initiative to help players experience a compelling need to change and grow. These lessons were not new, but they needed to be experienced by this team, at this time, for this purpose.

> "If you tell me, I will listen
> If you show me, I will see
> If you let me experience, I will learn"
> —Lao Tzu, ancient Chinese proverb

There are organizational initiatives that also facilitate stronger team performance. In the example of US volleyball, the team did not have the resources, dedication, commitment, culture, or aligned leadership to allow the players to excel. Once the US committed to providing full-time training facilities, using sports psychologists, arranging jobs for players, embracing a culture that valued teamwork above individual performance, and aligning leadership to team goals, the players could flourish.

Improving Workplace Teams

It is also useful to remember that team magic doesn't just happen automatically. Teams have to go through a process before they can function smoothly. Bruce Tuckman (1965) defined four stages of team development—forming, storming, norming, and performing—later adding a fifth stage, adjourning. The actual time it takes to go through these stages can range from days to four to six months, depending on a variety of factors including the context and dimensions of the gap between actual and desired team performance. Specific programs can be crafted to help teams get through each stage more expeditiously, but the passage of time is also an important factor—some experiences cannot be rushed. There is no way, for example, that the US volleyball team's transition could have been achieved in several days. The challenges and hardships had to be experienced and earned.

The pandemic has clearly influenced team activities. The rise of virtual teams presents its own challenges because it is more difficult to develop trust, commitment, and team work remotely. It can be done, but it needs to be done differently than when body language can be observed, informal conversations can be held, and adjustments can be made quickly. In virtual contexts it is even more important to be clear about goals, have frequent check-ins, be coaches for each other, and be as transparent as possible. If possible, there is great advantage in having virtual teams meet face-to-face, even briefly. Once personal relationships are established (typically in the team forming stage), virtual communication functions much more smoothly.

Another option is to be intentional about the roles that team members play. This step is taken to counteract biases, conformity, and groupthink as well as to ensure as complete an analysis as possible. This also focuses team member contributions so that they don't feel like they have to try to be or do everything. These roles have a direct bearing on the recruiting and selection of team members as well as on L&D developmental initiatives to expand these strengths. Dating back to Raymond Belbin's work in the 1980s, this approach has helped teams be successful in many different situations. Michael Fishbein (2014) outlined seven different types of roles that can make important contributions to a fully functioning team:

- **Connectors** have strong personal networks and enhance visibility.
- **Experts** enhance credibility and depth.
- **Visionaries** see around corners.
- **Rising stars** are more likely to be innovative and forward-looking.
- **Peers** are more likely to be reality based.
- **Realists** are not swayed by hype or rhetoric.
- **Outliers** challenge standard practices.

The Report Card: Organizational Outcomes and Accountability

Business leaders at all levels must focus on results and outcomes. If they don't, they won't be leaders much longer. As Dave Ulrich has said, the purpose of HR (to whom both L&D and OD usually report) is not human resources; it is to drive business results. Teams exist for a purpose, this purpose should yield results that are monitored, and team members should be accountable for those results.

One useful way to demonstrate business outcomes and results for a team project is to demonstrate the time savings of the proposed solution. Many team projects should result in time savings, such as work being done faster, more efficiently, and with leaner resources. It is not difficult to then turn time savings into money savings.

If, for example, a team was able to reduce the time it takes to bring a product to market by four days (and 5,000 products were produced in a year), this time savings would result in a savings of more than $8 million (using the rates for a $100,000 fully burdened salary; Table 15-2). Are you surprised? The money adds up very quickly and is a powerful statement to fellow business leaders.

Table 15-2. Weekly, Daily, and Hourly Compensation by Salary Level

Burdened Salary	Weekly	Daily	Hourly
$100K	$2,083	$416	$52
$125K	$2,604	$520	$65
$150K	$3,125	$624	$78
$200K	$4,167	$832	$104

Let's examine another example of the impact of stating results in money using the case of unwanted turnover of capable employees. There are at least two ways to report turnover data:

- Our turnover rate is 15 percent (which is about the norm for large organizations).
- The cost to the organization of losing a quality engineer is $215,000 per person.

Which version do you think is more likely to garner the attention of team and business leaders? Money talks and people listen.

There are at least five ways in which teams can drive business results and they all should be monetized whenever possible (Forman 2020). When business results are specific and monetized, they gain visibility and credibility throughout the organization. Let's look at some examples for each of the five business outcomes.

Optimizing Talent

Are we leveraging the talent in the organization effectively? This parameter should be true wherever people are expected to perform, whether on athletic teams, dramatic productions, orchestras, or business endeavors. There needs to be an extraordinarily strong fit between what is required for success and the talent deployed. If not, individuals and organizations both suffer. OD practitioners should seek to remove barriers so that people can be on the teams they want to be on. Open talent marketplaces enable individuals to make their own choices, which means they will be more likely to stay committed and, data shows, get up to speed faster and more efficiently than people appointed otherwise. In fact, people who self-select become ready 25 to 33 percent faster than their appointed colleagues (Forman 2020). These time savings can be easily monetized.

Cost Savings

It is important to streamline processes so that waste, inefficiencies, old practices, and extra costs are identified and eliminated. Because cost savings hit the bottom line quickly, they are spotlighted by executives. Cost savings are usually the easiest business impact to monetize.

A core principle of high-performing teams is that they operate with high trust. Stephen Covey (2006) studied the business impact of trust and found that higher trust brings faster decisions and lower costs. This leads to what he calls a "trust dividend," which can be two to three times the cost of doing business. It takes longer to do things if there are needless safeguards built in. Too many layers slow down decisions, limit responsiveness, and hamper agility.

Productivity Improvements

Productivity pertains to doing the same or better work, faster. It's an efficiency measure that can be affected by automation, intelligent technology, smarter and more committed employees, informed practices, and better methods. A key workforce factor is how quickly employees become proficient, especially in such a rapidly changing world.

Engaged teams are more productive than teams that are not so committed. Gallup's research has clearly demonstrated the relationship of engagement to the level of productivity.

On a four-point engagement scale in which being engaged is level 3, productivity increases or decreases by 20 percent per level. This data can be monetized by ascertaining a team's engagement level through a survey, using salary as a proxy measure for productivity, and then multiplying the number of team members by average salary.

Better Outcomes

This outcome pertains to improving business performance in such areas as revenue, profit, innovative new products, product quality, brand credibility, supply chain effectiveness, quality of new customers, and faster time to market. The vitality index is a measure of the creative capacity and market execution of teams and the organization in general. It measures the amount of revenue generated from new products in N (usually two or three) prior years. The number of prior years is dependent on the life cycle and time to market for the product.

This measure is significant because many organizations rely on legacy products for the majority of their revenue. However, this is not sustainable over time. If, for example, at least 25 percent of yearly revenue does not come from new products, the organization's future may be in doubt.

Leveraging Communities, Resources, and One Another

One of the great frustrations of leaders is that organizations rarely learn from past mistakes and are less than the sum of their very capable parts. Leaders yearn for a company where the genius happens among people and social capital becomes a vital competitive advantage. When trust, collaboration, and commitment occur in a team, the power of professional networks becomes apparent. People with robust and extensive professional networks are 25 percent more productive than people who do not have these connections (Forman 2020).

Summary

As we have seen, the world changes in a blink of an eye. Just think about the disruptive external forces that might have occurred over the past several months, let alone before the COVID-19 pandemic. Large organizations, however, are slow to adapt to these changes because they're designed to protect themselves from risk and preserve the status quo. But small, focused communities of people and teams have the potential to be different. When properly constituted, teams can change as fast as the world around them and stay resilient. L&D and OD play vital roles in developing high-performance teams by improving the workplace so the workforce can flourish.

Key Takeaways

Here are a few things to remember about developing high-performance teams:

- **Work is now increasingly a team sport,** especially in a world characterized by unrelenting change, growing interdependence, and uncertain futures. Organizations that respond and adapt to these challenges will be successful; those that don't, won't.
- **The greatest chance for success today is for small, agile, flexible teams** that are focused on purpose, represent diverse communities, demonstrate effective team practices, and are self-forming and self-governing.
- **Teams don't just magically happen.** They must be built on the foundation of trust, collaboration, and commitment. Upon these foundations, effective team practices can emerge and flourish.
- **Teams are formed for a purpose** and will be judged by achieving outcomes and improving the organization in measurable ways. Results and business outcomes matter.

Comprehensive Succession Planning with a Diversity, Equity, and Inclusion (DEI) Lens

MAKIYA MUSGROVE WOODS

IN THIS CHAPTER

♦ Explore the importance of comprehensive and integrated succession planning efforts to ensure sustainability

♦ Establish a strong infrastructure for succession planning that is linked to DEI strategy

♦ Broaden the identification and assessment of succession candidates can lead to more differentiated development plans

The future of work is causing many in the L&D field to pivot and reshape their approaches to developing talent in their organizations to meet the pressing needs of today, while keeping a clear view on the needs of tomorrow. This evaluation has signaled a need for something different than what's been done in the past for several reasons—associates' changing desires, organizations' shifting strategies, prevalent and prominent social justice challenges, and, of course, the great reshuffle and resignation. This presents a great moment for those responsible for and tasked with organization development, including L&D professionals who are interested in OD efforts, to think critically about integrating aspects of HR, talent management, and diversity, equity, and inclusion (DEI) to help their associates and organizations thrive.

This is obviously easier said than done. Having had a chance to integrate talent, learning, and DEI in a prior role, I found that traditional L&D professionals were only starting to extend their learning efforts beyond the classroom to focus on development that happens on the job. For example, the L&D team hadn't considered including succession planning—the focus of this chapter—in their learning strategy. In many cases, they did not have visibility to the process. That's changing.

Succession planning has evolved over the years as organizational talent agendas have shifted. Historically focused on ensuring business continuity through talent readiness for the most senior roles in the organization, the succession planning process has shifted in terms of the depth and breadth of focus. Many organizations are now actively succession planning for director and vice president roles in addition to those in the C-suite. This deepening of succession planning efforts has prompted a need to focus on identifying talent earlier in their careers with the potential to take on these roles. The pool is also broadening—organizations are looking internally and externally to build this talent pipeline. This shift in the process requires a fresh look at the talent management practices feeding the succession planning process, such as talent development.

L&D and OD practitioners can play an important role in the comprehensive succession planning process. Ensuring this change requires leveraging key skill sets including change expert, strategic leadership and planning, business acumen, emotional intelligence, and collaboration. In this chapter, I'll guide you through a process to bring these capabilities to life to design or enhance a comprehensive and future-oriented succession planning approach. Whether you are a seasoned OD practitioner looking to broaden your skill set or an L&D professional currently focused on creating learning and onboarding programs, I'll share a plan for getting started that's designed to encourage different thinking about how to approach succession planning with a DEI lens. But first, let's dive deeper into the rising importance of succession planning.

The Importance of Succession Planning

Ensuring the continuity of critical leadership positions has long been a focus of organizations, and this became even more prominent as the nature of work changed in several ways in the years following the COVID-19 pandemic and the Great Resignation. According to ZipRecruiter, there were 40,000 active C-Suite level job openings across the network in October 2021, which is twice as many as before the pandemic (White 2022). Beyond that, companies are also finding it hard to fill roles at every level. The Bureau of Labor Statistics (BLS) reported in April 2022 that the US had 11.4 million job openings (BLS 2022). This extreme need to find talent at all levels underscores the importance of comprehensive succession planning that reaches deeper in the organization. While senior leader succession planning is often owned by senior leadership and HR teams, organizations should continue to broaden their succession planning efforts to include critical roles at multiple levels in the organization.

In addition to ensuring continuity for critical positions, modern organizations are also working to diversify their most senior leadership teams as part of their DEI strategy. Because diverse talent tends attract diverse talent—and play a critical role in retaining and developing that talent—achieving sustainable success with DEI starts with incorporating more diversity in the most senior ranks. This is an extremely important nuance that can get lost. While we've realized the importance of diversity of thought on innovation and growth, it's important to note that the organizational culture needs to allow people to safely share those thoughts. Many organizations are focused on helping leaders become more inclusive to combat this, and rightly so, but they are often starting from a diversity representation deficit. Leadership diversity can help fill in the gap.

As important as DEI has become, HR and talent leaders responsible for succession planning may not think about how to ensure leadership diversity and process equity when creating or revamping their succession planning processes. More organizations are adding chief diversity officers—senior leaders who think more holistically at about extending a DEI strategy to all levels in the organization. For example, they can leverage L&D's expertise to embed opportunities to practice and learn about inclusive behaviors into all learning initiatives while leaning on OD's role in supporting organizations to achieve their goals through sustainable change efforts.

Going forward, organizations should focus their succession planning efforts on preparing for critical roles while also ensuring their leadership has the necessary diversity to innovate and grow the businesses. The path to success in this endeavor will require focus in two important areas: Establishing or enhancing a strong infrastructure for succession planning, and ensuring a broad and unbiased assessment of all talent development plans.

Establishing or Enhancing a Strong Infrastructure

Whether you are starting a new succession planning program or introducing a focus on leadership diversity to your current program, both require a change in process, thinking, and behaviors. In many ways, this requires a large-scale OD and change effort and L&D professionals can and should leverage their diagnostic skills to understand the current state as an initial step. This will help you identify and articulate the vital importance of leadership diversity in succession planning.

Assess the Current State

You can begin your diagnostic journey by looking at what metrics your organization might use to evaluate their succession planning efforts. Unfortunately, a 2022 ATD study found that only 28 percent of respondents measured the effectiveness of their succession planning efforts with internal candidates. While these organizations were significantly more likely to be high performers, the fact that less than a third measured the effectiveness is a challenge that good diagnostic work can help solve. If the organization has identified metrics for succession planning, reviewing those will be an initial step. If no metrics have been identified this is a great opportunity to use your L&D skills, think from the end, and establish metrics based on the pain points identified in the diagnostic phase.

Start by talking to those who create the process (HR or talent management), drive the process (leaders), and benefit from the process (recent successors), as well as those you want to include in the process (diverse talent). Because transparency about the succession planning process is not standard practice in many organizations, attempting to diagnose the formal process may prove challenging. Leaders will be more likely to associate succession planning with the pain points they've experienced, such as extended time to fill critical roles, poor transitions into more senior roles, surprise loss of top talent, and lack of an internal, diverse bench to fill roles. Meanwhile, associates can help you understand where the process currently stands by sharing their own pain points, which may include a desire for more career development conversations with leaders, missed opportunities to take on new assignments, few development opportunities, and an overall lack of visibility into talent processes. Listening to key stakeholders will also help you gather powerful insight into any potential lagging indicators of the pain points including regrettable attrition, team instability, lack of engagement, short length of time in top talent roles, and lack of accountability or follow through.

One other note to make on listening during the diagnostic phase: It may be tempting to try to learn from all associates at once in a listening session or group discussion, but this will likely skew the results. Remember, the experiences of diverse talent may be different and conversations with those groups may require a deeper level of listening. In addition, I've seen how the dynamics shift if a group includes a cross section of individuals at different hierarchical levels (such as a leader with individual contributors)—people tend to fall in line with the person in the room who holds the most power. I have found a similar dynamic shift when doing listening sessions with a cross section of majority and underrepresented individuals. Power dynamics are at play in both settings, and while it may take and enhanced level of facilitation and a bit more time, you'll be better able to truly understand their experiences if you speak with like groups.

Link Succession Planning and Your DEI Strategy

As organizations shift their succession planning focus to leadership diversity, it is critically important to understand where the organization is on its DEI journey. This will be different for each, but here are a few critical questions you can ask to aid your understanding:

1. **Is there a balanced focus on external efforts and workplace diversity?** The last few years have seen an increased public focus on DEI efforts organizations are doing in the community. However, it's important to ensure the organization is taking a balanced approach of external community efforts and remaining committed to fostering an internal diverse workforce as you focus a DEI lens on succession planning. This organizational alignment between words and actions is becoming an increasingly important part of the employee brand promise.

2. **Is DEI connected to the talent strategy?** This question is helpful to understand if the organization has articulated its "why" for a more diverse, equitable, and inclusive workplace. If there is a connection between DEI and the talent strategy, you'll see more organizational buy-in to intentionally focus on leadership diversity. If that connection is missing, more work will be required to ensure your efforts for leadership diversity are not seen as less important.

3. **Has the organization established representation goals?** If the organization has publicly declared representation goals, the natural next step is to extend this effort to leadership development and succession planning.

4. **Are employee resource group (ERG) leaders considered to be part of the pool of top, diverse talent?** Asking this seemingly disconnected question helps

you understand whether there's a true connection between DEI strategy and succession planning. ERGs are typically grassroots groups designed to create safe spaces for underrepresented talent within an organization; many support their external communities as well. They are an important tool for advancing DEI goals, and ERG leaders should be an equally important part of the broader talent strategy. Their efforts require leadership skills such as strategic planning and influencing without authority. When their work is connected to the business, ERG leaders can and should provide a pool of diverse talent ready to be tapped as successors.

5. **Is inclusion part of the leadership profile and is the organization modeling and fostering accountability for demonstrating inclusive behaviors?** The demographics of the workforce are changing rapidly—by gender, generation, ethnicity, and a host of other unseen diversity dimensions. Leaders will require new leadership skills and as we plan for successors it's increasingly important to ensure we are equipping them with the tools they need to collectively lead their businesses and teams.

These questions will be critical to ensuring buy in and ultimately the sustainability of a more comprehensive succession planning program.

When the goal of increased diversity and representation is clearly and frequently communicated from senior leadership it's much easier to gain buy in from all involved in the process. I experienced this firsthand as the talent partner for senior executives. During our early discussions about the importance of diversity, no one questioned it or their desire to do things differently. The bigger concern was how we could do it with the leaders already in place. Because our diversity strategy was embedded in our talent strategy, we were able to anchor our messaging in the change to the talent strategy, which included a focus on lateral versus vertical moves to broaden the experience of leaders slated for critical roles. We also knew that it was important to start at the top (with the most senior executive leadership team) to model the right behaviors.

The effort to diversify the executive leadership team was surgical and well planned. Our strategy included a mix of organization design, lateral moves at a level more senior than we had done before, and a rigorous executive search in which we told the recruiters we were looking specifically for diverse talent. We weren't able to pull through diverse internal talent to take on the senior roles because we had a very sparse pipeline, which is a problem for many organizations. While a lack of internal successors was only cited by 18 percent of respondents to a recent ATD study as a key challenge in succession planning efforts, adding the dimension of diverse internal successors will likely shift those results.

Identify What Leadership Behaviors Your Organization Needs

Furthermore, a commitment to more diverse representation in leadership and a robust succession pipeline should also signal a commitment to more inclusive leadership behaviors. An ATD 2022 research report found that 70 percent of organizations' succession plans included positions at the vice president level, 67 percent were at the director level, and 62 percent were for C-suite positions other than the CEO. It is becoming increasingly important to prepare potential leaders to take on these roles in a more modern way for a more modern workforce. With this knowledge at the forefront, organizations will need to think beyond the technical capabilities required for their most critical roles. While leadership qualities—such as leading change courageously, nurturing all talent, and harnessing differences for impact—may have been articulated in the past, their renewed importance will require a refresh and stronger accountability.

As L&D professionals form strategic and collaborative partnerships with the OD or HR leader currently in charge of the process, they will be able to draw on their diagnostic and change management skills to support the successful roll out of these new leadership behaviors. A good start is to understand which behaviors are currently being rewarded, the impact of those behaviors, and if they represent the behaviors the organization will need in the future. You may find that prior experience and technical capabilities are given top priority; if that happens, you'll want to round them out with the softer leadership capabilities necessary for your organization. Reviewing which leaders are being promoted and understanding what sets them apart is an effective way to see which behaviors your organization values—and then use that knowledge to identify which skills succession candidates have strengths in and which they do not. It can be tempting to review the latest leadership development research and use that to choose which leadership capabilities to adopt; however, simplicity will serve organizations most effectively.

If the organization is smaller or doesn't have access to large amounts of data, you can instead draw upon feedback from leaders during the diagnostic phase to help pinpoint the behaviors that helped or hindered an individual's successful transition into a new role. Because there aren't many roles that need a succession plan it's easier to monitor them, so it's advisable to keep an ongoing listening strategy to support continuous improvement of the process.

Prior to introducing a formal new role acceleration process for leaders at an organization, I did some very informal continuous monitoring. I simply checked in with recent transfers at the 30-, 60-, and 90-day mark and asked a standard set of questions to understand how they were approaching their role and their perceived effectiveness. I listened for leadership behaviors versus technical capability to see if their approach in leadership style mattered. At one point, I realized that two of the recent transfers were receiving very different feedback. So, I decided to continue monitoring them beyond the 90-day mark. The first person was new to the leadership position but had been identified as a high potential. The second person was transitioning into this position after leading another business unit. They were both identified as potential successors for the senior leadership team. I asked them questions such as:

- How do you know what's most important in your current role?
- How are you getting access to the unspoken knowledge about the role?
- Do you have the right people on your team to deliver your results (if not, do you have a plan)?
- Is your team engaged and how do you know?
- Have you identified a potential successor on the team?

I used two measurements to evaluate their success in their roles: growth in their business and their team's engagement scores. During my interviews, the behaviors that came out as important were curiosity about process and people, collaboration, shared leadership, and talent and team development. Possibly because she had never held this role before, the first leader showed up as curious and vulnerable enough to ask her team and peers questions, she pulled her full team into decision making, and became known as a leader who could attract top talent internally due to her leadership style. Conversely and likely because the second leader had performed the role before, he spoke more about tried-and-true methods, took a much more hierarchical approach with his team, and struggled to attract internal top talent to his team.

At the end of 18 months, both business units had achieved double digit growth; however, the engagement on the first leader's team was exceedingly higher than that of the second. Eventually the impact of the second leader's team's poor engagement proved disastrous. Both leaders moved on to different roles after two years, and the impact of how the second leader led the team was felt by his replacement. The second leader's lack of curiosity and, frankly, arrogance to maintain his usual approaches instead of having the team help design an effective team structure led to extreme burnout, which ultimately led to a record level of attrition and subsequent business loss. This is not a unique story, but had we not dug deeper to really understand not only the necessary leadership behaviors, but also the business impact of demonstrating them effectively we may not have had the courage to recalibrate the second leader and provide the feedback and support needed to round out his capabilities.

Plan How You Will Onboard Internal and External Successors

When thinking about succession planning, organizations often have to consider whether to build internal successors or bring in external talent. I think both options are valid because they'll both support your longer-term succession planning efforts. And there is much you can learn by observing how external candidates are brought in and onboarded that you can then apply to your internal succession process.

When brining in external successors for senior-level talent, additional care needs to be taken to ensure an effective transition. It's important to consider their entry point, how to effectively onboard them to the culture, and which senior leader they're paired with as a mentor or guide. This becomes even more important when introducing diverse talent into a homogeneous leadership team (such as one that's majority white male).

In a prior experience where we worked to diversify the senior leadership team, we found the most success when the entry point for our external hires was a role where they had a broader vantage point of the business, such as a strategy or a functional role that partnered with multiple business units. We also found success with focused and strategic onboarding. For another external hire, we decided to bring them in at a functional role prior to taking on a business role so that this person could get a well-rounded exposure to every business unit and senior leader at the organization and the challenges they faced. As this individual onboarded to the organization, I (as the talent leader) had to find a mentor to help her acclimate to the culture. Because she was a Black female, the natural suggestion was to pair her with another Black female in the organization. While I agree that it's helpful to have another perspective from someone in the organization who looks like you, in this case I sought to get that for her more informally. As a potential successor starting in a functional role, I selected a White males senior executive to serve as her mentor because he would provide the right level of visibility and support influencing the business. This individual was not the leader of the entire organization, but he had been with the company for a significant amount of time and therefore had a much louder voice in a room full of his peers—he was an excellent influencer. This strategic pairing yielded fantastic results. By working with and learning from her mentor about multiple business units and the culture of the organization, this individual was able to move into a critical roles after only 18 months.

The right infrastructure for comprehensive succession planning includes creating space and formality for effectively onboarding and transitioning the senior leaders who have been selected to be potential successors. Providing a solid onboarding process for senior leaders who are new to the organization as well as a well-planned transition for internal leaders should enable an accelerated path to growth for the business unit. Ensuring this is part of a healthy infrastructure for succession planning can also lead to more performance-based measurements. A 2022 ATD survey found that organizations were most likely to measure the effectiveness of their succession planning efforts by tracking the number of positions filled by succession candidates (76 percent), the number of candidates in the pipeline (58 percent), and retention rates for succession candidates (58 percent). New leader onboarding can be a great place to track these metrics to ensure the process is followed and working as it should. Measuring the early performance of new leaders' businesses and teams during the onboarding window provides another opportunity to determine the effectiveness of your selection process. Again, I believe OD practitioners can help by going deeper to understand the pitfalls for those who have recently transitioned into new roles and designing an onboarding process that aims to mitigate those pain points.

Determine Roles and Ownership of Succession Planning

When establishing or enhancing a succession planning process, understanding key roles and responsibilities will ensure the sustainability of the program. It can be challenging to gain the attention of senior leaders as they tackle multiple challenges to grow their businesses; however, it the effective execution of these discussions will bring talent development's value to the forefront of your leader's agendas. Typically, HR or talent management owns the process, which is helpful because they offer objective and more accurate views of the organization's talent, but I have found that it's more effective if the executive leadership team drives the process with heavy input and coaching from the HR and talent management teams.

Like many HR processes, succession planning is a proactive process that can get lost in the day-to-day challenges that are seemingly more pressing. To combat challenges with early identification of top talent, talent readiness, and overall program management, the frequency and consistency of talent discussions is critical. The current scramble for talent at all levels signals a need to think more broadly about succession planning. As organizations plan for roles deeper into the organization, managers and potentially all talent will be involved in the process by way of proactive career development. Ensuring they have the process knowledge and subsequent development tools will also aid in the success of your efforts. With ownership comes accountability, and having the executive leadership team drive the process will ensure a deeper level of accountability for effectively developing their talent for the enterprise.

Ensuring a Broad Assessment of Talent Development Plans

Effectively assessing whether talent has the potential to take on greater responsibility has long been a subjective process, and it becomes even more so when organizations rely on only one or two methods for assessment. When ATD's 2022 succession planning report asked about the methods organization use to identify potential succession candidates, 73 percent of respondents said they used performance reviews; other popular options were nominations from senior leaders (69 percent) and managers (50 percent). While understanding past performance is a good predictor of future success and senior leader and manager assessments have some level of effectiveness, these methods alone open the door to bias, including the halo effect, like-me bias, and recency bias. A comprehensive succession planning process should be as equitable as possible by incorporating a variety of ways to assess talent, a deeper understanding of which capabilities to assess, and a broader pool of assessors, such as the L&D function.

In some organizations, L&D and OD practitioners have designed initiatives that will help leaders identify skills gaps and then develop those skills. A more integrated approach to succession planning would not only allow these professionals to design more experiential development programs that are connected to business results, but also enable broader talent visibility and assessment deeper in the organization. Leveraging L&D professionals who have visibility to all levels of talent through the people who participate in TD programs could support these efforts.

To mitigate bias, these assessments would not need to define whether a person has potential; rather, they could help equip the person with a plan to enhance their potential for success in roles other than where they are currently. I had the opportunity to design a development program for diverse top talent in partnership with HR and L&D with successful results—70 percent of participants were promoted within a year of the program. Even though the participants nominated for the program had been deemed high potential by their managers, we took the additional step to use an external, industry-recognized objective assessment designed to evaluate leadership potential. This assessment helped us design content that was fit for purpose for those in the course broadly and helped us craft individual development plans more specific to what they needed to accelerate their readiness for their career aspirations.

When asked about the challenges in successful succession planning, 59 percent of organizations cited the lack of a robust development plan as a top challenge (ATD 2022). The difficulty with development plans for succession planning lies in identifying the focus of the plan and determining the most effective way to close the gap to accelerate readiness for critical roles. I personally believe that it is necessary to understand the role as well as the person before you can get differentiated development right. One of the most successful approaches is to clearly define role requirements and consistently use a standard or enterprise-wide leadership assessment. While I like 360-degree assessments, I prefer to couple them with personality assessments to deepen understanding for the individual. This pairing also enables richer feedback, which while critical for all talent is notably lacking for some diverse talent. For example, research in 2016 found that women not only received vague praise more often than men did, they were also more likely to receive feedback that was overly focused on their communication style, rather than their technical skills (Correll and Simard 2016). Once you understand these facets, the development planning becomes truly differentiated for the individual and supports succession readiness. In the past, this has been hard to achieve due to the volume of critical roles; however, as the succession planning pipeline widens, enhancing the development capability of the full organization will support scale and sustainability.

I once worked with an organization that partnered with an external firm to collate assessment data and themed coaching feedback for top leaders to understand gaps and focus areas. In addition, we reviewed manager-related themes from the most recent engagement surveys. The organization used this information to overhaul its internal leadership development programs to include organization-wide leadership capability building, while highlighting and leveraging where individual leaders were uniquely skilled and where they needed development. This development program also included a formal sponsorship component to help participants gain visibility. Sponsors play an important role in advancing participants' careers by getting closer to their work and advocating for them behind closed doors. We carefully selected the sponsors for our program from a pool of senior leaders currently on succession plans of their own. Formalizing their sponsorship also enabled us to assess these leaders' capability to coach and develop diverse talent, which they may not have had the opportunity to do in prior roles, but would have to do more of in the future. By building an iterative process to listen to both participants and their sponsors, we were able to tailor the development program to exactly what the groups needed.

It is important to note here that ATD's 2020 succession planning report found that many organizations that use more experiential methods for developing successors (such as custom training programs and job shadowing) were significantly more likely to be high performing.

Organizations can also turn to simulation-type development programs to identify potential successors earlier and equip them with the necessary skills that go beyond P&L management, marketing, or sales. Here, L&D professionals can offer their expertise in designing project-based development programs (versus training programs where the sole focus is imparting knowledge and assessing the retention of that knowledge), assessing learners, and providing real-time feedback throughout their participation. For example, if we know that leaders will need to be able to share leadership with their teams while managing constructive conflict, L&D professionals can help by designing experiential programs that allow leaders to practice these important capabilities in safe spaces. As succession candidates practice, the L&D professional becomes another assessor of the capability of these individuals while also providing the real-time feedback necessary to improve. This is potentially important feedback that is not always taken into consideration when assessing talent.

Broadening talent assessment to include a view of performance in customized and experiential leadership development programs will require greater focus, but organizations do not need to build new development programs for scratch. Here again, as L&D and OD practitioners we can partner with those in charge of succession planning to evaluate current leadership programs using richer criteria, especially criteria surrounding performance and team leadership.

Summary

There is a saying used by many required to influence, "To bring significant change we must meet organizations where they are." While I understand the comment's intent, I believe HR, talent, DEI, L&D, and OD leaders have an opportunity to more boldly bring organizations where they need to be by using rigorous and ongoing diagnostic methods to build a platform for their organizations. The phrase "War for Talent" was coined more than two decades ago and while talent has moved much higher up the CEO's agenda, we still have a way to go. As workforce challenges become increasingly more complex, we simply must accelerate our progress in succession planning to ensure we have the right leaders, equipped with the right capabilities to grow their businesses and teams. While a full integrated talent management strategy is ideal, comprehensive succession planning with a DEI lens is an excellent place to start when developing future-ready organizations.

Key Takeaways

Here are a few things to remember about integrating diversity into your succession planning strategy:

- The succession planning process needs to evolve to keep pace with the new talent agenda.
- Diversity, equity, and inclusion (DEI) is a key component of modern talent strategies and therefore succession planning strategies.
- This modernization requires a more integrated approach, which includes voices from previously siloed functions (such as L&D).
- OD professionals bring an end-to-end philosophical approach to succession planning that involves planned transitions for internal candidates, onboarding for external candidates, individualized development plans, and mentor or sponsor initiatives to aid organizations in defining a sustainable process.

Acknowledgments

First and foremost, a special thank you to Lisa Spinelli for sending me that cold email and taking a chance on me. My involvement in this book would not exist if not for her confidence in me, her guidance through the early stages, and her encouragement throughout.

As a first-time editor, I am grateful to the contributors for their collaboration and patience as we navigated this journey together. I am humbled by the knowledge and the wealth of experiences they have shared in this handbook.

Thank you to the ATD Press editorial staff, specifically Jack Harlow for coming in midway through the project, supporting with the edits, and keeping us on track, Mallory Flynn for guidance and encouragement through the final stages, Kay Hechler for her marketing insight and strategy, and Melissa Jones for guiding me through every step of the process.

I would like to acknowledge the leaders and mentors who gave me opportunities and experiences to grow my knowledge and skills in learning and organization development and whose influence contributed to the career that led me to this handbook.

From my inspirational and foundational years at Apple, thank you to Shawn Hoklas, James Knopf, Tracy Coleman, and Duke Zurek for countless opportunities to explore my curiosity and realize my potential in L&OD. And thank you to Jacy Escoffier, Cathy Heumann, Kati Lechner, and David Zygmont for leading by example and teaching me the highest standards of facilitation, design, and delivery of L&OD initiatives for the world's most admired company.

From my formative years at Performics, thank you to Chris Keating for leading and coaching me through my first leadership role in L&D, providing me every opportunity to expand my knowledge and allowing me the freedom to take risks and challenge the status quo. And to Cassie Yates and Scott Shamberg for being open to my thought leadership and providing many opportunities for me to contribute outside L&D.

From my time at Zoom, thank you to Jodi Rabinowitz for the opportunity to contribute to the development of our Zoomies and to Sarah Payne for teaching me new things about OD and beyond in every conversation we shared.

From my time at CommerceHub, thank you to Janay Jespersen for taking me out of my comfort zone and trusting me with high-visibility projects. And to Lexi Baldisseri and Jess Henning, thank you for allowing me to collaborate with you in initiatives that will forever influence my understanding and execution of OD.

Lastly, there are too many to name, but to those who believed in me enough to take the time to give me a kind word or a bit of feedback, I'm thankful for your generosity and wouldn't have made it here without you.

—Brian J. Flores

References and Recommended Resources

Chapter 1

Aaronson, J., and E. Hasan. 2018. "In Focus | HR Organizational Development & Change." Georgetown University School of Continuing Studies, December 13. youtube.com /watch?v=RG3s8MYLq8M.

Anderson, D.L. 2019. *Organization Development: The Process of Leading Organizational Change.* Thousand Oaks, CA: SAGE Publications.

ATD (Association for Talent Development). nd. "What Is Organization Development?" ATD Talent Development Glossary. td.org/talent-development-glossary-terms/what -is-organization-development.

Clark, R.E., and F. Estes. 2008. *Turning Research Into Results: A Guide to Selecting the Right Performance Solutions.* Charlotte, NC: Information Age Publishing.

Hasan, E., and I. Adeleye. 2021. "Advance DEI Using Talent Development Expertise." *TD at Work.* Alexandria, VA: ATD Press.

Michigan.gov. nd. "The Pros and Cons of Data Collection Methods." michigan.gov/-/media /Project/Websites/leo/Folder20/Data_Collection_Methods--pros_and_cons_2.pdf ?rev=8f397d02c9be4d45af6324ca01b4e241.

Stobierski, T. 2019. "The Advantages of Data-Driven Decision-Making." Harvard Business School Online, August 26. online.hbs.edu/blog/post/data-driven-decision-making.

Chapter 2

Allen, A. 2020. *Cynicism.* The MIT Press Essential Knowledge Series. Cambridge, MA: The MIT Press.

Banerjee, S.R. 2021. "Large-Scale Interventions." Chapter 10 in *Organization Development Interventions: Executing Effective Organization Change,* edited by W. Rothwell, S. Imroz, and B. Bakhshandeh. New York: Routledge.

Bhasin, H. 2021. "Organizational Politics—Definition, Meaning, Reasons and Effects." Marketing91, January 9. marketing91.com/organisational-politics.

Cady, S., and Z. Shoup. 2015. "Competencies for Success." Chapter 7 in *Practicing Organization Development: Leading Transformation and Change,* edited by W. Rothwell, J. Stavros, and R. Sullivan. Hoboken, NJ: John Wiley & Sons.

Ferris, G., and K. Kacmar. 1992. "Perceptions of Organizational Politics." *Journal of Management* 18(1): 93–116.

Janis, I. 1983. *Groupthink: Psychological Studies of Policy Decisions and Fiascoes,* 2nd ed. Boston: Wadsworth.

Jarrett, M. 2017. "The 4 Types of Organizational Politics." *Harvard Business Review,* April 27. hbr.org/2017/04/the-4-types-of-organizational-politics.

Jones, M.C., and W. Rothwell, eds. 2017. *Evaluating Organization Development: How to Ensure and Sustain the Successful Transformation.* New York: Routledge.

Kaplan, R., and D. Norton. 2003. *Strategy Maps: Converting Intangible Assets Into Tangible Outcomes.* Boston: Harvard Business Review Press.

Organization Development Network. nd. "Global OD Competency Framework." odnetwork.org/page/global-framework.

Phillips, J., and P. Phillips. 2011. *The Consultant's Scorecard: Tracking ROI and Bottom-Line Impact of Consulting Projects.* New York: McGraw-Hill.

Rothwell, W. 1999. *The Action Learning Guidebook: A Real-Time Strategy For Problem Solving, Training Design, and Employee Development.* New York: Pfeiffer.

Rothwell, W., B. Benscoter, M. King, and S. King. 2016. *Mastering the Instructional Design Process: A Systematic Approach,* 5th ed. Hoboken, NJ: John Wiley & Sons.

Rothwell, W., and C. Park, eds. 2021. *Virtual Coaching to Improve Group Relationships: Process Consultation Reimagined.* New York: Routledge.

Rothwell, W., A. Stopper, and J. Myers, eds. 2017. *Assessment and Diagnosis for Organization Development: Powerful Tools and Perspectives for the OD Practitioner.* London: CRC Press.

Smith, R., D. King, R. Sidhu, D. Skelsey, and APMG, eds. 2014. *The Effective Change Manager's Handbook: Essential Guidance to the Change Management Body of Knowledge.* New York: Kogan Page.

Varney, G. 1977. *Organization Development for Managers.* Boston: Addison-Wesley.

Webber, E. 2016. *Building Successful Communities of Practice: Discover How Connecting People Makes Better Organizations.* London: Tacit.

Wenger, E. 1999. *Communities of Practice: Learning, Meaning and Identity,* New York: Cambridge University Press.

Chapter 3

Acho, E. "Uncomfortable Conversations With a Black Man." Videos. uncomfortableconvos.com/watch.

Brown, B. *Dare to Lead.* Podcast. brenebrown.com/podcast-show/dare-to-lead.

Brown, B. *Unlocking Us.* Podcast. brenebrown.com/podcast-show/unlocking-us.

Brown, B. 2018. *Dare to Lead: Brave Work. Tough Conversations. Whole Hearts.* New York: Random House.

Gallup. nd. "Gallup's Employee Engagement Survey: Ask the Right Questions With the Q12 Survey." gallup.com/workplace/356063/gallup-q12-employee-engagement-survey.aspx.

Grant, A. *WorkLife.* Podcast. adamgrant.net/podcasts/work-life.

Kotter, J.P. 1995. "Leading Change: Why Transformation Efforts Fail." *Harvard Business Review* 73(2): 59–67.

Kotter, J.P. 1996. *Leading Change.* Boston: Harvard Business Review Press.

Kotter, J.P., and D.S. Cohen. 2012. *The Heart of Change: Real-Life Stories of How People Change Their Organizations.* Boston: Harvard Business Review Press.

Lorsch, J.W., and E. McTague. 2016. "Culture Is Not the Culprit." *Harvard Business Review Magazine,* April.

Parker, P. 2018. *The Art of Gathering: How We Meet and Why It Matters.* New York: Riverhead Books.

Chapter 4

Abbasi, S.M., and K.W. Hollman. 1991. "Managing Cultural Diversity: The Challenge of the '90s." *Records Management Quarterly* 25(3).

Ahmad, T. 2021. "Why Justice, Equity, Diversity, and Inclusion Matter for Climbers." Access Fund, March 18. accessfund.org/open-gate-blog/jedi-101-for-climbers.

Bortz, D. 2020. "Benefits of Having Affinity Groups at Work." Monster, March 21. monster .com/career-advice/article/affinity-group.

Brooks, L. 2020. "Certificate of Strategic Diversity, Equity, and Inclusion." Brooks Consultants. brooks-consultants.com/certificate-in-strategic-diversity-equity-and -inclusion.

Brooks, L. 2021. "Integrating Change Management in Your DEI Interventions." HR Exchange Network, June 2. hrexchangenetwork.com/hr-talent-management /columns/integrating-change-management-in-your-dei-interventions.

Burkett, E. 2022. "Women's Rights Movement." *Encyclopedia Britannica*, December 2. britannica.com/event/womens-movement.

Clark, T.R. 2020. *The 4 Stages of Psychological Safety: Defining the Path to Inclusion and Innovation.* Oakland, CA: Berrett-Koehler Publishers.

Corrigan, J. 2022. "Only 34% of Companies Have Enough Resources to Support DEI Initiatives." Human Resource Director–America, February 28. hcamag.com/us /specialization/corporate-wellness/only-34-of-companies-have-enough-resources-to -support-dei-initiatives/326842.

Edmondson, A.C. 1999. "Psychological Safety and Learning Behavior in Work Teams." *Administrative Science Quarterly* 44(2): 350–383.

Evans, F. 2020. "Why Harry Truman Ended Segregation in the US Military in 1948." History.com, November 5. history.com/news/harry-truman-executive-order-9981 -desegration-military-1948.

Gimenez, C., V. Sierra, and J. Rodon. 2012. "Sustainable Operations: Their Impact on the Triple Bottom Line." *International Journal of Production Economics* 140(1): 149–159.

Guild Education. 2021. "The ROI of DE&I: 7 Key Components for Business Leaders to Measure." Guild blog, December 7. blog.guildeducation.com/the-roi-of-dei.

Hall, S.H. 2022. "9 Ways to Measure the Success of Your DEI Strategy in 2023." Senior Executive, December 16. seniorexecutive.com/9-ways-to-measure-the-success -of-your-dei-strategy.

History.com Editors. 2021. "George Floyd Is Killed by a Police Officer, Igniting Historic Protests." A&E Television Networks, History.com, June 25. history.com/this-day -in-history/george-floyd-killed-by-police-officer.

Kirkpatrick Partners. nd. "The Kirkpatrick Model." Kirkpatrick Partners. kirkpatrick partners.com/the-kirkpatrick-model.

Kotter, J. 2022. "The 8-Step Process for Leading Change." Kotter, August 10. kotterinc .com/8-step-process-for-leading-change.

Min, Ji-A. 2016. "A Shortlisting Criteria How-To Guide for Identifying the Best Candidates." Ideal blog, October 13. ideal.com/a-shortlisting-criteria-how-to-guide-for -identifying-the-best-candidates.

Paluck, E.L. 2006. "Diversity Training and Intergroup Contact: A Call to Action Research." *Journal of Social Issues* 62(3): 577–595.

Papini, J. 2021. "Becoming a Champion for Diversity, Equity, and Inclusion." CIDIS, July 1. cidisconsulting.com/becoming-a-champion-for-diversity-equity-and-inclusion.

Pfeiffer, T., and J. Mayes. 2018. "D&G, H&M, Pepsi & More: Racist Ads Show Tone-Deaf Marketing Knows No Border." Business Standard, November 23. business-standard .com/article/companies/d-g-h-m-pepsi-more-racist-ads-show-tone-deaf-marketing -knows-no-border-118112300068_1.html.

Phillips, K. 2016. "How Much Is Scrap Learning Costing Your Organization?" ATD Insight, August 10. td.org/insights/how-much-is-scrap-learning-costing-your-organization.

Silverstein, J. 2021. "The Global Impact of George Floyd: How Black Lives Matter Protests Shaped Movements Around the World." CBS News, June 4. cbsnews.com/news /george-floyd-black-lives-matter-impact.

Taing, E. 2013. "A Toolkit for Recruiting and Hiring a More Diverse Workforce." University Health Services, Tang Center, University of California, Berkeley, April. diversity.berkeley.edu/sites/default/files/recruiting_a_more_diverse_workforce _uhs.pdf.

The Intersect Group. 2021. "How BRGs Can Benefit Your Organization." The Intersect Group blog, May 26. theintersectgroup.com/blog/how-brgs-can-benefit-your -organization.

van Vulpen, E. 2019. "What Is Organizational Development? A Complete Guide." Academy to Innovate HR, December 2. aihr.com/blog/organizational-development.

Chapter 5

Gallup. 2010. "Gallup Global Wellbeing: The Behavioral Economics of GDP Growth." Gallup.news.gallup.com/poll/126965/gallup-global-wellbeing.aspx.

Kuehner-Hebert, K. 2019. "Investing in Holistic Wellness Leads to More Productive Employees." BenefitsPRO, July 10. benefitspro.com/2019/07/10/investing-in-holistic -wellness-leads-to-more-productive-employees.

Lorsch, J.W., and E. McTague. 2016. "Culture Is Not the Culprit." *Harvard Business Review,* April.

Mehta, P. 2021. "Authenticity and Employee Wellbeing With Reference to Emotional Work: A Review." *Mental Health and Social Inclusion* 25(2): 146–158. doi.org/10.1108 /MHSI-11-2020-0077.

Morais-Storz, M., R.S. Platou, and K.B. Norheim. 2018. "Innovation and Metamorphosis Towards Strategic Resilience." *International Journal of Entrepreneurial Behaviour & Research* 24(7): 1181–1199. doi.org/10.1108/IJEBR-11-2016-0369.

Myles-Jay, L., P. Dieppe, and A. Medina-Lara. 2016. "Review of 99 Self-Report Measures for Assessing Well-Being in Adults: Exploring Dimensions of Well-Being and Developments Over Time." *BMJ Open* 6(7). doi.org/10.1136/bmjopen-2015-010641.

National Domestic Violence Hotline. nd. "Domestic Violence Statistics." thehotline.org /stakeholders/domestic-violence-statistics.

NWI (National Wellness Institute). nd. "NWI's Six Dimensions of Wellness." National Wellness Institute. nationalwellness.org/resources/six-dimensions-of-wellness.

Sull, D., C. Sull, and B. Zweig. 2022. "Toxic Culture Is Driving the Great Resignation." *MIT Sloan Management Review,* January 11. sloanreview.mit.edu/article/toxic-culture -is-driving-the-great-resignation.

Chapter 6

ATD (Association for Talent Development). 2020. Talent Development Body of Knowledge (TDBoK). Alexandria, VA: ATD Press.

Association for Talent Development (ATD). "What Is Organization Development?" ATD. td.org/talent-development-glossary-terms/what-is-organization-development.

Budden, R. 2021. "Managing the Business Risk of Climate Change." Geospatial World, July 6. geospatialworld.net/blogs/managing-the-business-risk-of-climate-change-2.

Center for Climate and Energy Solutions (C2ES). nd. "Business Strategies to Address Climate Change." C2ES. c2es.org/content/business-strategies-to-address-climate-change.

Deloitte. 2021. "Organizations Are Feeling the Pain of Climate Change: Here Are Five Ways It's Affecting Their Business." *Forbes,* April 16. forbes.com/sites/deloitte/2021/04/16

/organizations-are-feeling-the-pain-of-climate-change-here-are-five-ways-its
-affecting-their-business/?sh=56f73074e0c2.

Giles, S. 2018. "How VUCA Is Reshaping the Business Environment, and What It
Means for Innovation." *Forbes*, May 9. forbes.com/sites/sunniegiles/2018/05/09
/how-vuca-is-reshaping-the-business-environment-and-what-it-means-for
-innovation/?sh=24c6da21eb8d.

IBM. 2020. "COVID-19 and the Future of Business." IBM Institute for Business Value,
September. ibm.com/thought-leadership/institute-business-value/report/covid
-19-future-business.

Indeed Editorial Team. 2021. "What Is Business Alignment?" Indeed, April 29. indeed.com
/career-advice/career-development/business-alignment.

Kraaijenbrink, J. 2021. "Four Essential Trends for Every Post-Covid-19 Business Strategy."
Forbes, March 4. forbes.com/sites/jeroenkraaijenbrink/2021/03/04/four-essential
-trends-for-every-post-covid-19-business-strategy/?sh=6a4c4421c4a0.

McLaughlin, K. 2022. "COVID-19: Briefing Note #87, January 12, 2022." McKinsey, January
12. mckinsey.com/business-functions/risk-and-resilience/our-insights/covid-19
-implications-for-business.

Neilson, G.L., J. Estupiñán, and B. Sethi. 2015. "10 Principles of Organization Design."
Strategy + Business, March 23. strategy-business.com/article/00318.

Story, G. 2018. "Nemawashi or Groundwork in Business in Japan." LinkedIn, May 31.
linkedin.com/pulse/nemawashi-groundwork-business-japan-dr-greg-story.

Trevor, J. 2018. "Is Anyone in Your Company Paying Attention to Strategic Alignment?"
Harvard Business Review, January 12. hbr.org/2018/01/is-anyone-in-your-company
-paying-attention-to-strategic-alignment.

Chapter 7

Stewart, T.A., and A.P. Raman. 2007. "Lessons From Toyota's Long Drive." *Harvard Business
Review*, July–August. hbr.org/2007/07/lessons-from-toyotas-long-drive.

Chapter 8

Bryant, A., and A.L. Kazan. 2013. *Self-Leadership: How to Become a More Successful, Efficient, and
Effective Leader From the Inside Out.* New York: McGraw Hill.

Fechter, J. 2020. "What Is the Cost of Disengaged Employees?" HR University. hr.university/analytics/cost-of-disengaged-employees.

Ito, A. 2022. "My Company Is Not My Family." *Business Insider*, March 2. businessinsider.com/overachievers-leaning-back-hustle-culture-coasting-employees-work.

Chapter 9

Bersin, J. n.d. "The HR Capability Project." joshbersin.com/the-global-hr-capability-project.

Bersin, J. 2021. *The Big Reset Playbook: Change Agility*. Oakland, CA: The Josh Bersin Company. joshbersin.com/wp-content/uploads/2022/01/WT-Big-Reset-21_12-Sprint-6-Change-Agility-Report.pdf.

Biech, E. 2007. *Thriving Through Change*. Alexandria, VA: ATD Press.

Borysenko, K. 2019. "Burnout Is Now An Officially Diagnosable Condition: Here's What You Need To Know About It." *Forbes*, May 29. forbes.com/sites/karlynborysenko/2019/05/29/burnout-is-now-an-officially-diagnosable-condition-heres-what-you-need-to-know-about-it/#2d9692a42b99.

Burkett, H. 2015. "Talent Managers as Change Agents." Chapter 20 in *The Talent Management Handbook*, edited by T. Bickham. Alexandria, VA: ATD Press.

Burkett, H. 2017. *Learning for the Long Run: 7 Practices for Sustaining a Resilient Learning Organization*. Alexandria, VA: ATD Press.

Burkett, H. 2021. "Four Ways Leaders Can Build Team Resilience." *Forbes*, December 14. forbes.com/sites/forbescoachescouncil/2021/12/14/four-ways-leaders-can-build-team-resilience/?sh=19e1896d77ae.

Burkett, H. 2022. "Building Change Leadership From the Ground Up." *Talent Management*, August 2. talentmgt.com/articles/2022/08/02/building-change-leadership-from-the-ground-up.

CMI (Change Management Institute). 2017. "Change Manager Competency Models (Preview Document)." Change Management Institute. change-management-institute.com/wp-content/uploads/2022/06/cmi_change_manager_competency_models_preview_sept17.pdf.

Cummings, T.G., and C.G. Worley. 2016. *Organization Development and Change*, 10th ed. Boston: Cengage Learning.

Derler, A., and D. Baer. 2019. *How Four Companies Built a Growth Mindset Culture.* NeuroLeadership Institute Case Study. cdn2.hubspot.net/hubfs/1927708/Growth Mindset_CSCollection_US_FN%20(2).pdf.

Gartner. 2022. *Top 5 HR Trends and Priorities for HR Leaders in 2022.* Gartner. gartner.com /en/human-resources/trends/top-priorities-for-hr-leaders.

Herold, D., and D. Fedor. 2008. *Change the Way You Lead Change.* Stanford, CA: Stanford University Press.

Hoffman, M. 2020. "How to Build a Culture that Helps You Scale With Garry Ridge." Ptex Group, January 6. ptexgroup.com/build-culture-helps-scale-garry-ridge.

Holm, T. 2019. "Pardon the Disruption." *TD*, June.

Lutin, L. 2020. "Superlearning: Reskilling, Upskilling and Outskilling for a Future-Proof Workforce." Deloitte Insights, June 29. deloitte.com/us/en/insights/focus /technology-and-the-future-of-work/reskilling-the-workforce.html.

McLean & Company. 2022. "2022 HR Trends Report." McLean & Company. go.mcleanco .com/2022_hr_trends_ga.

Mitchell, C., R.L. Ray, and B. van Ark. 2014. *The Conference Board CEO Challenge 2014: People and Performance.* New York: The Conference Board.

Phillips, J.J., and E.F. Holton. 1997. *Leading Organizational Change.* Alexandria, VA: ATD Press.

Prosci. 2018. "Measuring the Effectiveness of Change Management." Prosci Thought Leadership, June 5. prosci.com/hubfs/2.downloads/thought-leadership/ Measurement-Metrics-TL.pdf.

Prosci. n.d. "What is Change Management and How Does it Work?" Prosci Thought Leadership. prosci.com/resources/articles/what-is-change-management-and-how -does-it-work.

Sutton, J., n.d. "Plan to Extinguish Organizational Burnout." McLean & Company. hr.mclean co.com/research/ss/plan-to-extinguish-organizational-burnout.

Chapter 11

Dyer, C., and K. Shepherd. 2021. *Remote Work: Redesign Processes, Practices and Strategies to Engage a Remote Workforce.* New York: Kogan Page.

GitLab. nd. "GitLab's Guide to All-Remote." GitLab. about.gitlab.com/company/culture /all-remote/guide.

Klahre, A.-M. 2017. "3 Ways Johnson & Johnson Is Taking Talent Acquisition to the Next Level." Johnson & Johnson, August 29. jnj.com/innovation/3-ways-johnson-and -johnson-is-taking-talent-acquisition-to-the-next-level.

Microsoft. 2021. "The Next Great Disruption Is Hybrid Work—Are We Ready?" Work Trend Index Annual Report, March 22. microsoft.com/en-us/worklab/work-trend -index/hybrid-work.

SilkRoad and CareerBuilder. n.d. *State of Recruitment & Onboarding Report.* SilkRoad Technology. hr1.silkroad.com/state-of-recruitment-onboarding.

Zapier. n.d. "The Ultimate Guide to Remote Work." Zapier. zapier.com/learn/remote-work.

Chapter 12

BR (Business Roundtable). "Placing a Greater Emphasis on Skills in Hiring and Advancement, Improving Equity and Diversity in Employment." Business Roundtable. businessroundtable.org/workforceskills.

Kande, M., and M. Sonmez. 2020. "Don't Fear AI. It Will Lead to Long-Term Job Growth." World Economic Forum, October 26. weforum.org/agenda/2020/10 /dont-fear-ai-it-will-lead-to-long-term-job-growth.

Markle. "Rework America." markle.org/rework-america.

Opportunity@Work. 2019. "Hire for the Skills It Takes to Do the Job." Opportunity@Work, December. opportunityatwork.org/wp-content/uploads/2019/12/Skills-Based -Hiring.pdf.

OSN (Open Skills Network). "Build the Skills Ecosystem of Tomorrow." openskillsnetwork .org.

Parker, K., and J.M. Horowitz. 2022. "Majority of Workers Who Quit a Job in 2021 Cite Low Pay, No Opportunities for Advancement, Feeling Disrespected." Pew Research Center, March 9. pewresearch.org/fact-tank/2022/03/09/majority-of-workers -who-quit-a-job-in-2021-cite-low-pay-no-opportunities-for-advancement-feeling -disrespected.

Roslansky, R. 2021. "You Need a Skills-Based Approach to Hiring and Developing Talent." Harvard Business Review, June 8. hbr.org/2021/06/you-need-a-skills-based -approach-to-hiring-and-developing-talent.

Skillful. nd. "Take Your Organization to the Next Level With Skills-Based Practices." Skillful. skillful.com/employers.

US Chamber of Commerce Foundation. "The T3 Innovation Network." uschamber
foundation.org/t3-innovation.

World Economic Forum. nd. "Workforce and Employment: Reskilling." Strategic
Intelligence. intelligence.weforum.org/topics/a1Gb0000000LJQ4EAO/key-issues
/a1Gb0000001hNYPEA2.

Chapter 13

Falcone, P. 2016. *75 Ways for Managers to Hire, Develop, and Keep Great Employees.* New York:
HarperCollins Leadership.

Falcone, P. 2017. *101 Sample Write-Ups for Documenting Employee Performance Problems,* 3rd
ed. New York: HarperCollins Leadership.

Falcone, P. 2018. *96 Great Interview Questions to Ask Before You Hire.* New York: HarperCollins
Leadership.

Falcone, P. 2019. *101 Tough Conversations to Have With Employees: A Manager's Guide to
Performance, Conduct, and Disciplinary Challenges,* 2nd ed. New York: HarperCollins
Leadership.

Falcone, P. 2022. *Workplace Ethics: Mastering Ethical Leadership and Sustaining a Moral
Workplace.* New York: HarperCollins Leadership.

Chapter 14

Anderson, R., and B. Adams. 2016. *Mastering Leadership: An Integrated Framework for
Breakthrough Performance and Extraordinary Business Results.* Hoboken, NJ: John Wiley
& Sons.

Anderson, R., and B. Adams. 2019. *Scaling Leadership: Building Organizational Capability and
Capacity to Create Outcomes that Matter Most.* Hoboken, NJ: John Wiley & Sons.

Bersin, J. 2010. "High-Impact Learning Culture: The 40 Best Practices for Creating an
Empowered Enterprise." Bersin by Deloitte.

Dyer, A., S. Dyrchs, A. Bailey, H.-P. Burkner, and J. Puckett. 2020. "Why It's Time to
Bring Learning to the C-Suite." Boston Consulting Group, July 14. bcg.com
/publications/2020/why-it-is-time-to-bring-learning-to-the-c-suite.

Edmondson, A. 1999. "Psychological Safety and Learning Behavior in Work Teams."
Administrative Science Quarterly 44(2): 350–383. doi.org/10.2307/2666999.

Edmondson, A. 2019. *The Fearless Organization: Creating Psychological Safety in the Workplace for Learning, Innovation and Growth.* Hoboken, NJ: John Wiley & Sons.

Hess, E., and K. Ludwig. 2017. *Humility Is the New Smart: Rethinking Human Excellence in the Smart Machine Age.* Oakland, CA: Barrett-Koehler.

Hess, E.D. 2014. *Learn or Die: Using Science to Build a Leading-Edge Learning Organization.* New York: Columbia University Press.

Kegan, R., and L.L. Lahey. 2016. *An Everyone Culture: Becoming a Deliberately Developmental Organization.* Boston: Harvard University Press.

O'Neil, J. 1995. "On Schools as Learning Organizations: A Conversation With Peter Senge." ASCD, April 1.

Offterdinger, E., and C. Allen. 2021. *Conscious, Capable, and Ready to Contribute: How Employee Development Can Become the Highest Form of Social Contribution.* Conscious Capitalism Press.

Petrie, N. 2014. "Future Trends in Leadership Development." Center for Creative Leadership. Whitepaper. cclinnovation.org/future-trends-in-leadership -development.

Senge, P. 1990. *The Fifth Discipline: The Art and Science of the Learning Organization,* 1st ed. New York: Penguin Random House.

Villiers, A. 2020. "Why We Should Stop Using 'Soft' Skills." Career Convergence Web Magazine, February 1. ncda.org/aws/NCDA/pt/sd/news_article/278124/_PARENT /CC_layout_details/false.

Wright, J. 2018. "The Origin of Soft Skills." Joe Jag, February 17. code.joejag.com/2018/the -origins-of-soft-skills.html.

Chapter 15

Arena, M. 2018. *Adaptive Space: How GM and Other Companies Are Positively Disrupting Themselves and Transforming Into Agile Organizations.* New York: McGraw Hill.

Boch, L. 2015. *Work Rules! Insights From Inside Google That Will Transform How You Live and Lead.* New York: Twelve.

Buckingham, M., and A. Goodall. 2019. *Nine Lies About Work: A Freethinking Leader's Guide to the Real World.* Boston: Harvard Business School Press.

Clifton, J., and J. Harter. 2019. *It's the Manager: Moving From Boss to Coach.* New York: Gallup Press.

Covey, S. 2006. *The Speed of Trust: The One Thing That Changes Everything.* New York: The Free Press.

Dignan, A. 2019. *Brave New Work: Are You Ready to Reinvent Your Organization.* New York: Portfolio.

Doshi, N., and L. McGregor. 2015. *Primed to Perform: How to Build the Highest Performing Cultures Through the Science of Total Motivation.* New York: HarperCollins.

Edmondson, A. 2018. *The Fearless Organization: Creating Psychological Safety in the Workplace for Learning, Innovation, and Growth.* New York: Wiley.

Fishbein, M. 2014. *How to Build an Awesome Professional Network.* Self-published.

Forman, D. 2015. *Fearless HR: Driving Business Results.* San Diego: Sage Learning System Press.

Forman, D. 2020. *Fearless Talent Choices: That Can Make or Break Your Business.* San Diego: Sage Learning System Press.

Hamel, G. 2012. *The Future of Management.* San Francisco: Jossey-Bass.

Hamel, G., and M. Zanini. 2020. *Humanocracy: Creating Organizations as Amazing as the People Inside Them.* Boston: Harvard Business Review Press.

Harari, N. 2018. *Sapiens: A Brief History of Humankind.* New York: Harper Perennial.

Kotter, J.P., and D.S. Cohen. 2002. *The Heart of Change: Real-Life Stories of How People Change Their Organizations.* Boston: Harvard Business School Press.

Lencioni, P. 2002. *The Five Dysfunctions of a Team.* San Francisco: Jossey-Bass

Mankins, M.C., and E. Garton, 2017. *Time, Talent, Energy: Overcome Organizational Drag and Unleash Your Teams Productive Power.* Boston: Harvard Business Review Press.

Murray, S. 2022. *If Gold Is Our Destiny: How a Team of Mavericks Came Together for Olympic Glory.* London: Rowman and Littlefield.

Pink, D. 2009. *Drive: The Surprising Truth About What Motivates Us.* New York: Riverhead Books.

Schwartz, T. 2010. *The Way We Are Working Isn't Working: The Four Forgotten Needs That Energize Great Performance.* New York: Free Press.

Suzman, J. 2021. *Work: A Deep History, From the Stone Age to the Age of Robots.* New York: Penguin Press.

Ulrich, D., D. Kryscynski, M. Ulrich, and W. Brockbank. 2017. *Victory Through Organization: Why the War for Talent Is Failing Your Company and What You Can Do About It.* New York: McGraw Hill Education.

Zak, P. 2017. *The Trust Factor: The Science of Creating High-Performance Companies.* New York: AMACOM.

Chapter 16

ATD (Association for Talent Development). 2022. *Succession Planning: Preparing Organizations for the Future.* Alexandria, VA: ATD Press.

Correll, S.J., and C. Simard. 2016. "Research: Vague Feedback Is Holding Women Back." *Harvard Business Review,* April 29. hbr.org/2016/04/research-vague-feedback -is-holding-women-back.

US Bureau of Labor Statistics (BLS). 2022. "Job Openings and Labor Turnover Summary," BLS, Economic News Release, June 1. bls.gov/news.release/jolts.nr0.htm.

White, M.C. 2022. "CEOs Are Joining the 'Great Resignation,' Trading Fatigue for Family Time." NBC News, January 18. nbcnews.com/business/business-news/ceos-are -joining-great-resignation-trading-fatigue-family-time-rcna12223.

About the Contributors

Catherine Allen

Catherine Allen is co-founder and CEO of AO People Partners, a company dedicated to inspiring and supporting the conscious practice of people development in the workplace. Catherine is passionate about helping leaders and organizations lean into the power of developing people to drive business success and meaningful social contribution. With more than 25 years of experience working as an organizational and people skills development practitioner and executive coach, Catherine specializes in helping executive leaders and teams own, model, and drive business and people development integration in their organizations. Skilled in conflict resolution, communications, business strategy, and change management, Catherine has extensive experience working with executive leaders seeking to take their business to the next level of conscious growth and senior leaders transitioning to executive level roles in private sector organizations in a range of industries. Catherine holds an MS in conflict analysis and resolution from George Mason University and is a certified professional coach. She also co-authored with Ed Offterdinger of *Conscious, Capable, and Ready to Contribute: How Employee Development Can Become the Highest Form of Social Contribution*. Catherine writes and speaks regularly on leadership and people development integration and why people development in the workplace should become a recognized and incentivized form of social contribution.

LaKisha C. Brooks

LaKisha C. Brooks, MSc, MEd, CDP, CDR, is the director of diversity, equity, inclusion, and justice at the International Coaching Federation and CEO and senior director of diversity and talent at Brooks Consultants. She's also a nationally recognized certified diversity professional and a columnist for *DimEnsIons of Organizational Development: The Bottom Line of Diversity, Equity, and Inclusion* at HR Exchange. LaKisha previously served as a coaching and mentoring advisory board member for HR.com and currently serves as a master of leadership of science administration professional advisory board member at Central Michigan University. A decorated talent management and leadership development consultant, LaKisha was a member of the Leadership Sandy Springs Class of 2017 and the Leadership Bartow Class of 2022. She was also recognized as ATD Central Florida Chapter's 2018 Trainer Showdown winner and a Top 100 HR Influencer in 2021 in Talent Management for Engagedly. LaKisha has more than 14 years of talent management, leadership development, and global diversity consulting experience, and has worked with organizations such as BioAgilytix, Thor Industries, Win Waste, and the National Hemophilia Foundation.

Holly Burkett

Holly Burkett, PhD, SPHR, SCC, is an accomplished talent builder, change leader, and organization development professional with more than 20 years' experience as a trusted business advisor to such companies as Apple, SEVA, and Premera Blue Cross. She is passionate about developing resilient leadership capabilities that enable high engagement, performance, and well-being. She serves clients as a Prosci certified change practitioner, a certified Marshall Goldsmith Stakeholder Centered Coach, a Senior Professional in HR, and member of Forbes Coaches Council. An associate of the ROI Institute, Holly has special depth in helping leaders measure the impact of strategic change efforts. The award-winning author of *Learning for the Long Run*, she contributes to the Conference Board as a Distinguished Principal Research Fellow and is a regularly featured author in industry resources including ATD's Talent Development Body of Knowledge (TDBoK) and HRCI's *The Rise of HR*. A sought-after coach, speaker, and facilitator, Holly has a doctorate in human capital development. You can reach her by email at holly@hollyburkett.com.

Brandon Carson

Brandon Carson is an award-winning global talent development leader with a proven record of success in learning and organization development, leadership training, coaching, change management, curriculum development, and performance consulting. He has authored two books, *Learning in the Age of Immediacy* and the award-winning *L&D's Playbook for the Digital Age*, both published by ATD Press. In 2020, Brandon created L&D Cares, a nonprofit dedicated to providing coaching, mentoring, and career resources for talent development professionals. He talks and writes about digital transformation, innovation, employee experience, and how the digital age is influencing workplace performance. Brandon has an MEd in educational technology, a BA in business, and a certification in advanced analysis.

Catherine W. Corey

Catherine W. Corey, MPA, SPHR, ACC, CAE, is chief goodness officer at Good for the Soul Consulting. With more than 20 years of leadership experience across industries, Catherine has a unique perspective on how to get the best out of people. She helps organizations cultivate talent and get results through coaching, facilitation, training, and HR and OD leadership. Her specialties include employee engagement, values-centered work, and mental health and wellness. She works with advocacy and service-based nonprofits, government agencies, and private sector corporations, as well as C-suite and emerging leaders. The common thread in Catherine's work is ensuring safe spaces for uncomfortable and necessary conversations, because from a place of genuine psychological safety, people can accomplish extraordinary things together. Catherine is a lifelong learner, having earned not only SPHR, ACC and CAE credentials, but also an executive certificate in leadership coaching and master of public administration. She is currently pursuing a PhD in clinical psychology, with a primary research interest in moral injury. Catherine also believes in active community involvement and has volunteered on a suicide prevention hotline for more than a dozen years. She and her husband split their time between the DC and Seattle areas.

Paul Falcone

Paul Falcone is principal of Paul Falcone Workplace Leadership Consulting, specializing in management and leadership training, executive coaching, international keynote speaking, and facilitating corporate off-site retreats. He is the former CHRO of Nickelodeon and has held senior-level HR positions with Paramount Pictures, Time Warner, and City of Hope. Paul has extensive experience in entertainment, healthcare, biotech, and financial services, including in international, nonprofit, and union environments. Paul is the author of a number of best-selling books, which been translated into Chinese, Korean, Vietnamese, Indonesian, and Turkish. His five-book Paul Falcone Workplace Leadership series was published in 2022. Paul is a certified executive coach through the Marshall Goldsmith

Stakeholder Centered Coaching program, a long-term columnist for SHRM and *HR Magazine*, and an adjunct faculty member in UCLA Extension's School of Business and Management. He is an accomplished keynote presenter, in-house trainer, and webinar facilitator in the areas of talent and performance management, leadership development, and effective leadership communication. For more information, visit PaulFalconeHR.com.

David C. Forman

David C. Forman's career, spanning four decades, has focused on improving the knowledge, skills, and performance of people. As a learning scientist, business leader, chief learning officer, adjunct professor at the Pepperdine Graziadio School of Business, and bestselling author, David's actions, courses, and writings have been recognized around the world. He has worked closely with such business clients as Apple, IBM, FedEx, Ford, American Express, SAP, Prudential, Deloitte, PwC, DuPont, and Allsate Insurance. In the nonprofit arena, David has worked with The Ford Foundation, Children's Television Workshop, Cedars Sinai Hospitals, Johns Hopkins University, AID, and many governmental agencies. David's latest books Fearless HR and Fearless Talent Choices are global bestsellers.

Deepti Gudipati

Deepti Gudipati, MPP, MSPD, ACC, is founder and principal consultant at DG Leadership Solutions. She brings nearly 20 years of experiences as a coach, organizational consultant, and facilitator into the work of systems change. She founded DG Leadership Solutions from a desire to help organizations and teams explore ways to work better, together. Deepti's approach is highly collaborative and experiential. She empowers clients with the strategy, skills, and tools they need to own the change process by leveraging their authentic strengths and values. She is adept at unlocking new levels of awareness, helping people feel comfortable taking risks, and aligning a company's talent pool with organizational need. Her clients span a diverse range of sectors and leadership levels, including advocacy and mission-focused organizations, philanthropic organizations, and government and private sector leaders. Equity and inclusion are at the core of all her work, because when we design systems that enable their people to be seen, heard, and empowered, we can be the change we envision in the world. Deepti has a master's degree in organizational dynamics from the University of Pennsylvania and public policy from Carnegie Mellon. She lives in Washington, DC, and spends her free time seeking adventures with her partner and dog.

Neal R. Goodman

Neal Goodman, PhD, is an internationally recognized authority on global leadership, global mindset, global OD, cultural intelligence, and DEI. He is committed to creating globally inclusive multicultural organizations through his work on corporate boards, executive coaching, mentoring, speaking, and writing. He has been leading programs that promote diversity and inclusion for more than 60 years. He worked with Dr. Martin Luther King and has delivered hundreds of diversity workshops that promote equity and inclusion. Neal has worked with many organizations—including AT&T, J&J, Citi, GE, Alcatel, Dow Jones, Prudential, Samsung, Bechtel, NBA, Hilton, Fujitsu, Philips, Conoco, HP, KLM, Delta, PwC, and the World Bank—to build and sustain their global and multicultural success. His expertise regularly appears in *The Financial Times, China Daily, The Guardian*, BBC, *WSJ*, CBS, and the *Christian Science Monitor*. He has also authored more than 140 books and articles on the globalization of organizations, cultural intelligence, and inclusion, equity, and diversity. A frequent speaker at professional meetings, Neal is the designated thought leader and expert on global talent development for ATD, SHRM, and The Economist Intelligence Unit. Neal is a professor emeritus at St. Peter's University, was a faculty associate at NYU's Stern Business School, and has been invited to be a senior fellow at the East-West Center in Hawaii three times. Neal can be reached at neal@nealgoodmangroup.com or through LinkedIn.

Ed Hasan

Ed Hasan, PhD, is the founder and CEO of Kaizen Human Capital and an adjunct professor at Georgetown University, where he teaches organization development and change. Additionally, he serves as a subject matter expert for the Association for Talent Development and Society for Human Resource Management (SHRM). An author, speaker, and coach, Ed was recognized as one of George Mason University's Prominent Patriots in Business, exemplifying his engagement as a well-rounded scholar and a person prepared to act through innovation. He was also a recipient of Georgetown University's Outstanding Faculty Award, which recognized him as a consummate professor and a role model for inclusive excellence. Ed's expertise includes organization development, change management, and workplace diversity, equity, and inclusion. He has a doctoral degree in education from the University of Southern California, where his research focus was religious inclusion in the workplace.

Randy Matusky

Randy Matusky is an innovative and dynamic talent development professional who is passionate about developing employees, upskilling teams, and partnering with senior leaders to help execute their strategic goals. He holds a master's degree in instructional design and leadership development; CPTD, PMP, and SPHR certifications; and is a certified Six Sigma coach. Randy is an associate director of organizational learning at Miltenyi Biotec, a global biotechnology company headquartered near Cologne in Bergisch Gladbach, Germany. He is also the founder and owner of Tomiko Consulting, which specializes in executive coaching and leadership development. Randy speaks and writes frequently on leadership, team development, change management, and how best to establish a culture of learning throughout the organization. He is an active member of the ATD DC chapter and the PMI DC chapter.

Beth Messich

Beth Messich is the principal and founder of Beth Messich Coaching and Consulting. A seasoned learning and development and talent management executive and leadership coach, Beth has spent the past 15+ years creating learning and talent solutions for companies ranging from early-stage startups to mature global brands. She collaborates closely with clients to create strategies, resources, and programs that are authentic to the organization and reach the best outcome. After years of coaching in her professional roles, Beth completed her formal coaching training at Georgetown's Institute for Transformational Leadership. She uses that experience to coach individuals and help incorporate coaching into organizational performance and development strategies to increase people leadership capabilities. Passionate about creating an inclusive culture, Beth believes that people are at their best when they can bring their whole selves to work. She offers a range of coaching engagements and human resources consultation. To contact Beth, email her at beth@bethmessich.com.

Sean Murphy

Sean Murphy is a director on the opportunity team at Walmart.org, where he supports Walmart's philanthropic efforts in developing the infrastructure needed to empower the development of a skill-based workforce system that enables all learning to count. In doing so, his work has led to investments in organizations such as the U.S. Chamber Foundation, Massachusetts Institute of Technology, National Governors Association, and Digital

Promise Global. Before joining Walmart.org in 2019, Sean was an associate director at a workforce board in Washington state, leading projects that focused on populations such as veterans and justice involved youth. He also worked within public policy and community engagement for US Senator Patty Murray and other congressional and statewide elected leaders in Washington state. Sean holds an AA from Highline Community College, BA in government from Eastern Washington University, and an MBA from both Queens University and Cornell University. He now resides in Rogers, Arkansas.

Neha Lagoo Ratnakar

Neha Lagoo Ratnakar, CPTD, MBA, MA, leads education and content for LEAD Network Europe, where she works with large CPG and retail companies across Europe to bring gender parity in leadership positions. But that alone doesn't define her career. She's also a part-time entrepreneur, an improvisor who has worked in a variety of fields around the world, and the best-selling author of *Back on Your Feet*. She brings a unique perspective from her global career successfully building teams and delivering results in remote settings. Her writing and talks nudge people to rethink their careers and work arrangements and to challenge their limiting beliefs. In her spare time, you'll find her trying to convince people that remote work is the best and being obnoxious about her impact on the environment. Her life in a nutshell: seven languages, eight countries, nine careers, and a 10-year-old.

William J. Rothwell

William J. Rothwell, PhD, DBA, SPHR, SHRM-SCP, RODC, CPTD Fellow, is president of Rothwell & Associates, partner in the Rothwell Partnership, and Distinguished Professor of Workforce Education and Development in the department of learning and performance systems in The Pennsylvania State University. He leads Penn State's online master's degree in organization development and change and also advises residential PhD students at the university. William is a frequent international traveler and teaches, consults, and trains globally online. Among his most recent books are *Organization Development Interventions*, *Virtual Group Coaching*, *Transformational Coaching*, *Successful Supervisory Leadership*, *Rethinking Organization Diversity, Equity, and Inclusion*, and *Succession Planning for Small and Family Businesses*. William earned the Lifetime Achievement Award from the Organization Development Network in 2022 and the Distinguished Contribution to Workplace and Performance Award from ATD in 2011.

Makiya Musgrove Woods

Makiya Musgrove Woods is an executive coach and influential talent leader who brings innovative talent strategies to organizations. Prior to founding Affinia Development Solutions, she served in a variety of talent management, leadership development, and HR business partner roles for Fortune 500 companies across multiple industries. In her last role as VP of talent, learning, and DEI she successfully integrated the previously siloed functions. A winner of the Top 100 Diversity Officers award, Makiya centers her work at the intersection of talent, DEI, and leadership development. Her breadth of expertise in these functions, as well as her extensive background in change management are ideal for helping companies connect their DEI strategy to their talent strategy for sustainable impact. In addition to leading the operations at Affinia Development, Makiya also serves as an executive board advisor for two nonprofit organizations dedicated to building the self-esteem of young girls. She has a BS in psychology and an MBA in organization development. Her certifications include Certified Master Coach, Korn Ferry 360, Korn Ferry Assessment of Potential, Hogan Leadership Forecast Series, Intercultural Development Inventory, Prosci Certified Change Practitioner, and CliftonStrengths Assessment Coach.

Heather R. Younger

Heather R. Younger is the world's foremost expert on active listening. She's a dynamic, uplifting speaker who harnesses humor, warmth, and relatability to instantly engage audiences and inspire them into action. As a proven expert in employee engagement, retention, and workplace culture, Heather has worked with countless organizations to create cultures where employees feel heard and valued, which causes them to become more engaged and improve retention. Her presentations energize teams, leaders, and organizations to create supportive cultures of care by improving how they listen to, communicate with, and empower one another in the workplace. Heather's latest book, *The Art of Active Listening: How People at Work Feel Heard, Valued, and Understood*, published in April 2023. To learn more, visit HeatherYounger.com.

Index

A

accountability, 259, 266–267, 281
achievable goals, 95
action, taking, 130–131
active listening, 124–125, 128–133, 238
Adams, Bill, 239, 247
adaptive changes, 139
ADKAR model, 140
ADP Research Institute, 257
advocacy, 192
affinity groups, 67
after action review (AAR), 159
Agile Manifesto, 115–116
Agile methodology, 114–118, 142–143, 153
Allen, C., 249
American Society of Training Directors (ASTD), v
Anderson, Robert, 239, 247
anger, 221
Apple, 176–177
Association for Talent Development (ATD),
    v, 59, 105, 274, 277, 281
authenticity, 80, 81
Avery Manufacturing, 60–61

B

BANI environments, 193–194
barriers to change, 69, 144, 149–151, 241–242
behavioral lens for soft skills development,
    238–240
Behavior level, in Kirkpatrick's method, 70
beingness, 219–220

Belbin, Raymond, 265
belonging, 58–59, 71. *See also* diversity, equity,
    inclusion, and belonging (DEIB)
Bersin, Josh, 240
big picture, connecting plan to, 126–127
Biogen, 154
black belts, Six Sigma, 112
Bloom's Taxonomy, 59
Boose, Michael, 106
Bridges, William, 140
Brooks Consultants, 63
Bryant, Andrew, 123
Buckingham, Marcus, 216, 257, 261
buddy system, 171
budget constraints, 101
Bureau of Labor Statistics (BLS), 273
business alignment, 91–103
    adjustments to improve, 101–103
    defined, 92
    designing organization for, 97–98
    human element of, 98–99
    information gathering for, 95–97
    mission, vision, and values in, 92–94
    retaining top talent with, 99–100
    sharing plan for, with leaders, 100–101
    strategic plan and yearly goals in, 94–95
    team structure in, 98
business case, 146
business resource groups (BRGs), 67
business strategy, L&D's role in, 242–243
buy-in, 11, 17, 151

C

O

observations, 10
Offterdinger, E., 249
Ohno, Taiichi, 106
onboarding, 171, 182–183, 212–215, 279–280
one-on-one conversations, 48
one-size-fits-all approaches, 11, 17
operating managers, OD by, 25–26
Opportunity@Work, 196
Optum, 75
organizational lens for soft skills
    development, 240–242
organizational outcomes, teams driving,
    266–268
organizational performance metrics, 158
organizational politics, 29–31, 35
organizational values. *See* values
organization chart, 19–26
    OD practitioners' work within, 32–34
    responsibility for OD on, 20–26
organization design, 27–28, 97–98
organization development (OD), 3–17
    defined, x, 5
    disciplines contributing to, 6
    effect of politics on, 29–31
    evolution of DEIB in, 58
    L&D and, x–xi
    organization design vs., 27–28
    process of, 3–17
    remote work and, 180–181
    and soft skills, 237–238, 252
    TD professionals in, vi, 122
    for teams, 257–258, 262–263
    training in, 66
organization development and culture
    (capability), v–vi
organization development (OD) practitioners
    evaluating results of, 34
    organizational politics for, 30–31
    responsibilities of, 27–29, 177

in succession planning, 271–272, 281, 283
    work within organization chart by, 32–34
organization norms, 81, 243–244
Outlier (team role), 265
overprocessing, 111
overproduction, 111
Own+Model+Drive model, 247–248

P

partnerships, 67
Patagonia, 93–94
patience, 6, 17
PBS, 196
PDCA cycle, 109–110
Peer (team role), 265
people skills, 236, 237, 252–253
PepsiCo, 64, 186
perception management, 221
performance evaluations, 51
performance management, remote, 185–186
performance metrics, 158–159, 224–227
performance tracking, skills-based, 203–204
Perkbox, 184
Perkspot, 184
permission, for self-care, 84–85, 87
Pew Research Center, 203
Phillips's ROI Methodology, 70
physical ability, DEI focused on, 174
physical well-being, 77
political approach to evaluating OD, 34
productivity, team, 267–268
professional development, xi
progressive discipline, 222–224
progress reports, 153
Project Aristotle, 260
project plan, 147, 148, 153
Prosci, Inc., 140
psychological safety, 58–59, 65–66, 240, 259, 260
pulse surveys, 153
purpose, ix, 243, 269

About the Editor

Brian James Flores is a distinguished expert in the field of learning and development, with more than 15 years of experience in the industry. He holds a degree in math and computer science from the University of Illinois–Chicago and a master's in education in human resource development from the University of Illinois–Urbana-Champaign.

Brian's career began at Apple, where he discovered his passion for adult learning theory and instructional design. He quickly rose through the ranks, leading and growing the training team and contributing to a multiyear project as part of a global training initiative. During this time, he gained invaluable experience in architecting engaging learning experiences and designing effective learning programs. After almost a decade at Apple, Brian joined Performics as a learning and development leader, where he designed and implemented innovative onboarding programs and industry-specific curriculum. He also discovered the overlap between learning and organization development, working closely with executive leadership to drive company-wide change management efforts.

Brian is a respected thought leader in the industry and has been invited to speak at various live and virtual events for universities, professional groups, and industry organizations. His expertise in both L&D and OD led him to subsequent roles as a talent and organizational development consultant at Zoom Video Communications and a senior manager of organizational development at CommerceHub.

Throughout his career, Brian has remained committed to the development and experience of employees. He believes that the combination of L&D and OD efforts is crucial to the success of any organization and is passionate about sharing his knowledge and expertise with others.

In his free time, Brian enjoys exploring new places and trying new foods with his wife, Ariel, and their three children, Noah, Nell, and Naia. He is grateful for their support and encouragement throughout his career, including in the development of this book.

About ATD

atd The Association for Talent Development (ATD) is the world's largest association dedicated to those who develop talent in organizations. Serving a global community of members, customers, and international business partners in more than 100 countries, ATD champions the importance of learning and training by setting standards for the talent development profession.

Our customers and members work in public and private organizations in every industry sector. Since ATD was founded in 1943, the talent development field has expanded significantly to meet the needs of global businesses and emerging industries. Through the Talent Development Capability Model, education courses, certifications and credentials, memberships, industry-leading events, research, and publications, we help talent development professionals build their personal, professional, and organizational capabilities to meet new business demands with maximum impact and effectiveness.

One of the cornerstones of ATD's intellectual foundation, ATD Press offers insightful and practical information on talent development, training, and professional growth. ATD Press publications are written by industry thought leaders and offer anyone who works with adult learners the best practices, academic theory, and guidance necessary to move the profession forward.

We invite you to join our community. Learn more at td.org.